IMAGES
of America

BARROW COUNTY

PHOTOGRAPHS FROM THE STELL-KILGORE COLLECTION

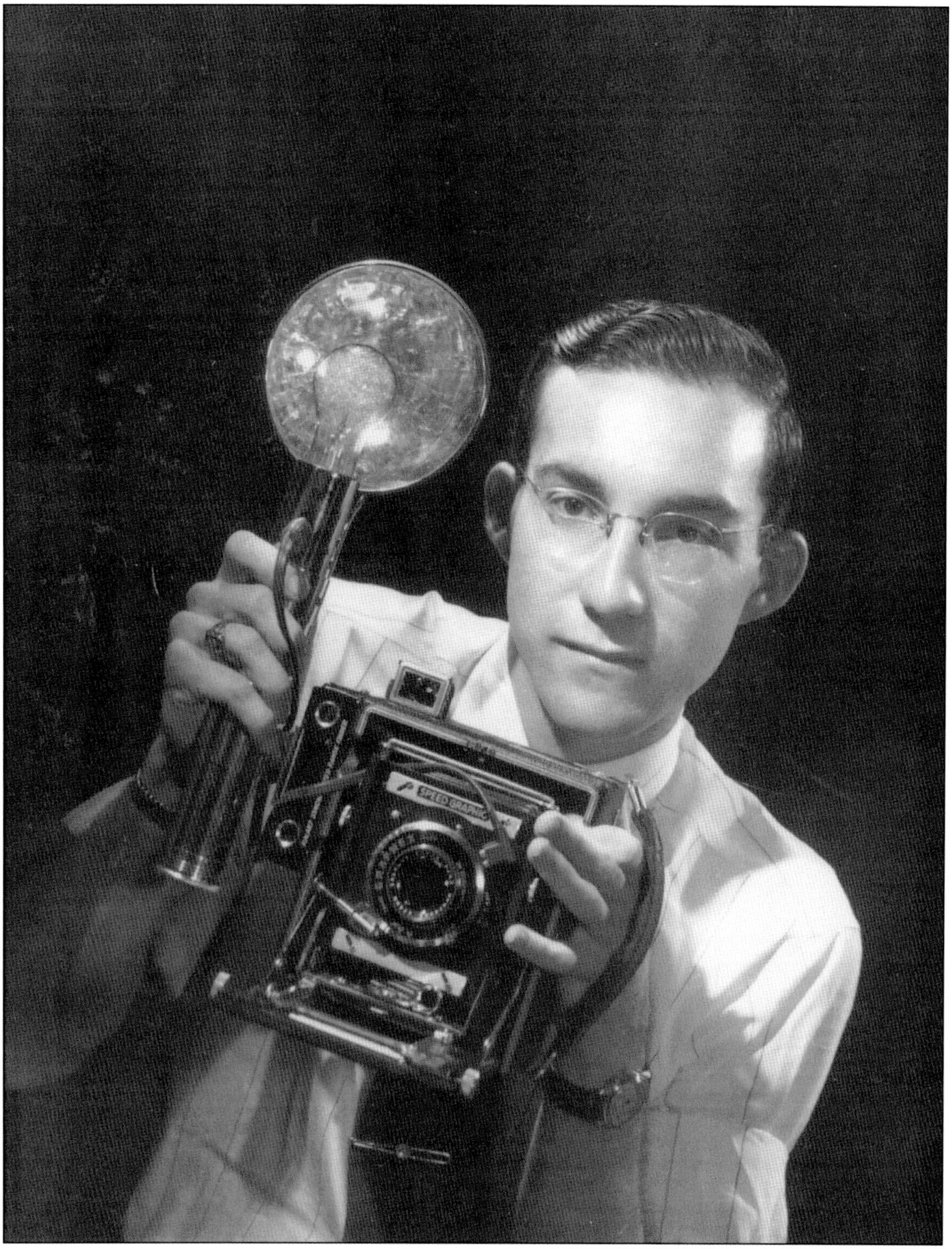

Pierson Stell.

IMAGES
of America

BARROW COUNTY
PHOTOGRAPHS FROM THE STELL-KILGORE COLLECTION

Myles R. Godfrey

ARCADIA
PUBLISHING

ISBN 978-0-7385-0627-2

Published by Arcadia Publishing
Charleston, South Carolina

Printed in the United States of America

Library of Congress Catalog Card Number: 00-107282

For all general information contact Arcadia Publishing at:
Telephone 843-853-2070
Fax 843-853-0044
E-Mail sales@arcadiapublishing.com
For customer service and orders:
Toll-Free 1-888-313-2665

Visit us on the Internet at www.arcadiapublishing.com

Contents

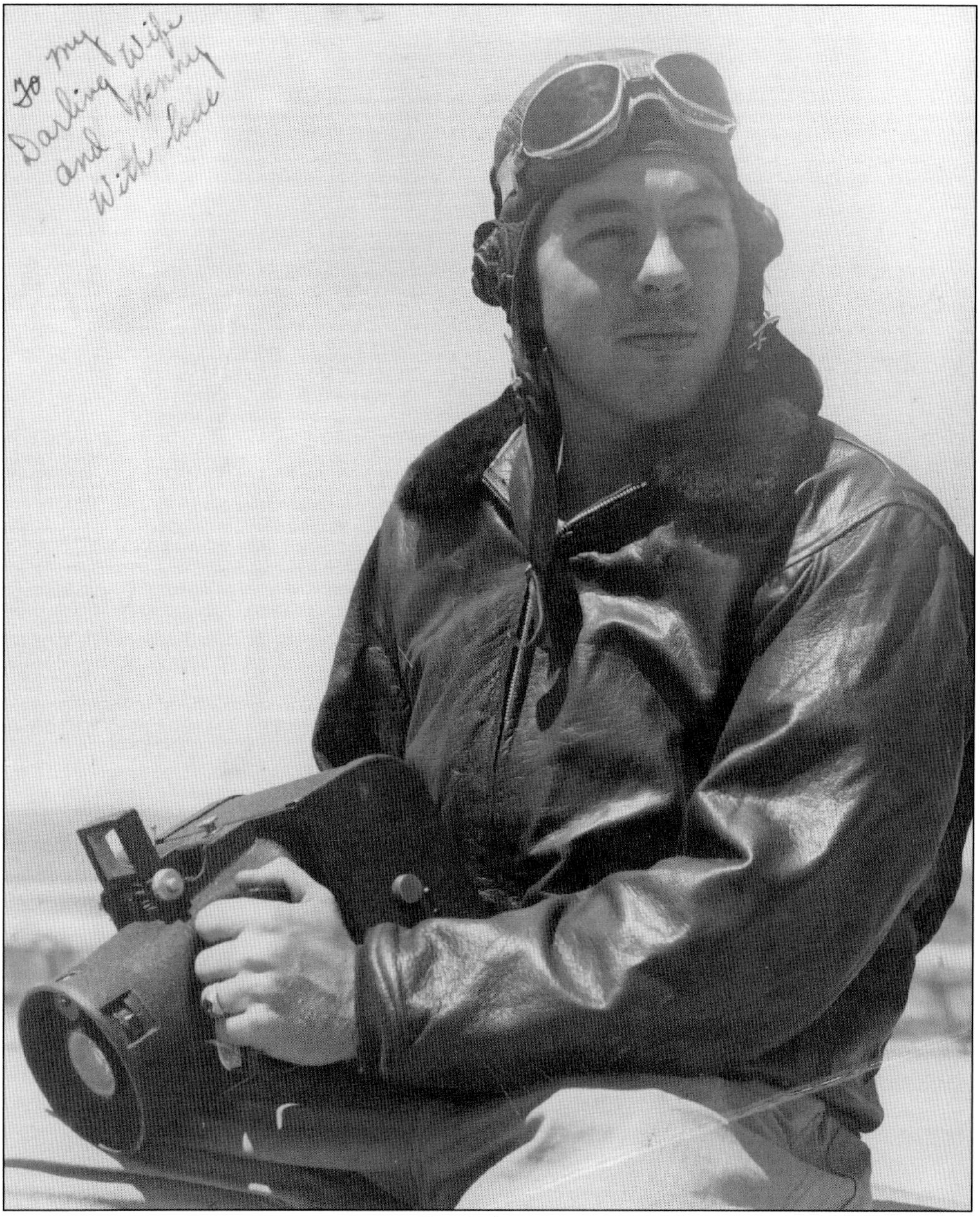

Ray Kilgore.

INTRODUCTION

This is not a history book. Instead, it is a tribute to two remarkable photographers and their work in Barrow County over almost 40 years.

When Pierson Stell opened Stell Photographic Services in 1946, World War II had just ended. Shortly thereafter he hired Ray Kilgore, who had received his photographic training in the Navy during the war. For the next four decades, until Ray retired in 1980 (and died in 1981), and until Pierson retired in 1987, the two photographed the mundane and the monumental in Barrow County life. Their precious files document in many ways what life was really like during those years.

When I undertook the task of preparing this book it seemed easy. After all, I had thousands upon thousands of high-quality images from which to choose. That turned out to be part of the problem. As I went through the files I chose only images I thought were artistically superior or historically important. Before I even reached the 1970s I had far too many photographs for only one book. As a result, the latest images you'll see here are from about 1969, even though the studio operated for almost 20 years after that.

But that didn't bother me. From a historical perspective, the older the better. I didn't think it would add to the importance of this book to include photos of things that have not changed all that much. Instead, it will offer buildings that are long gone, folks who are no longer with us, and some of the simple things that were an important part of life 30 or 40 years ago.

The biggest problem turned out to be identifying the faces. Some of the people pictured died decades ago, and it is a fact of life that none of us look like we did in the 1940s. Some of the organizations no longer exist. Some of the people photographed lived here for a short time and then moved on. We have done our best to identify them correctly. If there are errors, it is not because a lot of folks didn't try.

When you look at these photographs, don't just look at the faces or what is pointed out in the captions. Instead, look at the small details captured in their large-format negatives. See the signs, the food on the tables. Look at the earth, notice the forests or lack of trees. The small details are the things that really capture the time and place. From the air you'll see cultivated fields that are now forests or subdivisions. From the ground you'll see the way people really lived almost 50 years ago.

Most of all, don't forget that this is not just a collection of random photos from dozens of sources. Two very talented men created every image in this book.

ACKNOWLEDGMENTS

If everybody who "wrote" this book signed it, there wouldn't be enough room on the title page, and I would certainly need to sign somewhere near the bottom. Dozens of folks have taken their valuable time to help me in identifying the places and people shown in these images.

I started out with Dr. C.B. Skelton, John Mobley, and Louis Lovin. Then I added B-Bomb Smith, Jim Forrester, Larry Jones, Dorothy Jones, Ernest Graham, Joanna Mosley, Ella Ruth Price, Bob Wimberly, Rachel Wimberly, James Barnes, Myron Skinner, Sam Dunaway, Jack Segars, Shirley Segars, Hillman Patrick, Betty Patrick, Dr. Quentin Randolph, James Lay, Tootsie Lay, Donnie Canup, Linda Harris, Maria Lay, Mary Sims, Larry Holland, Phyllis Holland, Colleen Williams, Buddy Ouzts, Frank Dunagan, Gerald Moon, Alan Pentecost, John R. Pentecost, Gordon Blackwell, Ronney Massey, and many others. I am grateful to all of them.

Thanks also to *The Barrow County News*, for allowing me complete access to back issues of *The Winder News*.

Most of all, I wish to thank Myron Garrett, who acquired the Stell-Kilgore photo and negative files in order to ensure their preservation. This book would not have been possible without his generous help and cooperation.

—Myles Godfrey

One

Home from the War

Stell and Kilgore captured many images during the years just after World War II. There are family photographs with men in uniform, just returning from the war, and proud studio portraits of soldiers and sailors. Only five years later the country was at war again, this time in Korea, and once again the two photographers were there to chronicle the local scene. Again there are portraits, and this time photos of draftees leaving Winder for training. Most would come back, but some would not. Finally, there was the Vietnam era and more photographs of draftees, soldiers, and sailors.

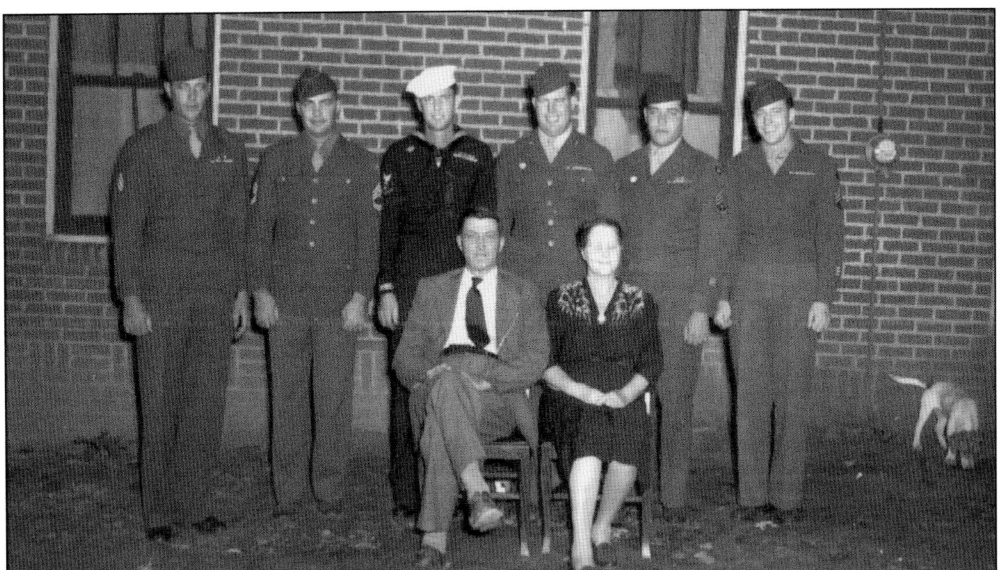

The six sons of Dave and Abbie Smith (seated) proudly served their country during World War II. Standing, from left to right, are Delmar, Doyle, Paris, D.S., Arthur (Buster), and Artis (Finnie). Paris, who was married and had children, had a draft deferment; however, when his two younger brothers were called, he decided that he should also serve. He joined the Navy.

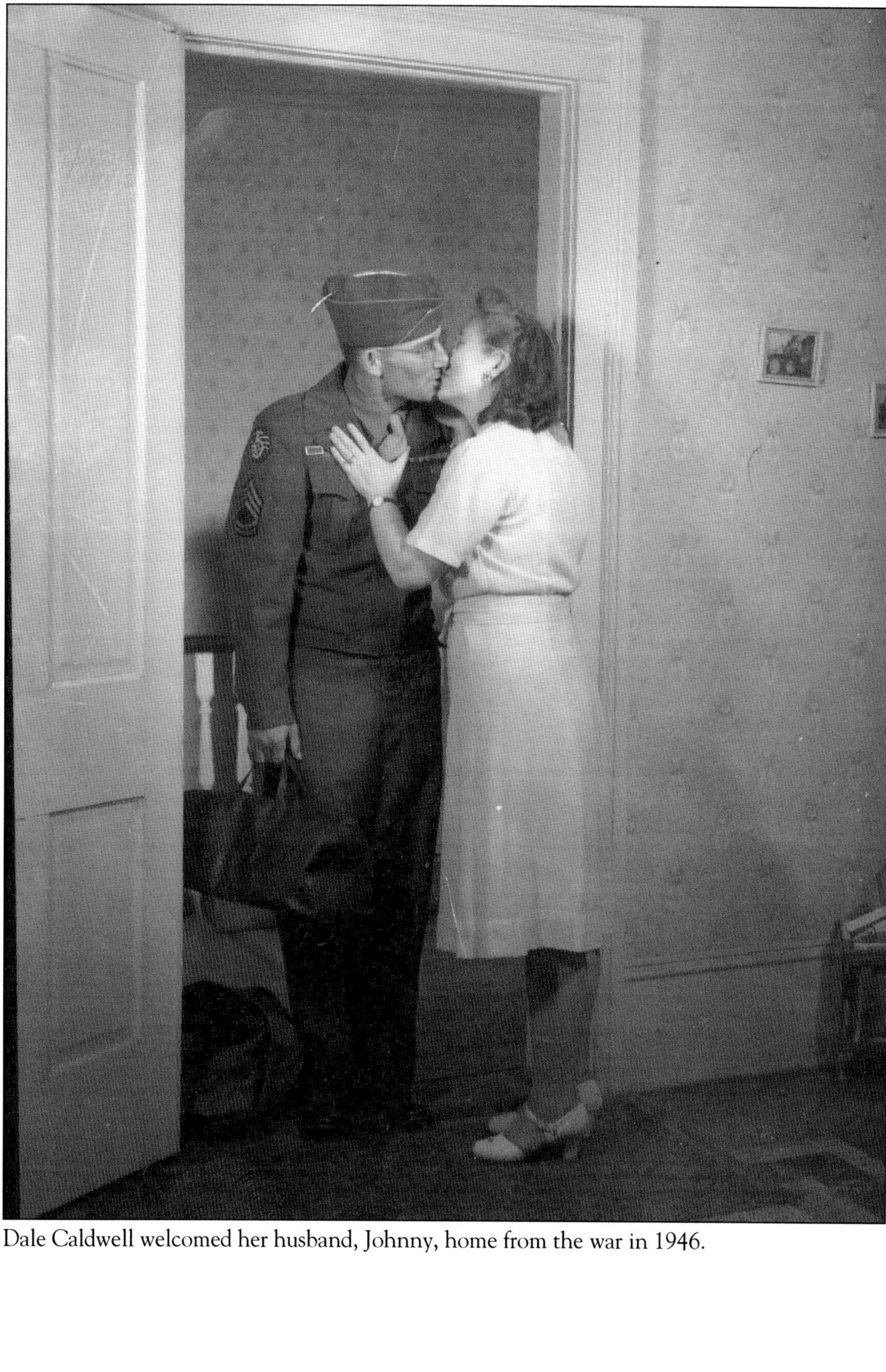
Dale Caldwell welcomed her husband, Johnny, home from the war in 1946.

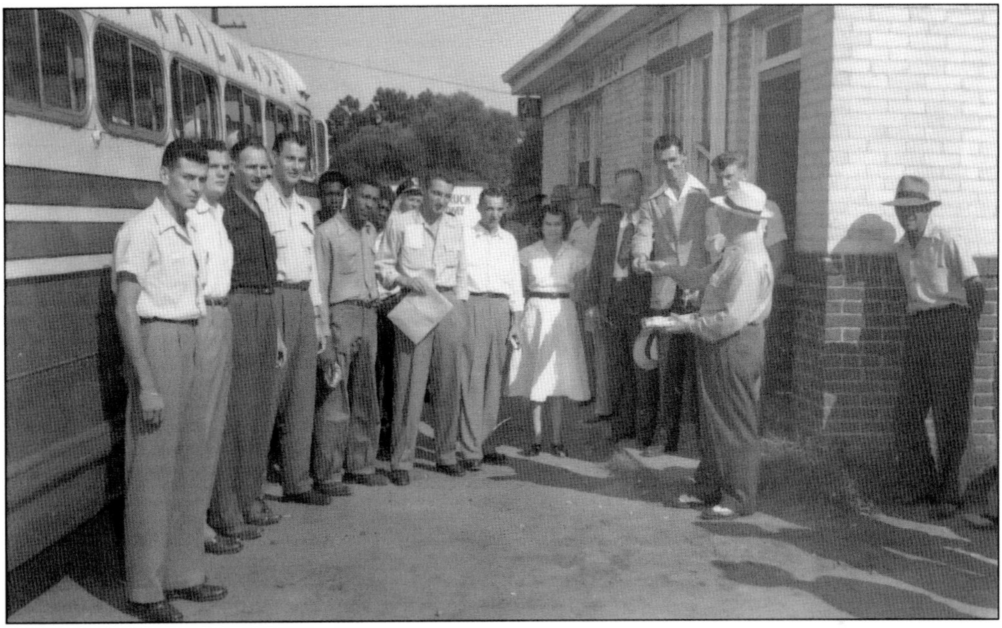

In August 1950, the first local men drafted to fight in the Korean War boarded a bus at Healan's Café on May Street. Shown here, from left to right, are Ernest Harold Miller, Winford Orr, Harvey Woodward (of the local draft board), Carlton Jackson Pentecost, Will Henry Peters, Robert G. Reid, Will Usher Hammonds, Rufus Winfrey Rogers, Chandler L. Aaron, Mary Page (draft board clerk), Paul Hosch (draft board chairman), William Hoyt Harwell, Lester Manders, and local merchant Henry Peskin. Peskin was continuing his tradition, begun during World War II, of seeing off each group of draftees with a carton of cigarettes and his sincere hope for their safe return.

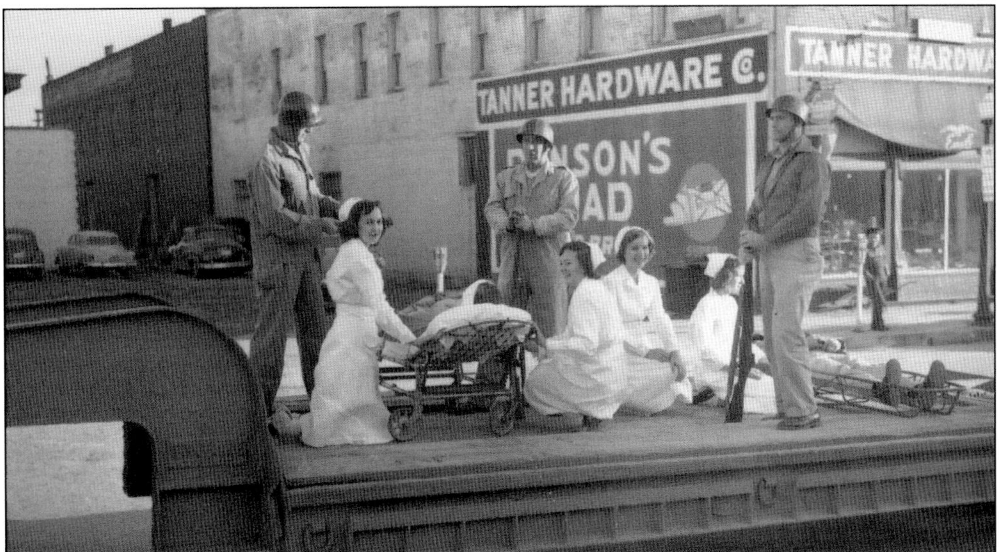

During the Korean War, the American Red Cross faced a blood shortage. This parade through downtown Winder helped to publicize the need for donors. The "nurses" (who were actually high school students), from left to right, are Barbara Guest, Sybil Gresham, Janet Tanner, and Barbara Lanthier. The men are unidentified.

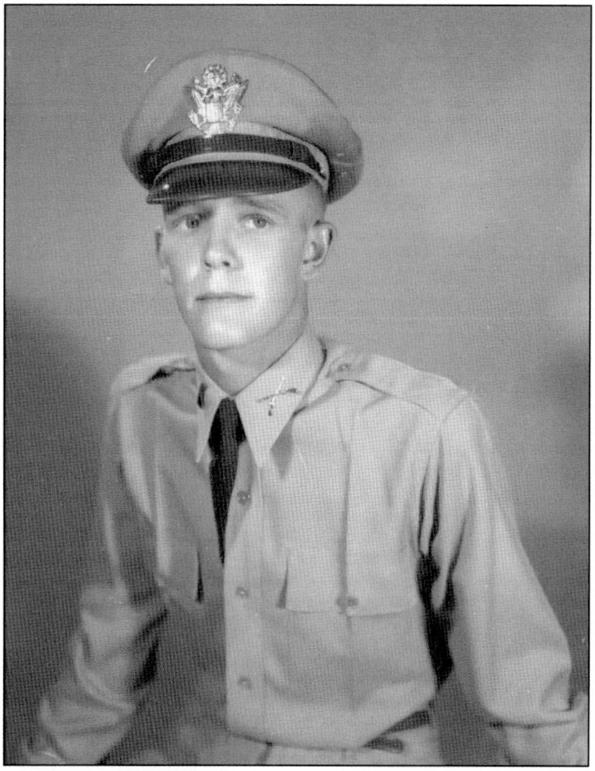

Army Lt. Clay Camp Jr. came to Stell Photographic Service for a formal portrait in July 1950, just before he left for Korea. Unfortunately, he would not return. Word reached Winder in February 1951 that he had been killed while leading a patrol. He was 22 years old. Two weeks later his friend Ernest Graham Jr. received a letter from Camp. In the letter, written between attacks, Graham said Camp wrote of his weariness: "He said if he could find a peaceful place to lay down, he could sleep forever . . . I guess that's what he did."

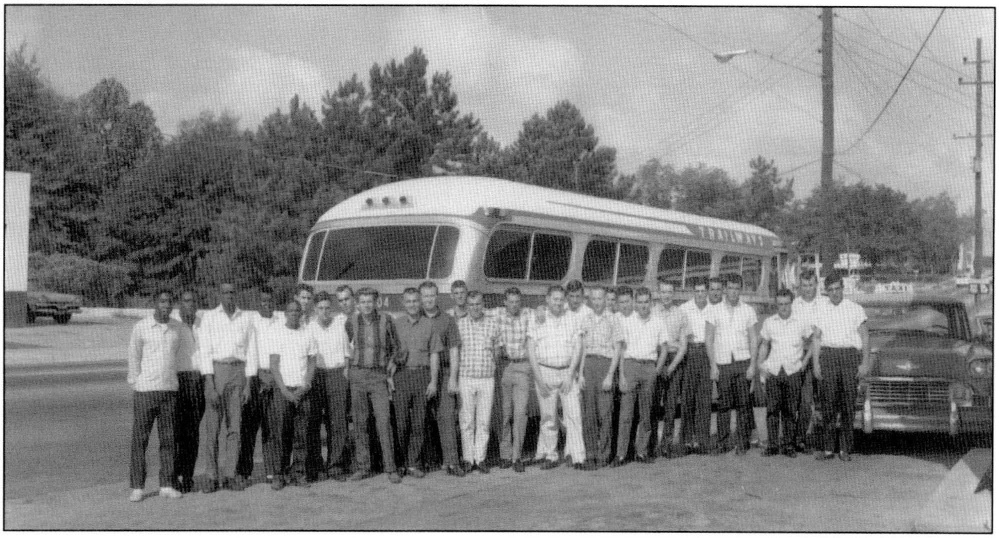

These Barrow County men boarded a bus to Atlanta for their pre-induction physical exams in July 1965. Pictured among them are Ollie Massey, Willie Berry, William Huff, Charles Satterfield, Joe Ford, Roger Maddox, Dillard Metcalf, Dennis Littleton, Buddy McDaniel, Ralph Womack, Roy Gilreath, William Johnson, Tony Sims, Benjamin Mathis, James Lee, Randall Rockmore, Harvey Shedd, Jessie Day, Willie Witt, Larry Reynolds, Gene Wall, Jimmy Hays, Winfred Segars, Willis Wells, Homer Deaton, Ronald Chancey, and Wilburn Pentecost. The men would know within a few weeks whether or not they would be drafted to fight in Vietnam.

Two

Doing Business

Stell and Kilgore captured hundreds of images of the interiors and exteriors of Barrow County stores and businesses. They show friendly, old-fashioned merchants who were loved and trusted by their customers. Most of these businesses are gone now, due to the invasion of huge chain discount stores.

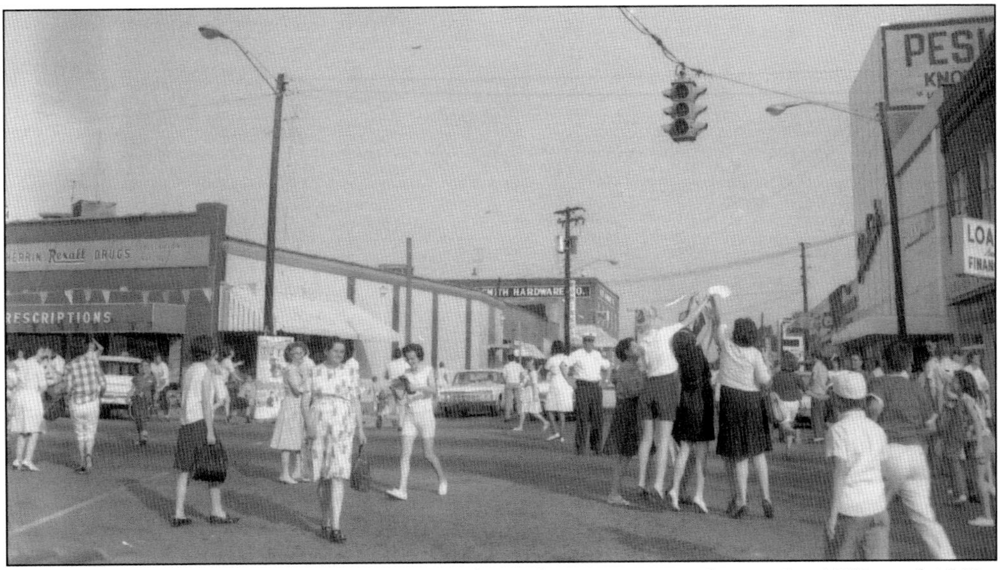

Winder merchants had some innovative and popular promotions during the 1950s and 1960s. For example, this is a photo made in May 1965 of folks chasing paper plates that were sailed from atop the Peskin's Department Store building. Some plates had prize certificates taped to them and some had cash. Even more exciting was another prize toss in which guinea hens with money taped to their legs were released from the same spot. Some flew right to the ground to be chased by onlookers. Others, with stronger wings, flew several blocks. During one event, a hen landed on the metal awning at Larry's Easy Pay. Several young people climbed up on the awning to capture it, but instead brought the awning crashing to the sidewalk.

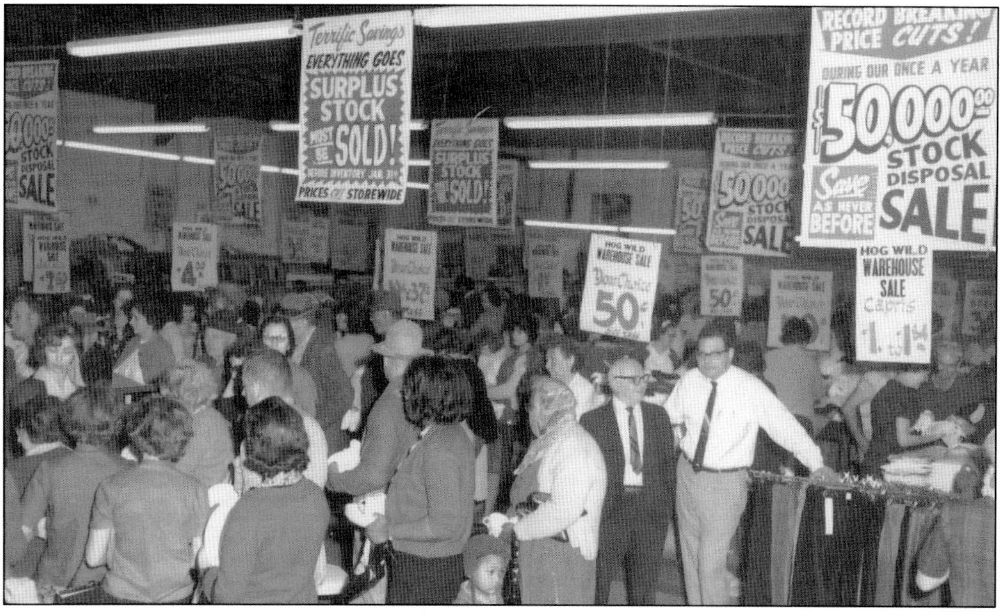

In 1929, during the depths of the Depression, Dave Hancock of Winder met a man named Henry Peskin while on a trip to Florida. He persuaded Peskin to come to Winder and open a store, and Peskin took his advice. He came to Winder, persuaded C.O. Maddox of The Peoples Bank to loan him $500, and opened a clothing store. An immigrant from Poland, he was the only Jewish man in Barrow County at that time. It was the beginning of a wonderful relationship between a community and a kind, generous, honest man that would last until he died on July 5, 1978, at age 80. In this photo, Henry Peskin (to the right, in a dark suit) is shown with his son Phillip (to the right, in a white shirt) during one of his sales events.

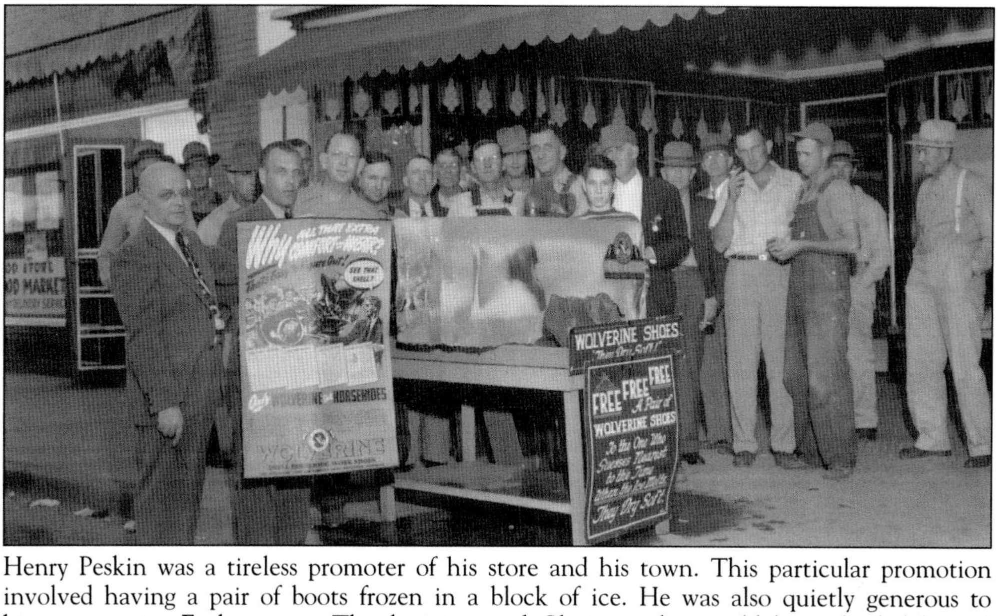

Henry Peskin was a tireless promoter of his store and his town. This particular promotion involved having a pair of boots frozen in a block of ice. He was also quietly generous to his community. Each year at Thanksgiving and Christmas he would have food delivered anonymously to the disadvantaged by a local grocery store. He also secretly helped many young people attend college.

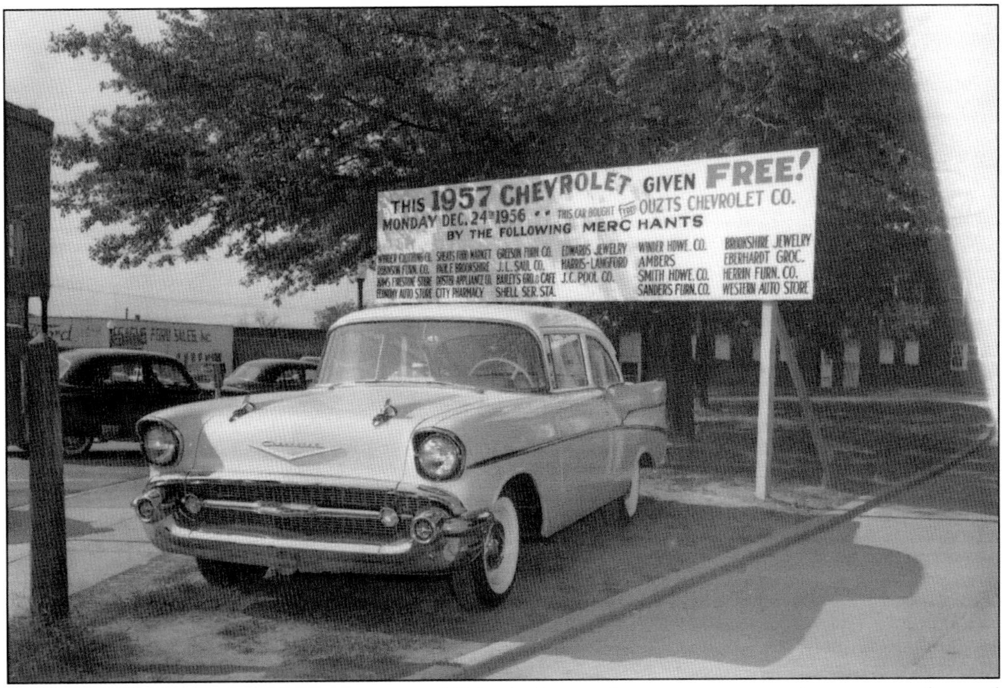

One of the biggest annual promotions of Winder's merchants was a car giveaway at the end of the Christmas shopping season, such as this one (above) given away in 1956. During the season, customers would accumulate numbered tickets from local merchants and bring them to a drawing held on the courthouse steps on Christmas Eve (below). Obviously, you had to be present to win the new car, so the event always drew huge crowds.

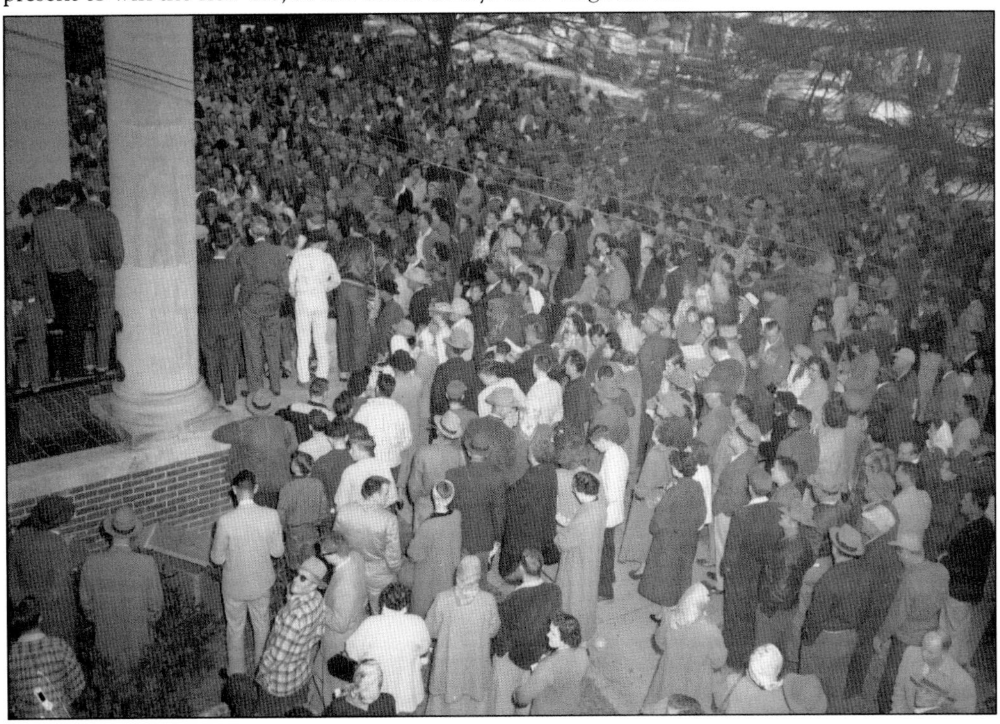

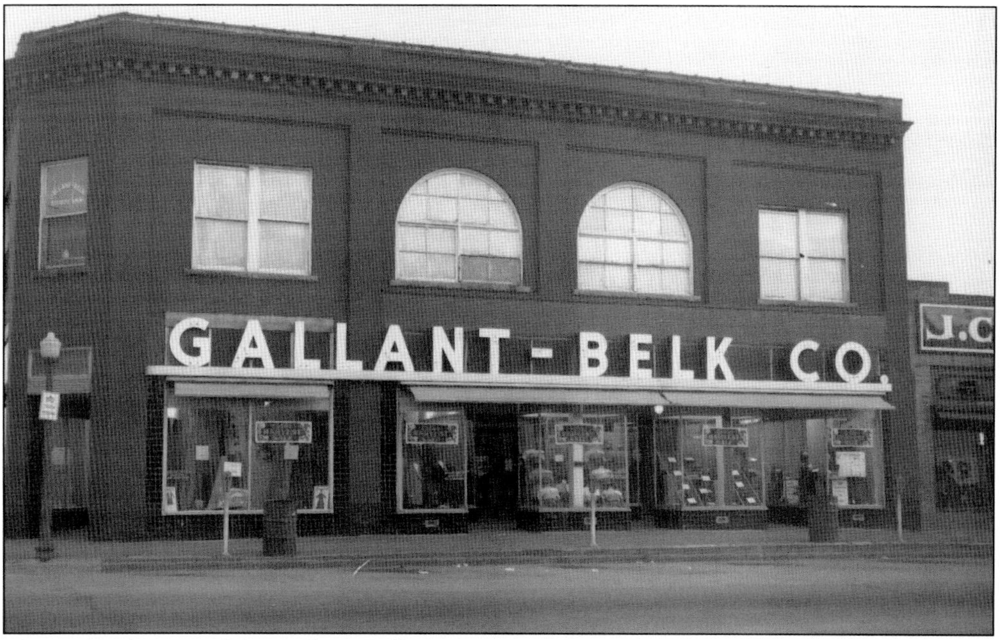

This 1952 photo is of the Gallant-Belk Company in downtown Winder. It occupied the space that now contains the city's gazebo and parking lot, at the corner of North Broad and Candler Streets. The store later moved to Holly Hill Mall and this building became a furniture store. The building was later destroyed by fire.

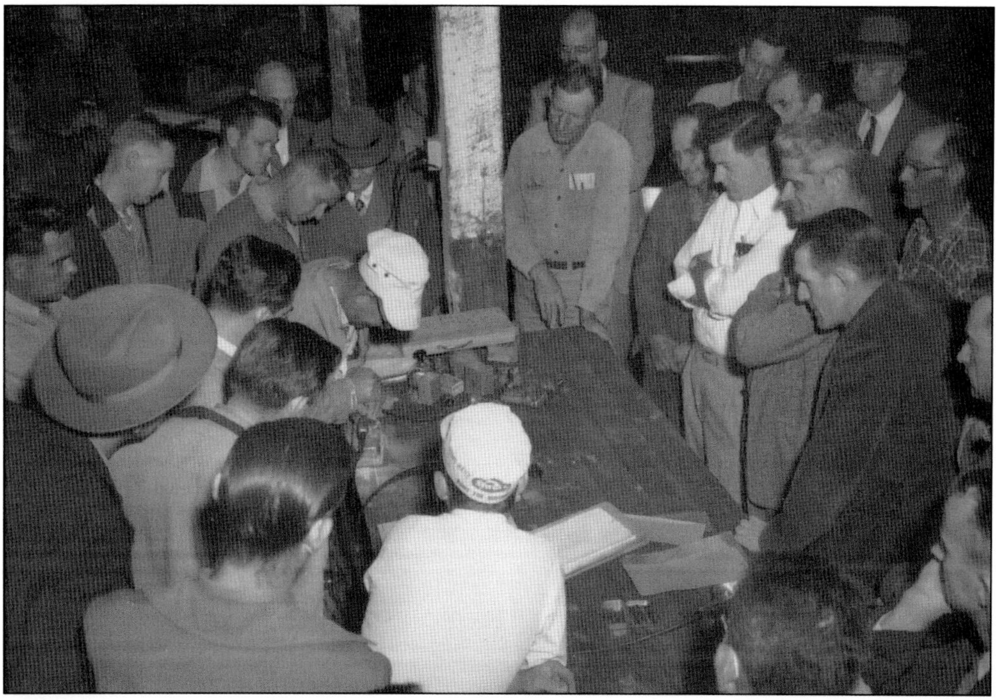

It's hard to imagine now, but electric tools were something new in 1954. This photo, taken at Smith Hardware Company in Winder, shows interested onlookers at a demonstration of an electric sander.

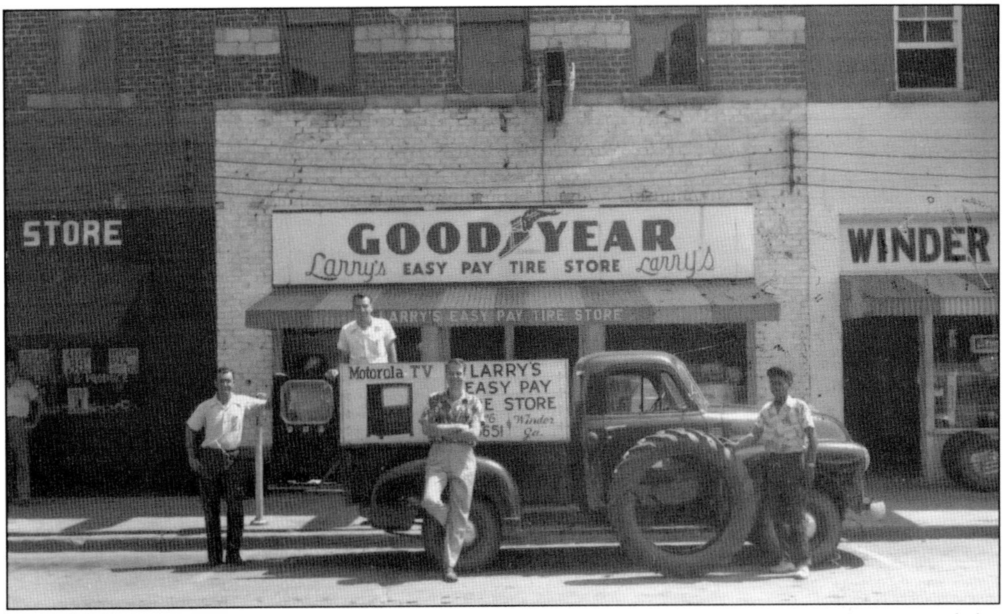

Tires and television sets were the big sellers at Larry's Easy Pay in 1951. Larry Jones opened the store in 1948 and it is still in operation in downtown Winder, having been purchased by long-time employees G.W. Steed and Sammy Everett. The tire business was later sold to Bob Jones and is now Bob's Tire Service. In the photo, from left to right, are Marion Holliday, Bob Jones, Larry Jones, and Howard Johnson. Larry, having served the community for more than 50 years, still operates a large furniture store in downtown Winder.

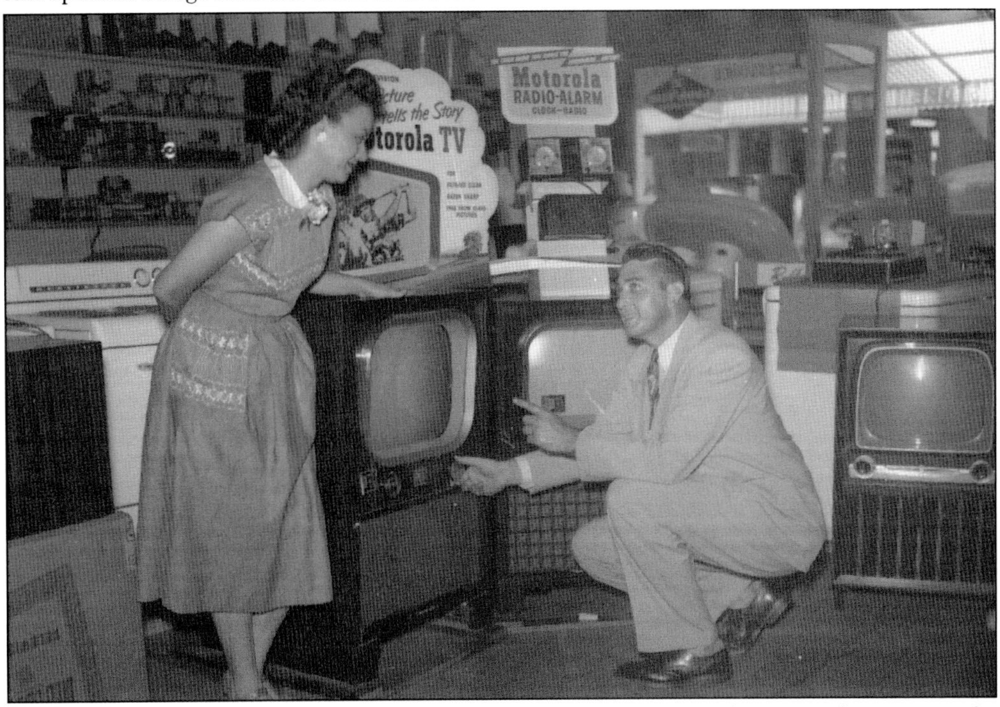

Lamar Murphy of Larry's Easy Pay demonstrates the advantages of a new television set for Evelyn (Mrs. Haase) Arnold in this photo taken in 1952.

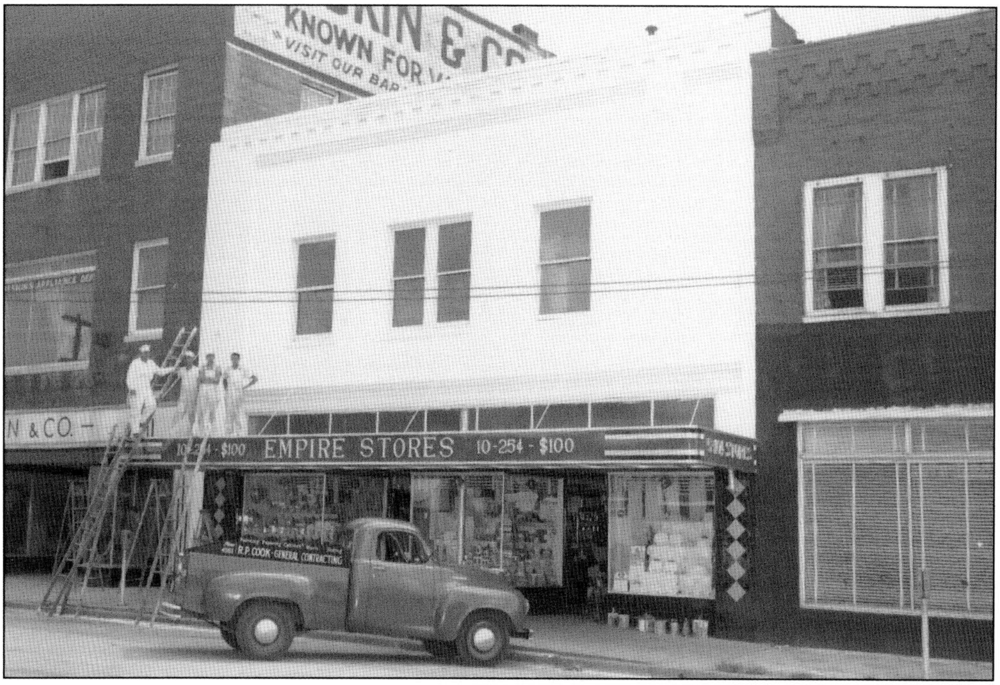

Empire 5&10¢ Store operated for years from this building on East Athens Street in Winder. It was later sold to Jim Griffith Sr., and became the Barrow 5&10¢ Store.

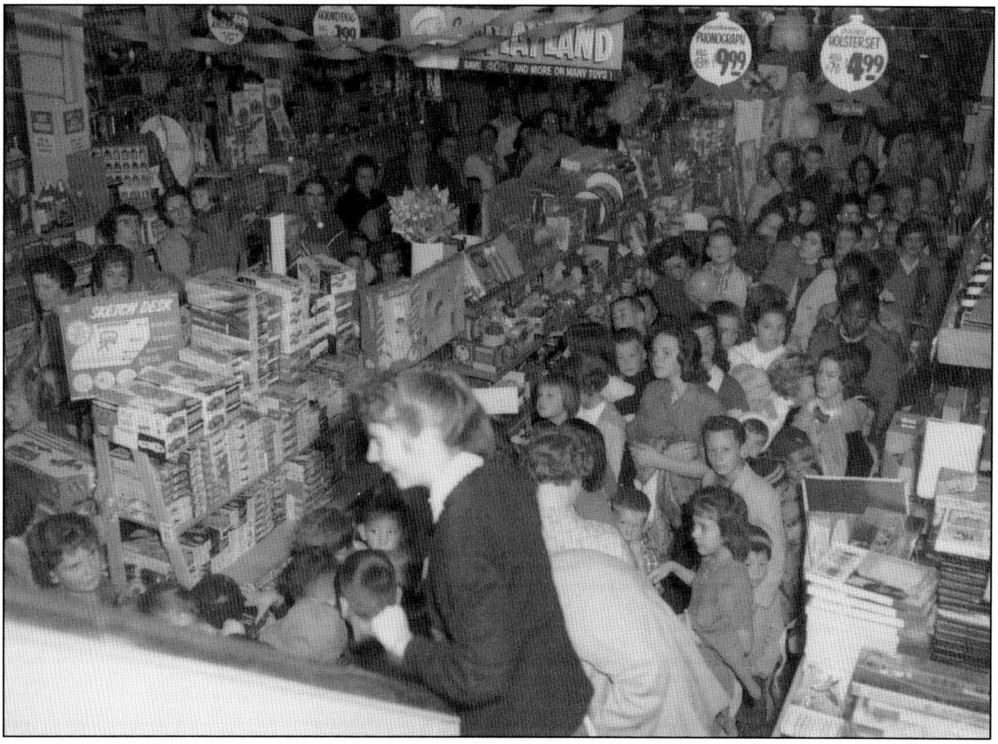

More than 500 children jammed the Barrow 5&10¢ Store for a visit by "Mr. Toymaker" in early December 1949.

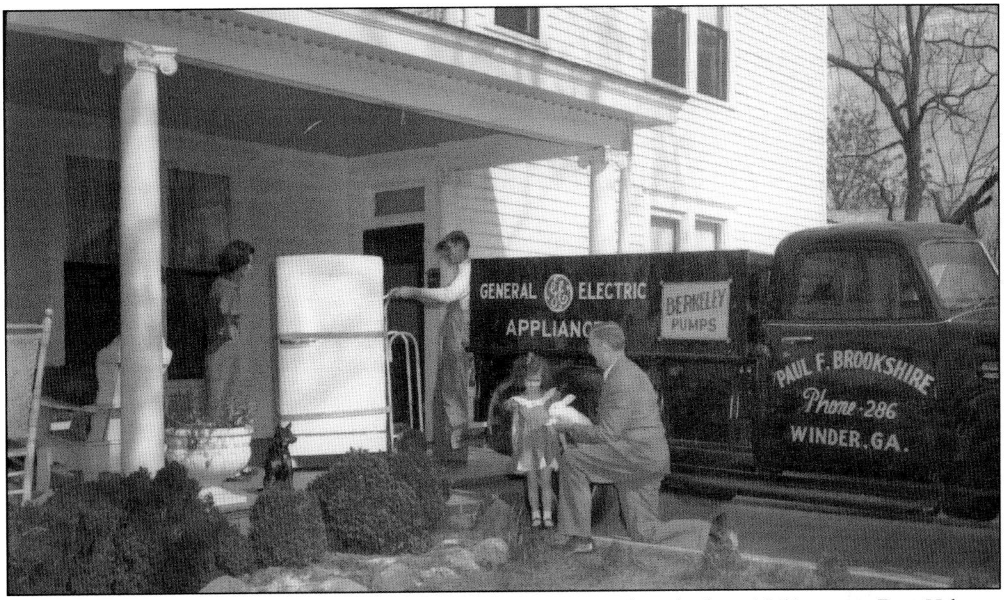

It would appear that getting a new refrigerator was a very big deal in 1950, since Ray Kilgore was on hand to photograph the event. Actually, this photo was probably made for promotional purposes, since Paul Brookshire (kneeling) is shown making the delivery to his own home. The house, at the corner of Midland and Center Streets, is still one of Winder's most beautiful. The deliveryman is Wes Bradberry. The woman is Brookshire's daughter, Johnnie Parks, and the child is his granddaughter, Lynn Parks.

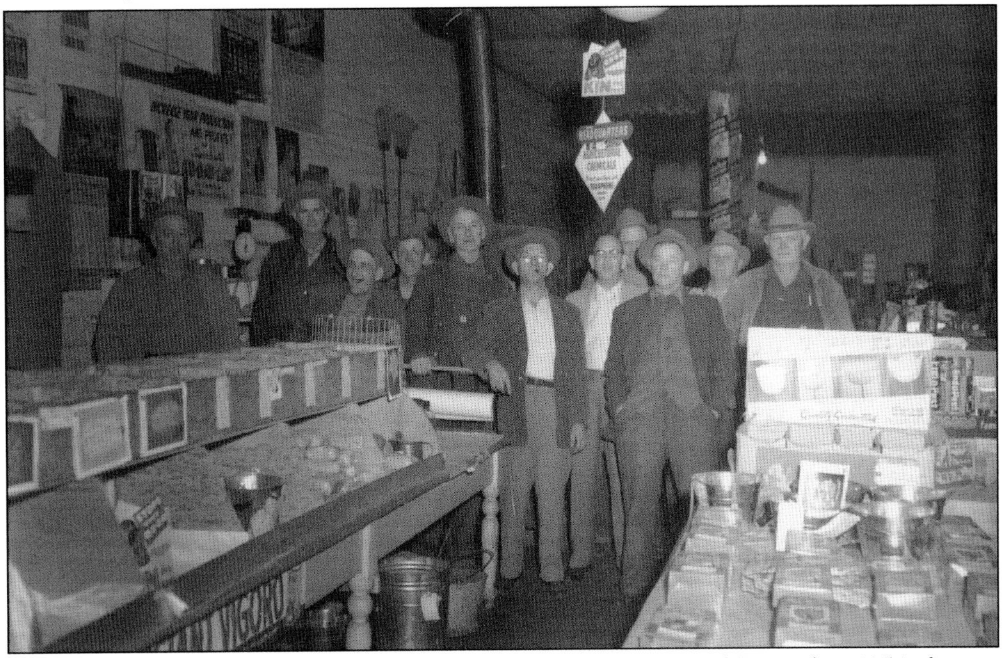

As shown by this photo taken at Winder Seed Company in mid-December 1954, farmers didn't have a lot to do in late winter. Fortunately, they did have several good places to hang out around a warm stove. The man in the center of the photo with a pipe in his mouth is Vasco Osborne.

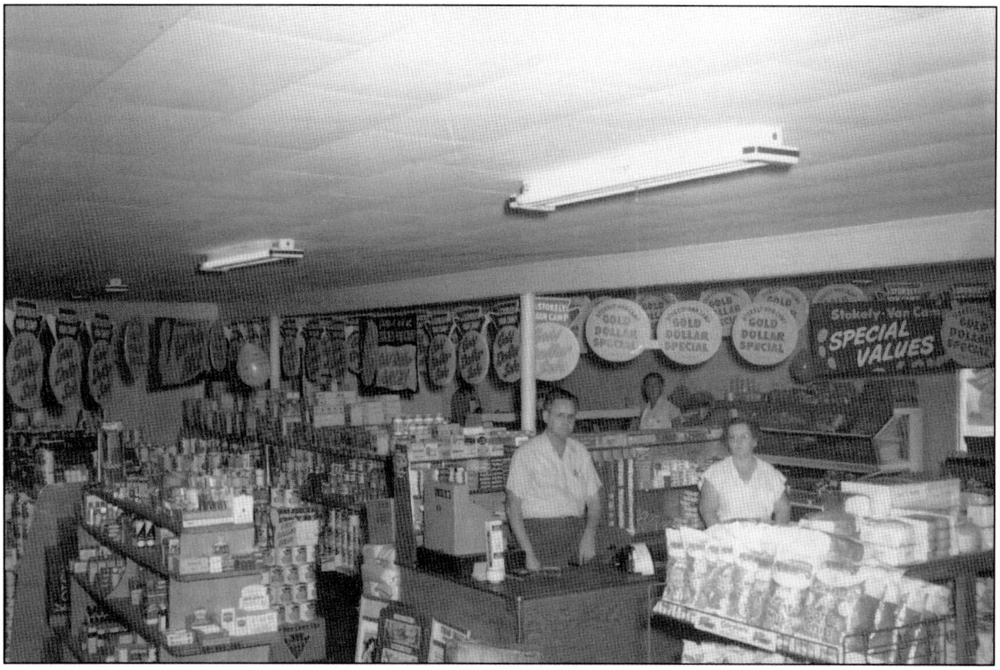

Bailey's Grocery, which also contained a popular café, stood on East Athens Street across from Sachem Mills. Shown in the foreground are Homer and Dora Bailey. The man in the background is probably their son Dean.

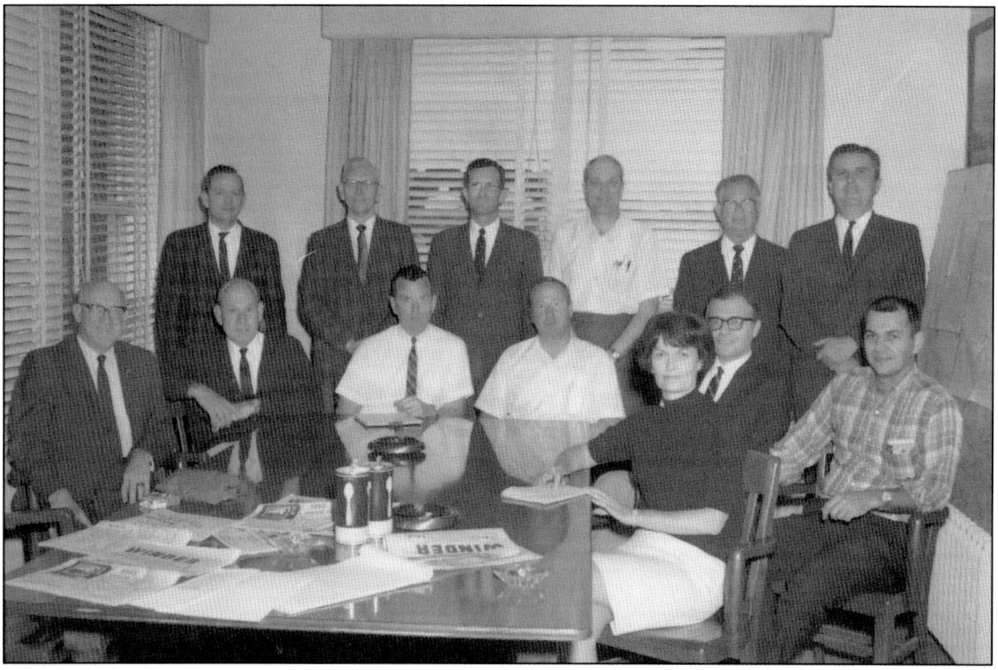

Some of Winder's leading merchants are shown here at a committee meeting at the chamber of commerce office in 1968. They are, from left to right, as follows: (seated) W.E. Atkinson, Cecil Grider, Bud Curry, unidentified, Helen Bentley, Sandy Schwartz, and Paul Stallings; (standing) John Bottoms, Claude Tuck, Maurice Sims, Larry Jones, Grady Good, and Charlie Sanders.

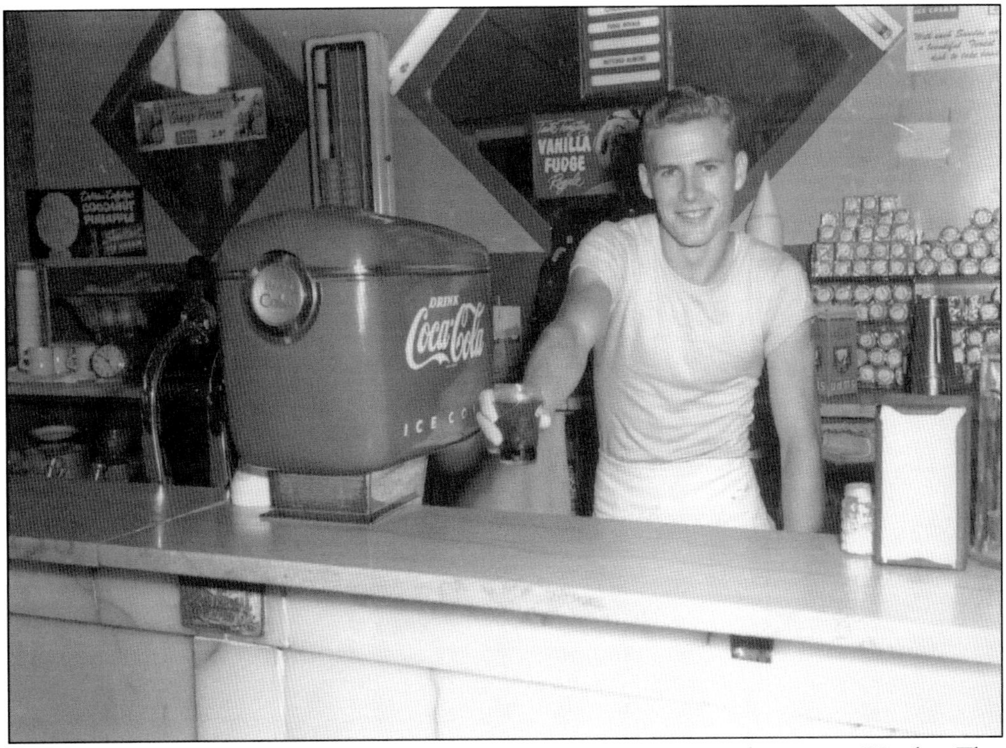

John Bennett was among the last "soda jerks" at City Pharmacy in downtown Winder. This photo was made July 5, 1951. Pharmacist and store owner Haase Arnold closed the soda fountain for good in January, 1952.

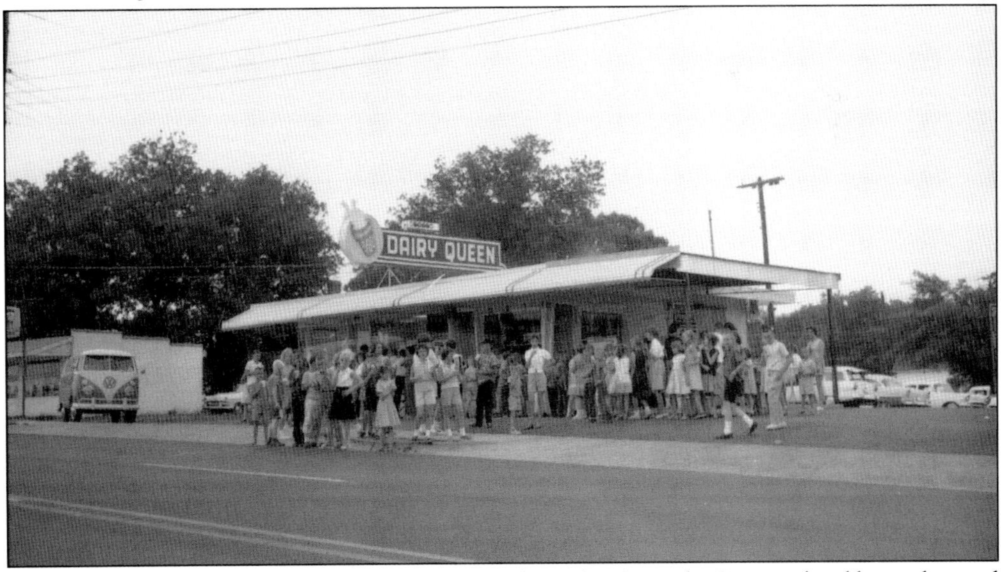

In 1962, children celebrated the end of school with one last bus ride. Seven school buses dropped off children at the Dairy Queen in Winder. The Walters family and their employees were swamped, but happy to sell so much ice cream in such a short time. The business, established in 1956, was Winder's first franchised fast food establishment. It is still in the family, owned today by Robert Walters.

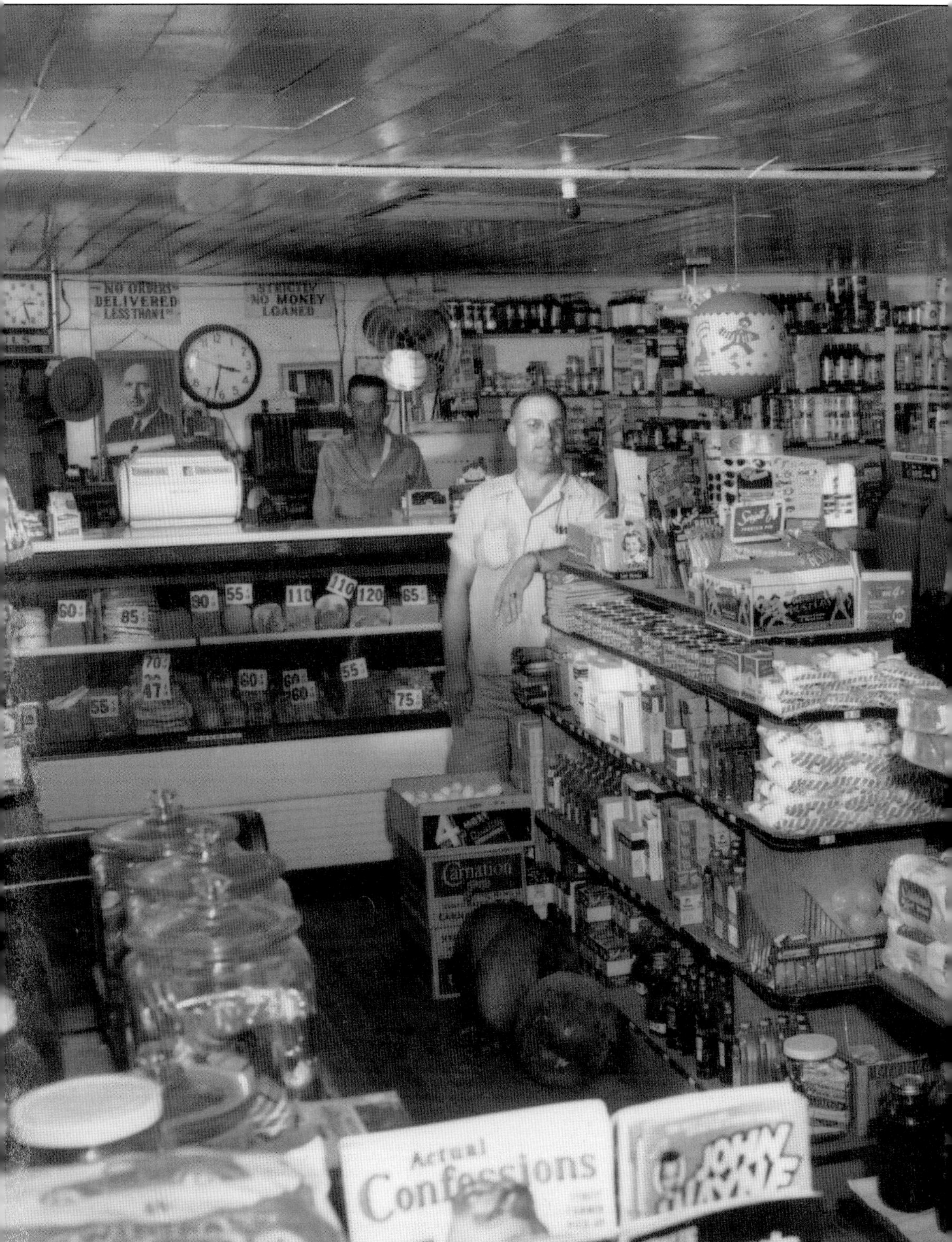
NO ORDERS DELIVERED LESS THAN 1
STRICTLY NO MONEY LOANED
Carnation
Actual Confessions

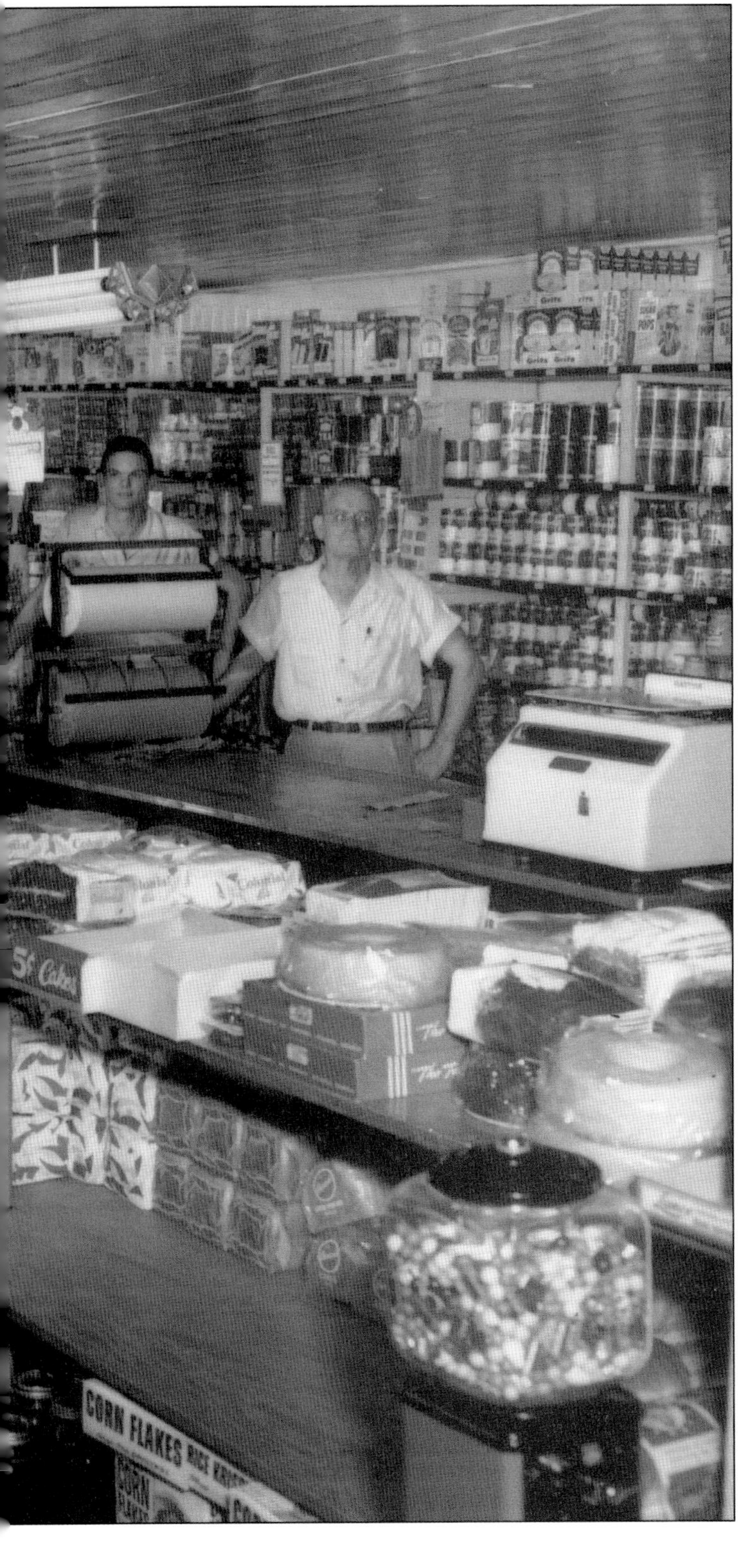

C.L. Sauls operated this store on East Midland Avenue for many years. When he died without any heirs, he willed it to longtime employee Howard Wilburn, who continued its operation well into the 1980s. Shown in the photo, from left to right, are Wilburn, Sauls, Otis R. Wallace, and Carey Sauls. The site of this store is now occupied by an addition to Winder Wesleyan Church. This photo is particularly remarkable for its clarity and depth. You can read the covers of the comic books and magazines in the foreground, as well as the signs on the back wall.

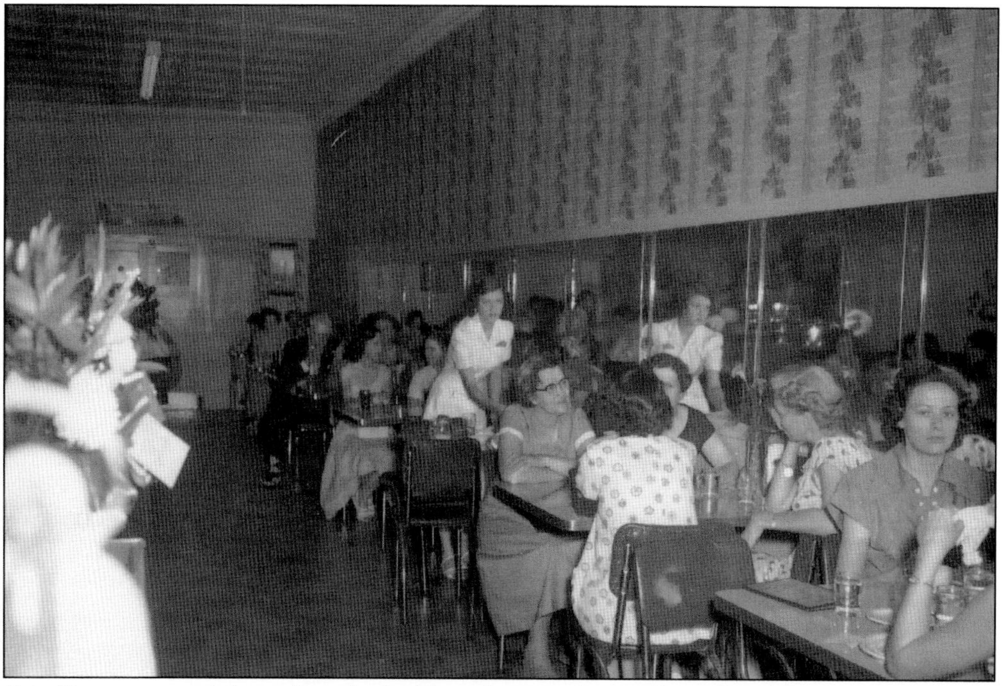

Orin Evans operated this café in the building that now houses Evans Jewel Box on North Broad Street in downtown Winder. The customer in the foreground is Sara Chandler, and the waitress is Nelda Hardy. This photo was made June 30, 1955, during the restaurant's grand opening.

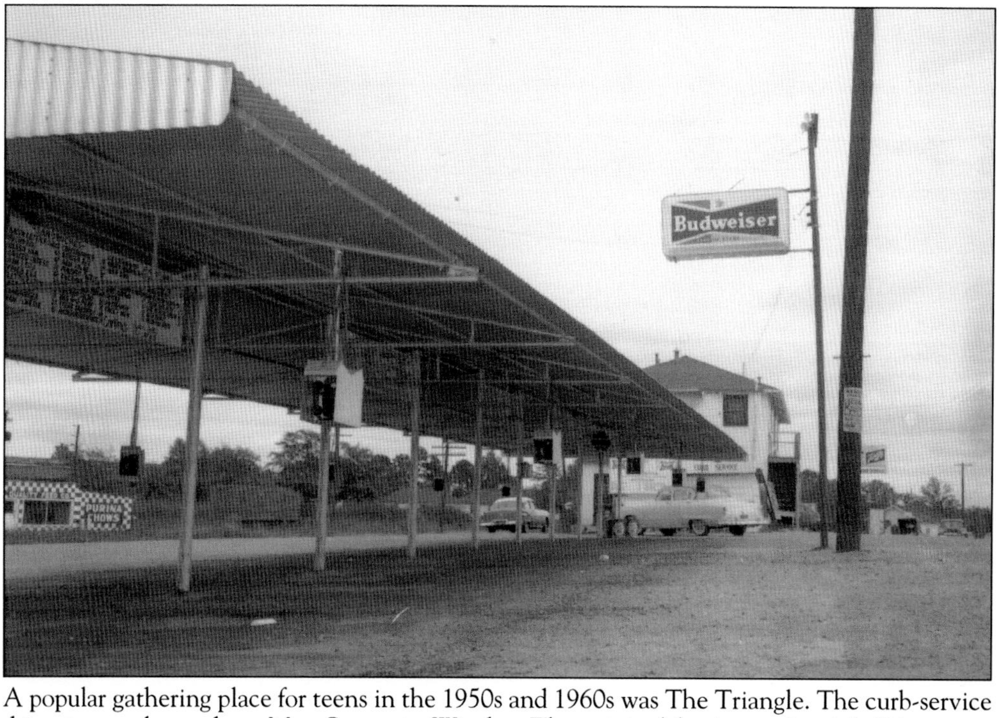

A popular gathering place for teens in the 1950s and 1960s was The Triangle. The curb-service drive-in was located on May Street in Winder. The original business, Austin's Diner, was founded in April 1950 by Mrs. G.L. Austin.

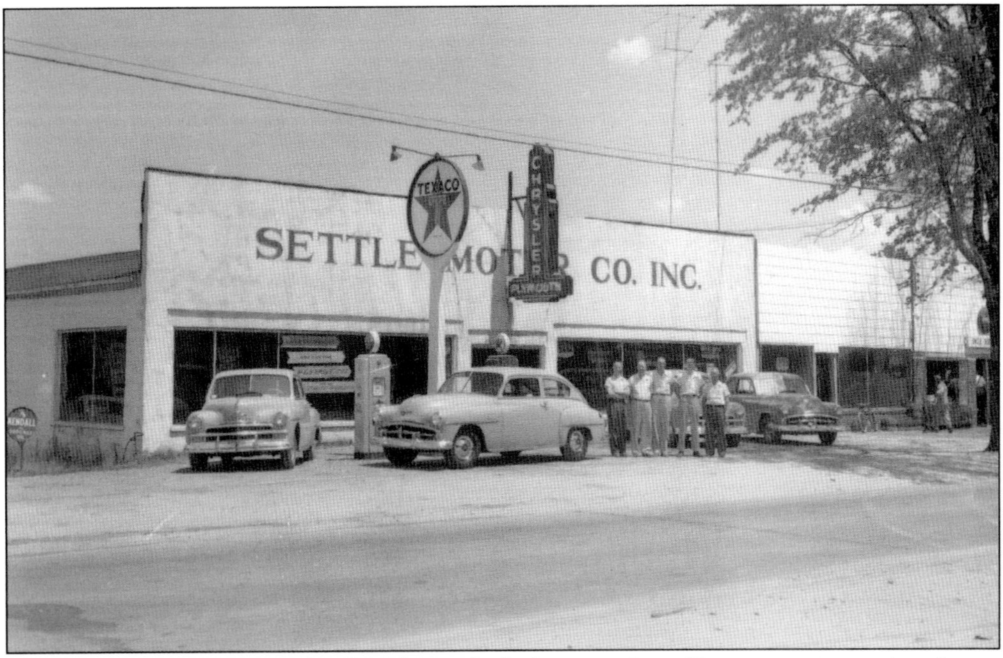

Settle Motor Company, a Chrysler-Plymouth dealer, was also a Texaco service station. It was located on North Broad Street in Winder.

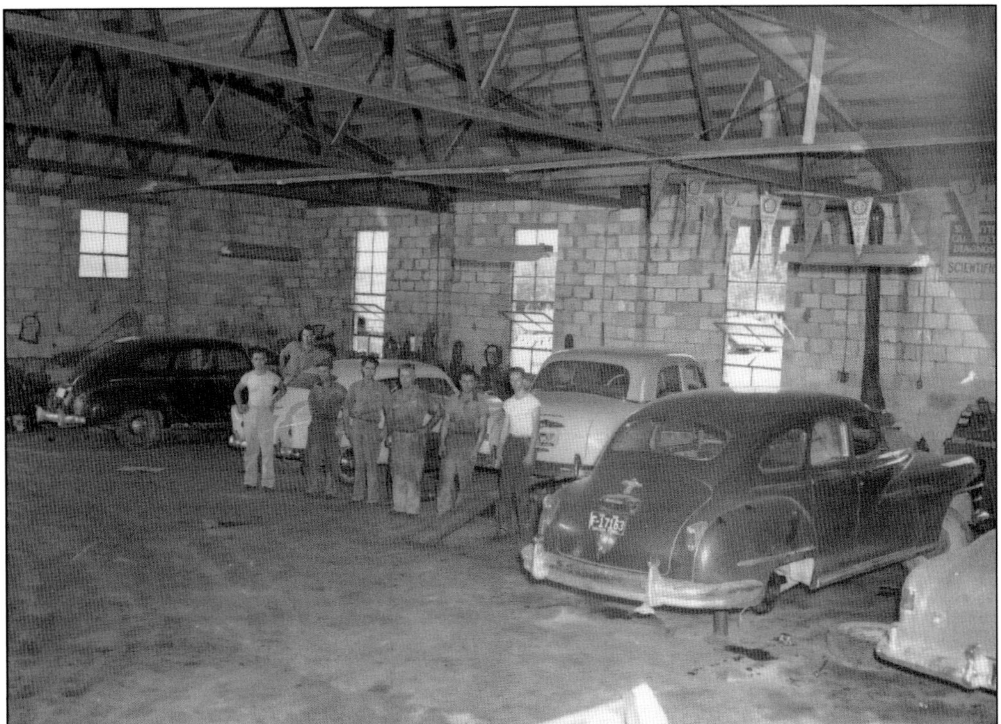

This is a view of the shop area in Settle Motor Company; it is much different from today's computerized automobile repair facilities. In those days mechanics actually repaired automobiles instead of just replacing parts.

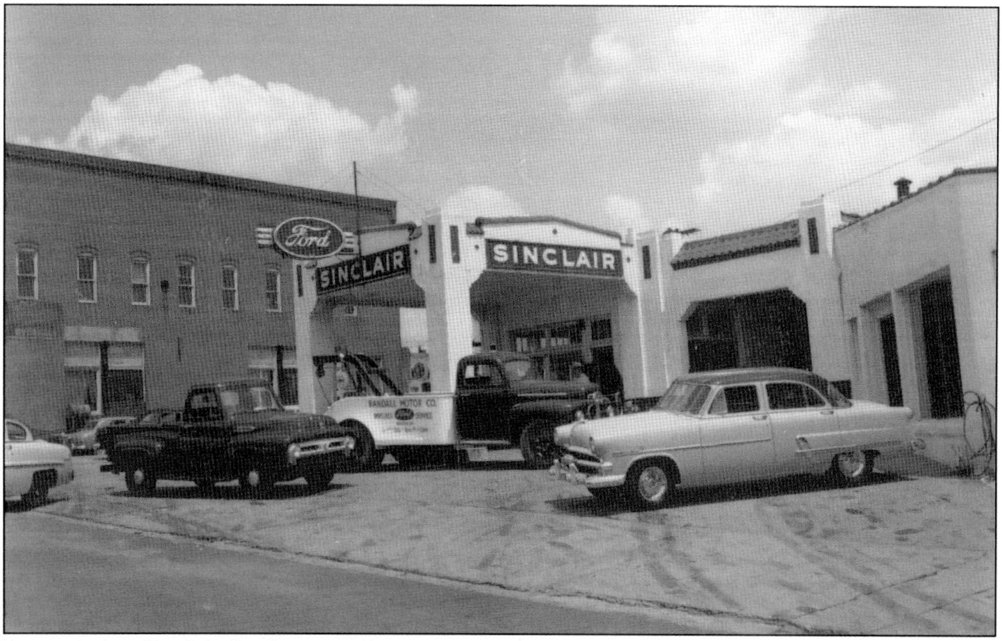

Barrow's first Ford dealership was also a service station. It was located on Broad Street near the old Sharpton Opera House, visible in the background.

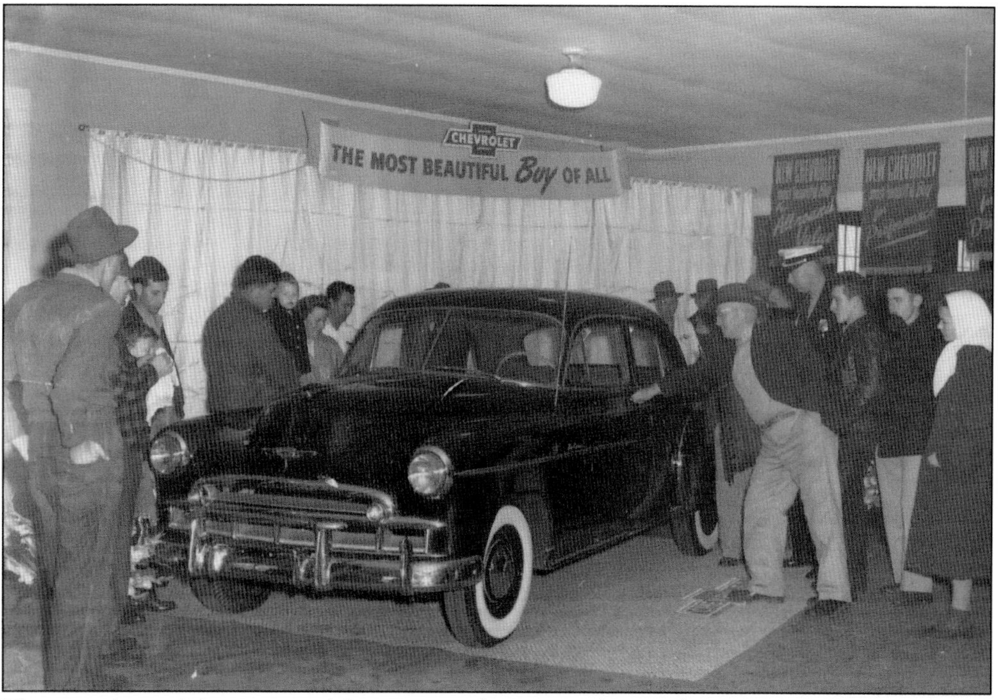

The unveiling of the new model cars was a big event during this period. Folks would flock to showrooms to see the latest changes in style from auto manufacturers. This photo, taken in January 1949, shows a crowd admiring the new Chevrolet. The man leaning over is Than Skinner, who liked this particular new car so much that he bought it. The policeman in the photo is "Tweet" Phillips.

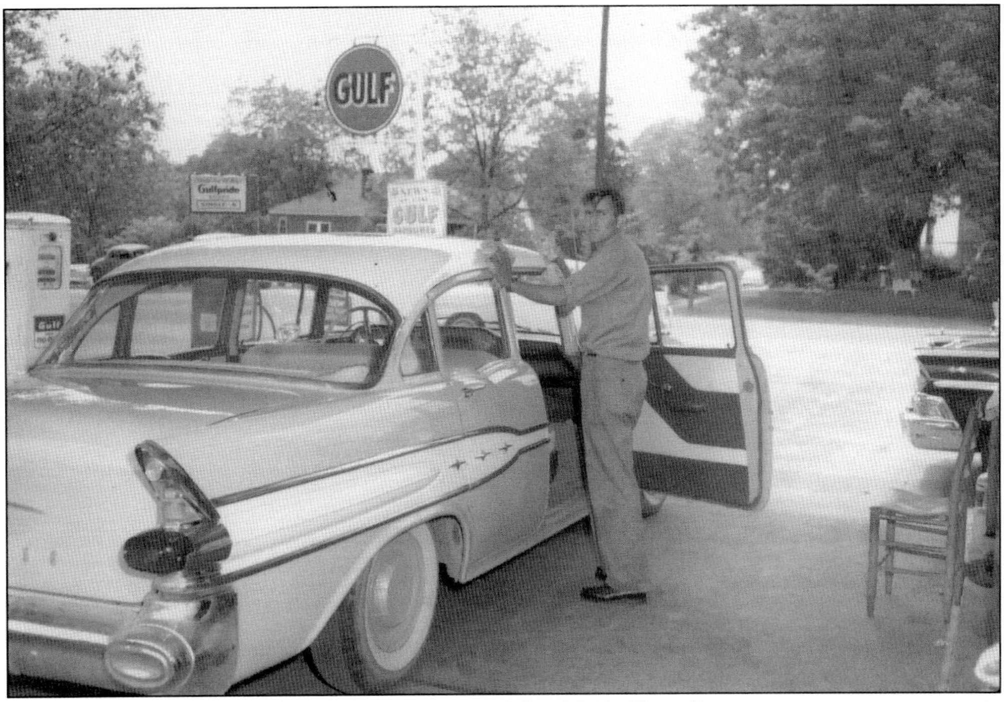

John Partee is pictured at his service station in May 1961. He still operates a service station in the same spot, on West Athens Street across from the old jail. In today's world of self-service convenience stores, he'll still pump your gas and check your oil.

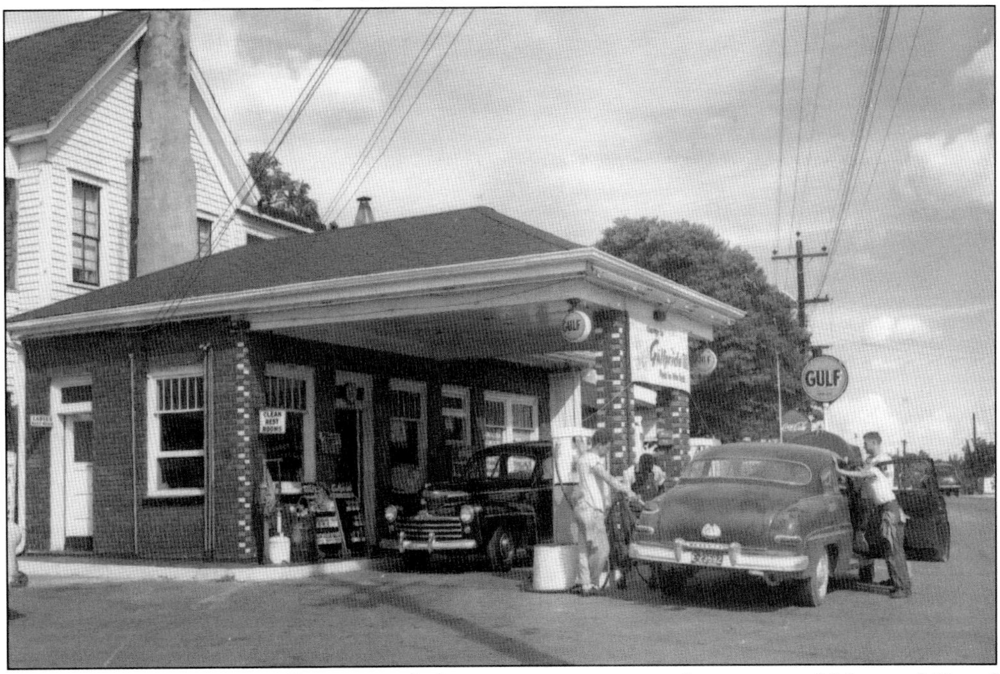

Freddie Wilkerson originally operated this service station at the corner of May and Broad Streets. Velma Reynolds opened a new station on this site in 1948. He sold the station to Jack Patrick in 1970, and that family still operates the "full service" station today.

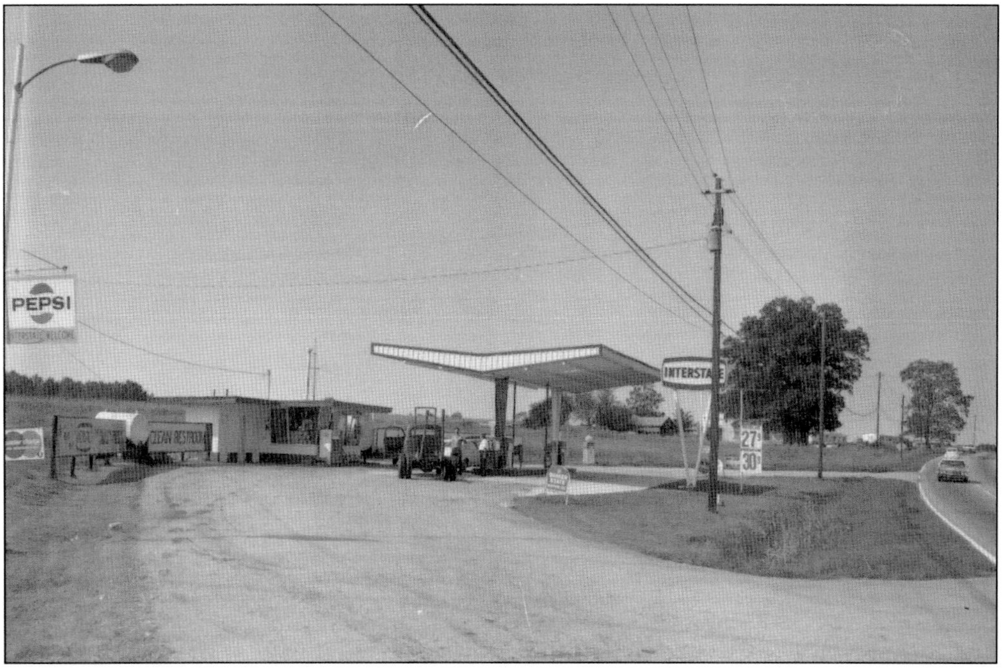

This building still stands on Highway 8 between Winder and Auburn. Note that regular gasoline is priced at 27.9¢ per gallon in this September 1969 photo. The sign at left originally said "clean restrooms," but the "s" has been covered.

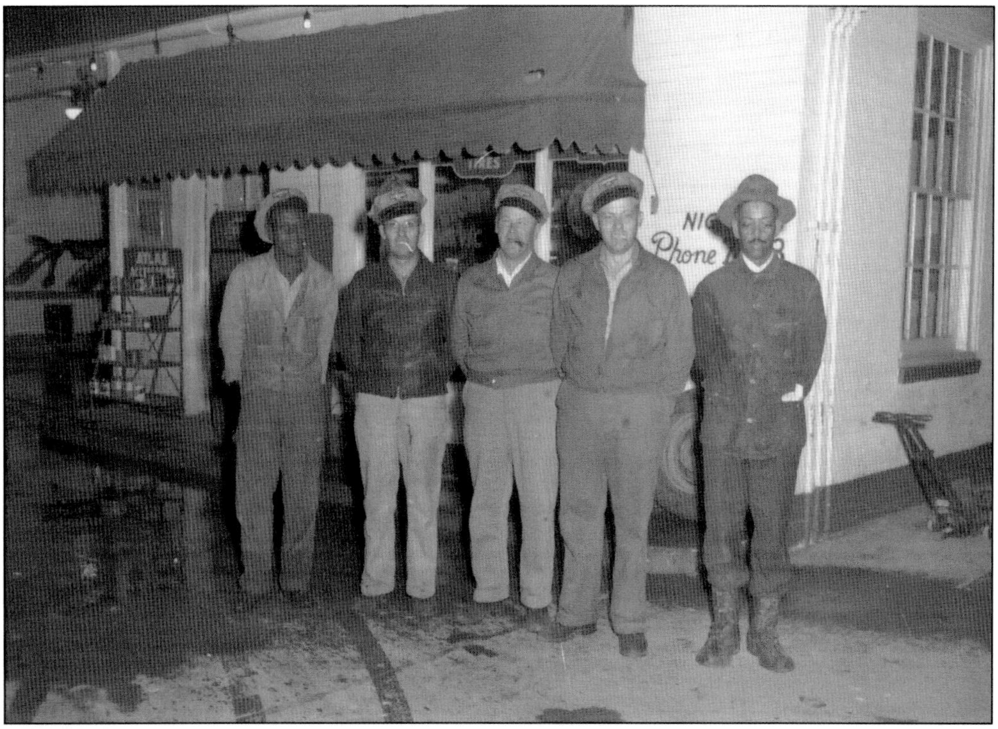

This photo was taken at Broad Street Service Station, which stood next to what was then the Winder Post Office and is now city hall.

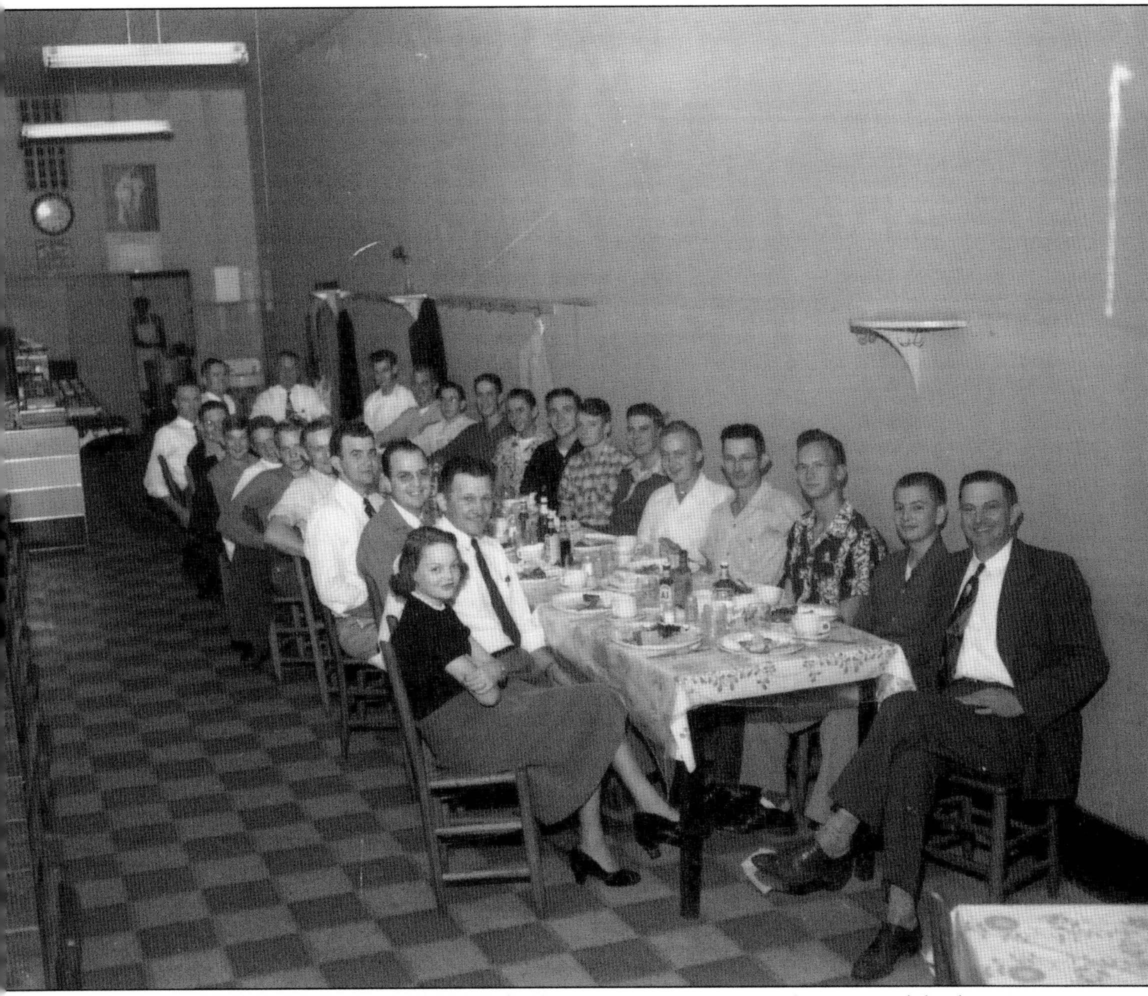

For many young men, working at Massey's food stores was not just a job, it was a life-changing experience. Many of Barrow County's most successful citizens received valuable training in customer service and developed a positive work ethic while working for Herbert Massey and store manager Bozo Bailey. In this photo of a holiday dinner in November 1952, Mr. Massey is at the right front of the table. Next to him is Ambrose Jackson, Marvin Conner, Pete Steed, Carl Healan, Jack Thomas, Paul Marlow, Bobby Lundy, Buddy Ouzts, Jack Chidsey, Max Williams, Mack Haney, and store manager James Randolph "Bozo" Bailey. At the end of the table are Gordon "Poss" Bowen and Ed Segars. Then, from back to front on the left side are Henry Edge, Lee Elrod, Jimmy Patrick, Scott Williamson, Ken Thornton, Ralph Massey, Gifton Thomas, Delmous Venable, Lester Steed, and Mr. Massey's daughter Glenda Massey Brown.

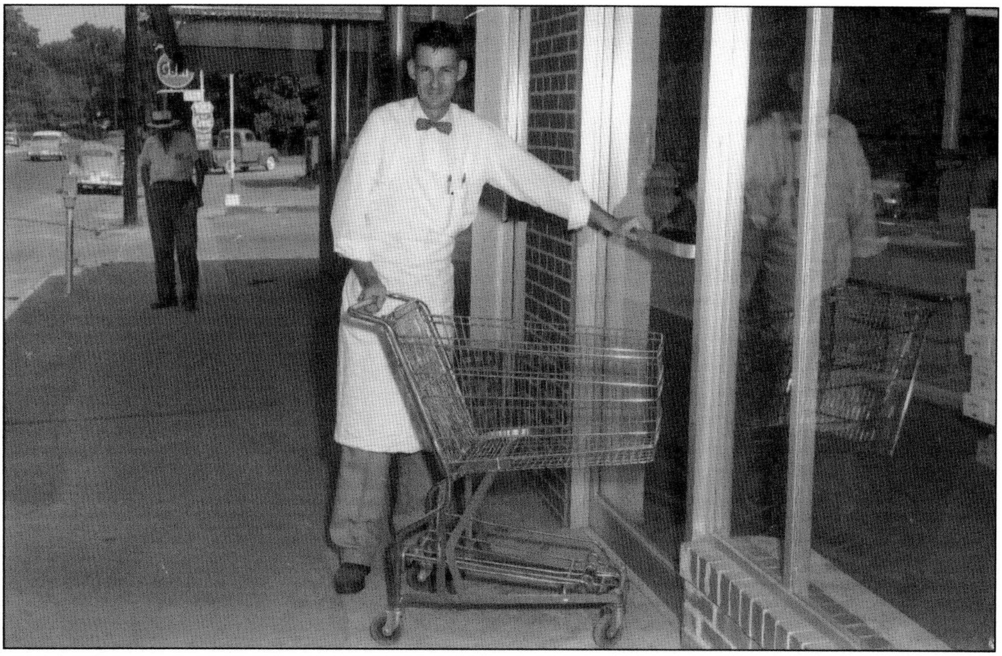

Bozo Bailey is shown entering Massey's Food Store when it was located on West Athens Street, across from the courthouse. "You learned customer service from Bozo," said Winder Mayor Buddy Ouzts. "You had to be polite. We couldn't even sweep while a lady was in an aisle. Bozo said the didn't want us kicking up dust while a lady was trying to shop." This photo was made in June 1958.

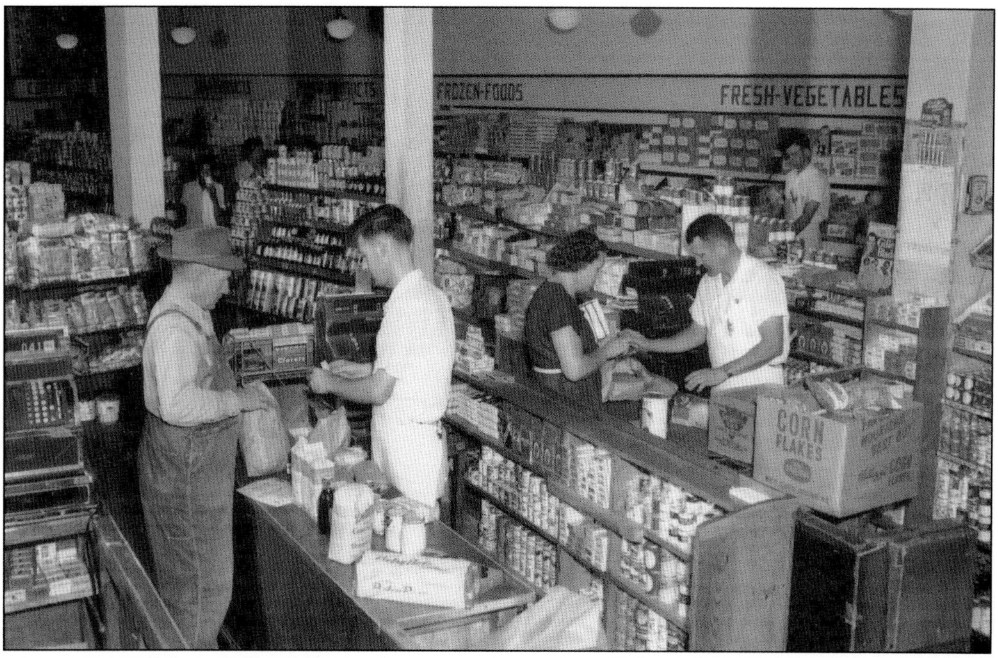

This view is of Massey's Food Store when it was located on Jackson Street in downtown Winder. Bozo Bailey is helping the customer on the left, while Lester Steed waits on the woman at right. This photo was made in July 1952.

Three

Working Life

When Stell and Kilgore began photographing Barrow County, most of the jobs were at Sachem Mills or at the numerous clothing manufacturing plants in the county. Their images capture memories of those long-gone workplaces, as well as some of the industries that ultimately replaced them.

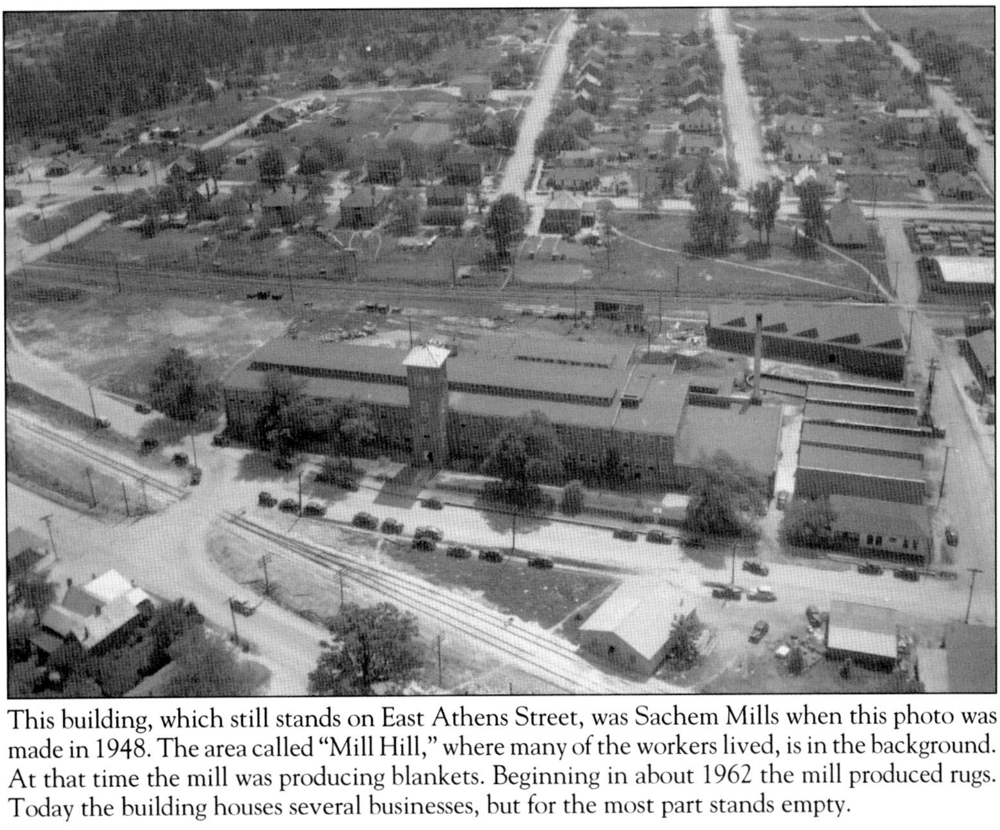

This building, which still stands on East Athens Street, was Sachem Mills when this photo was made in 1948. The area called "Mill Hill," where many of the workers lived, is in the background. At that time the mill was producing blankets. Beginning in about 1962 the mill produced rugs. Today the building houses several businesses, but for the most part stands empty.

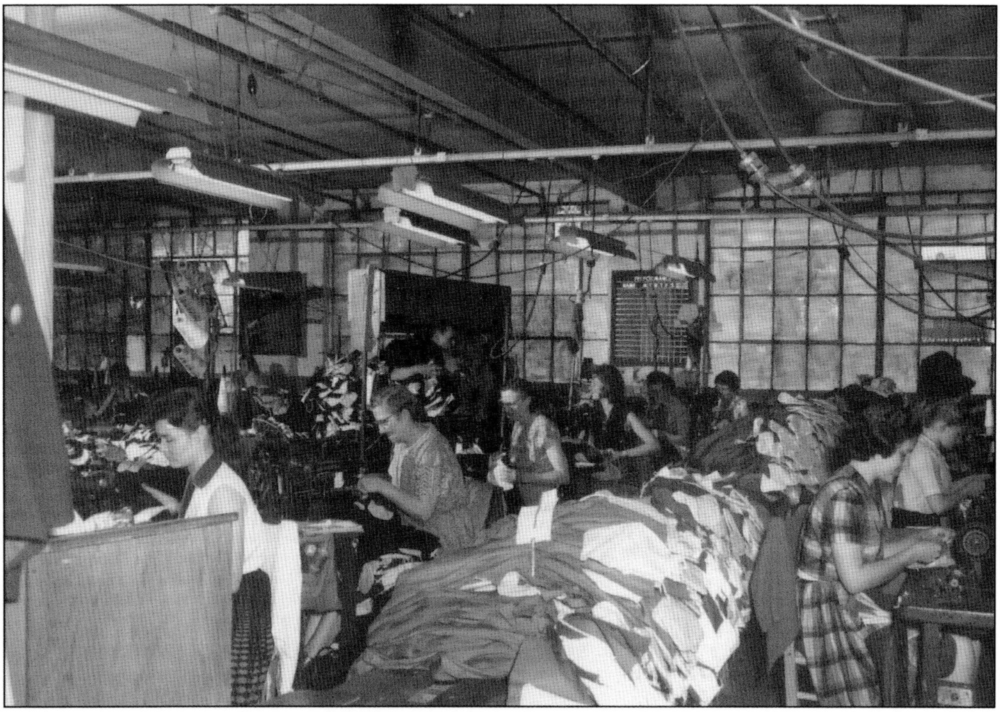

These women are shown sewing pants at Carwood in 1961. The photo gives a good view of the inside of the plant and shows the intensity of the workers at their machines.

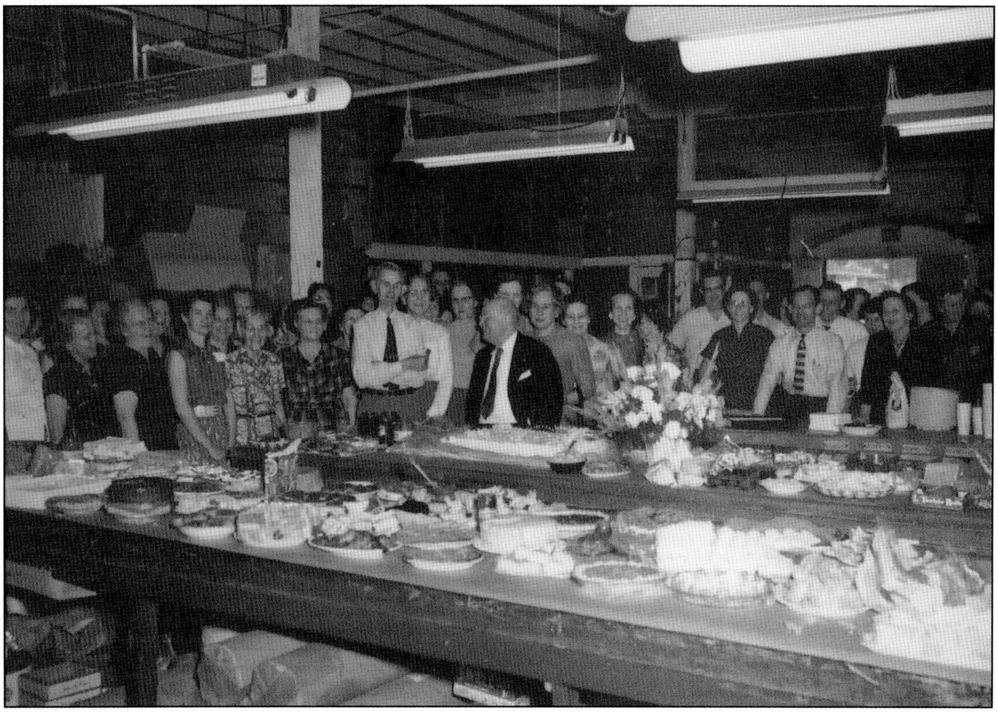

In March 1955, the Bellgrade Manufacturing Company threw a birthday party for "Uncle Deb" Wilkins and the employees brought covered dishes.

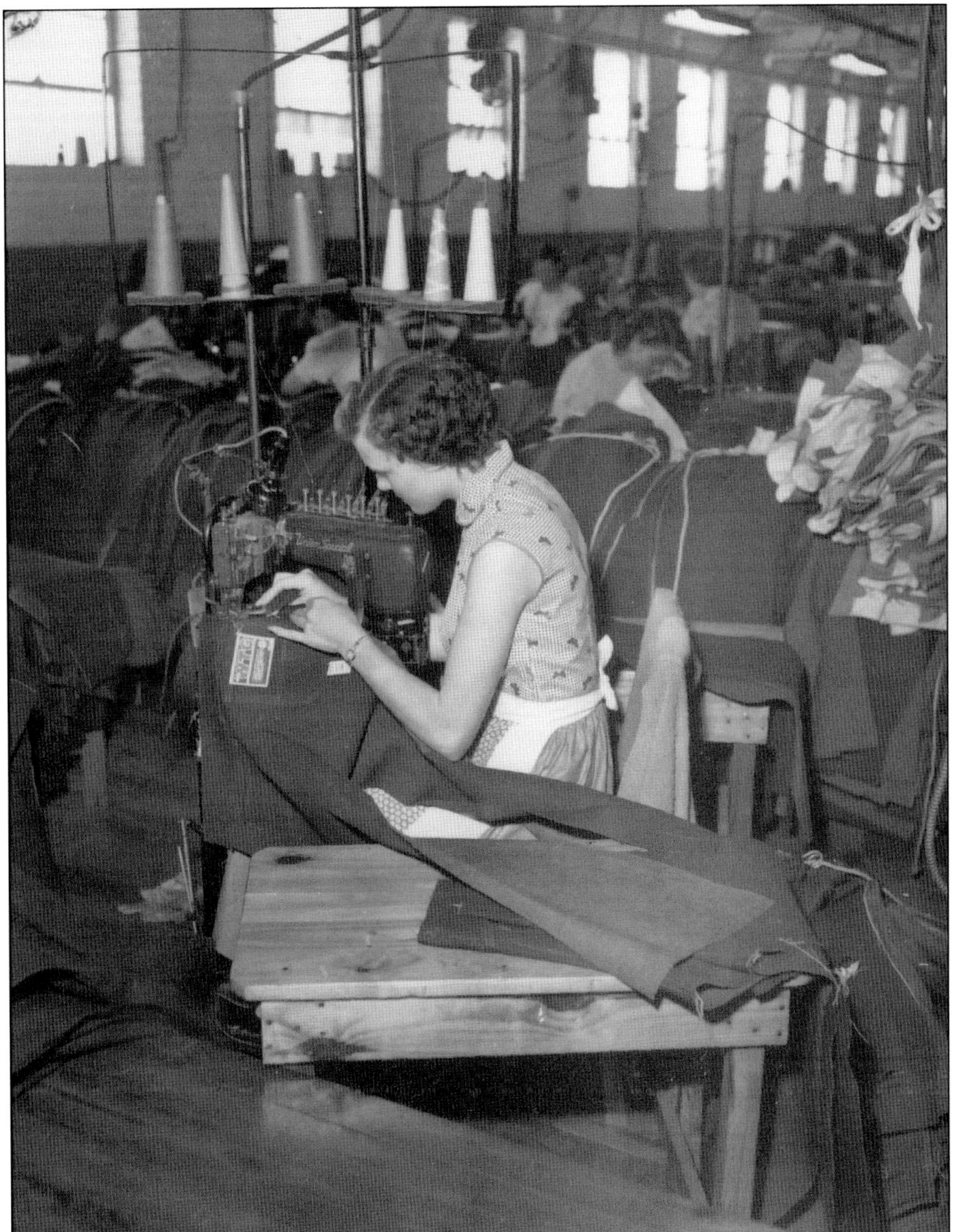

This young woman is shown sewing dungarees at the Carwood Manufacturing Company in March 1953. Work in "the plants" was hard, and the pay was not good, but it put a lot of food on Barrow County tables.

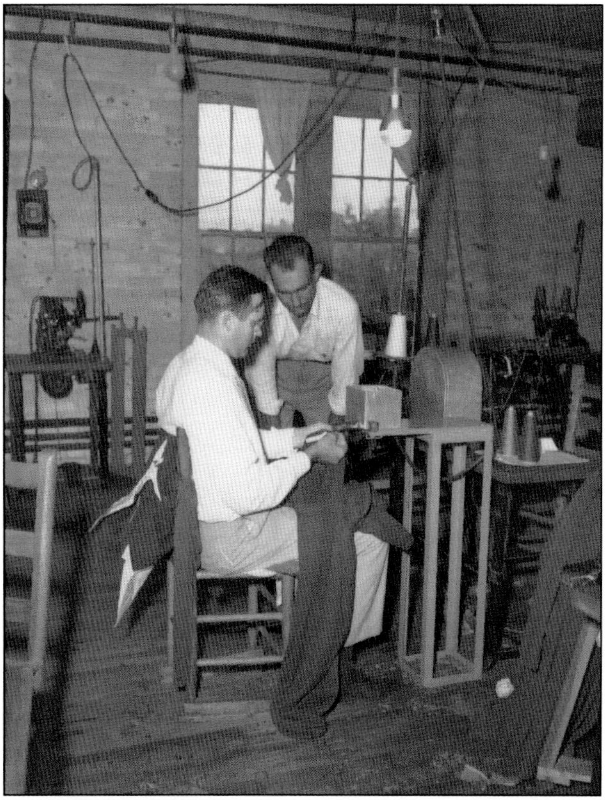

Many of the sewing plants made their own modifications to equipment, and sometimes invented new parts for them. The Stell-Kilgore files contain numerous photos of machinery parts that may have been made for patent applications or for protection against the copying of ideas. Here J.D. Withers of R&R Manufacturing in Auburn is shown working on a machine while an employee looks on.

This view of Carwood Manufacturing on East Athens Street was made just after "quitting time" on May 27, 1952. Many people recall meeting their parents on Friday, which was payday, to go shopping.

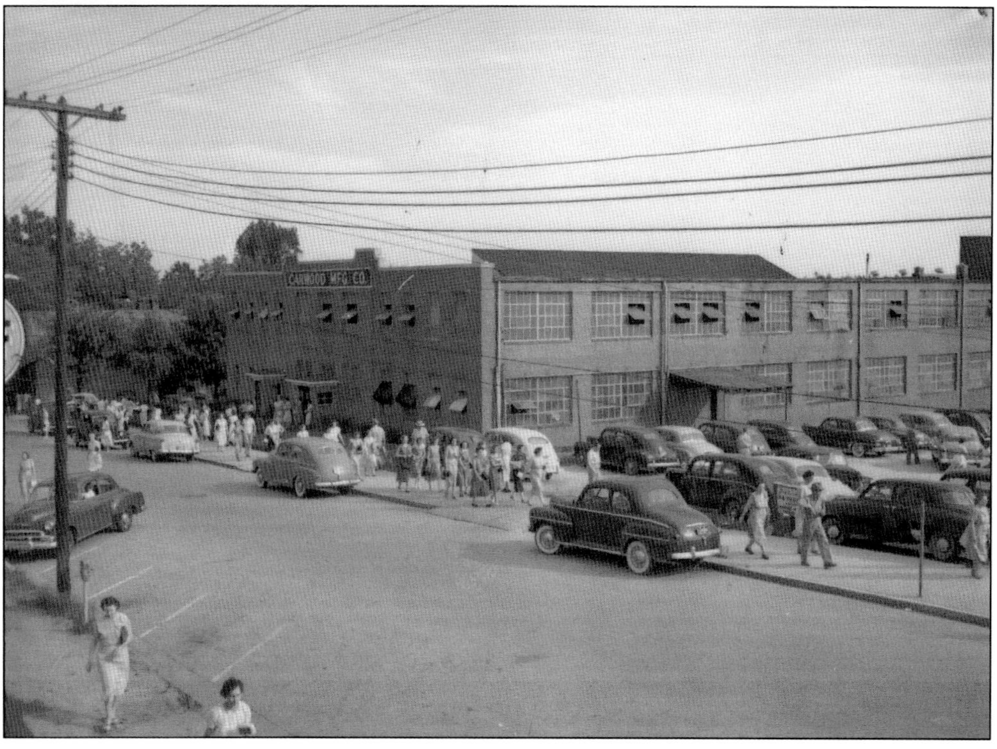

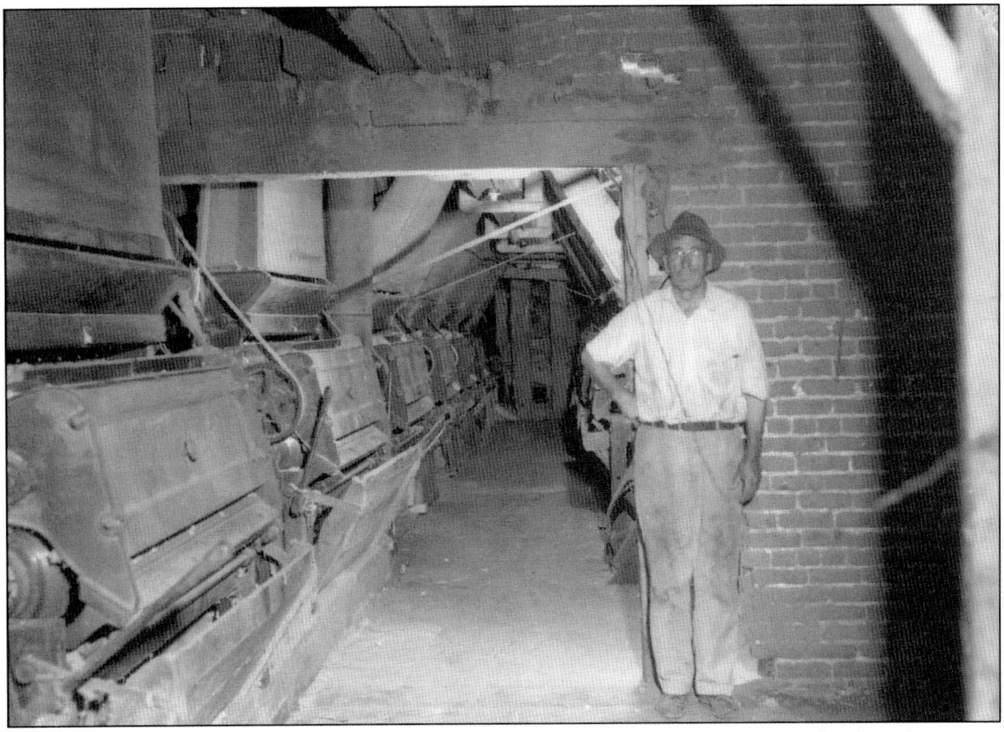

This is a view of the machinery used to crush cottonseed for oil, made inside the Thompson Oil Company on East Athens Street. Most of the buildings in that complex were burned or demolished. The city of Winder now owns the property.

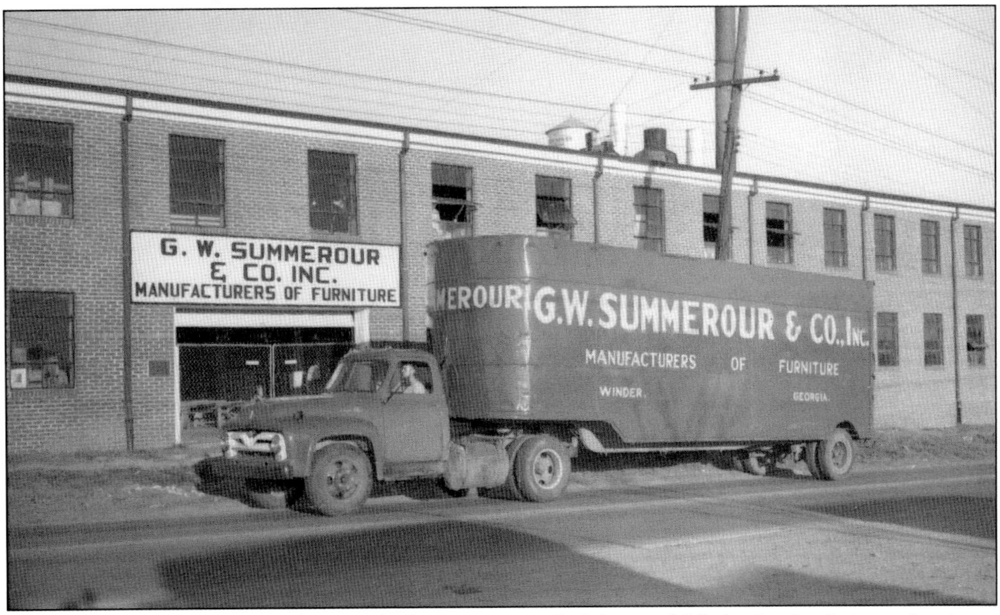

Winder, known for years as the "work clothing capitol of the world," also had a thriving furniture manufacturing industry during the 1940s and 1950s. G.W. Summerour & Company was located on May Street at the present location of Zaxby's. Another local manufacturer was the National Furniture Company.

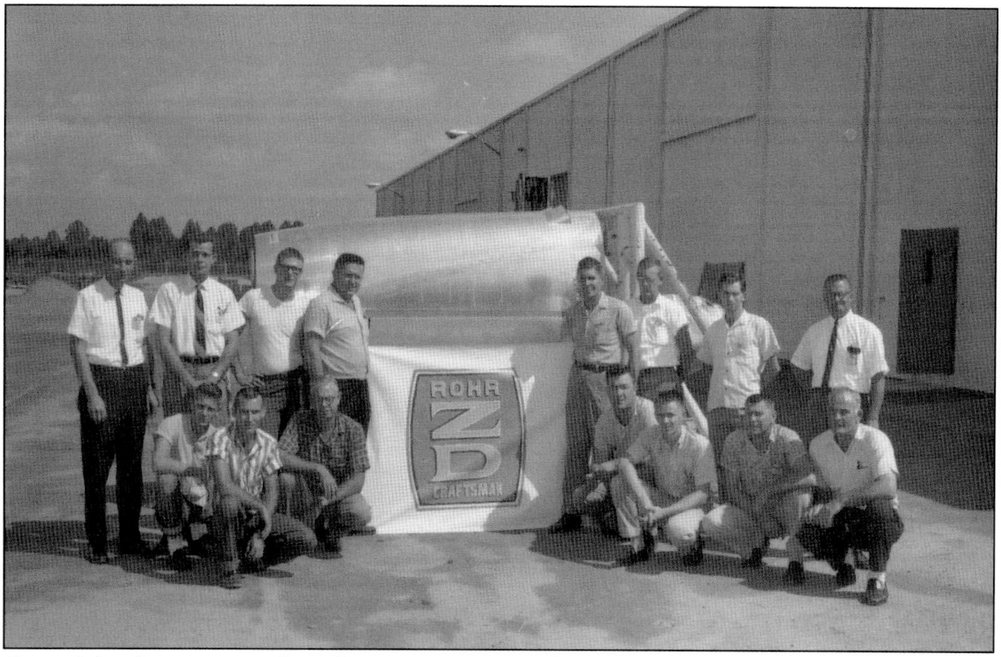

One of the first non-textile industries to move to Barrow was the Rohr Aircraft Company, which built engine cowlings for the Lockheed plant in Marietta, GA. These employees were part of a "zero defects" quality control program at the plant. They are, from left to right, as follows: (kneeling) Robert Warren, Eugene Nash, "Hoss" Craft, Royce Sims, unidentified, Guy Cooper, and Ernest Adams; (standing) Bruce Olson, Lynwood Callahan, Larry Holland, Ronnie Deaton, Billy Elder, Bill McLendon, Billy Simmons, and Dick Mingus.

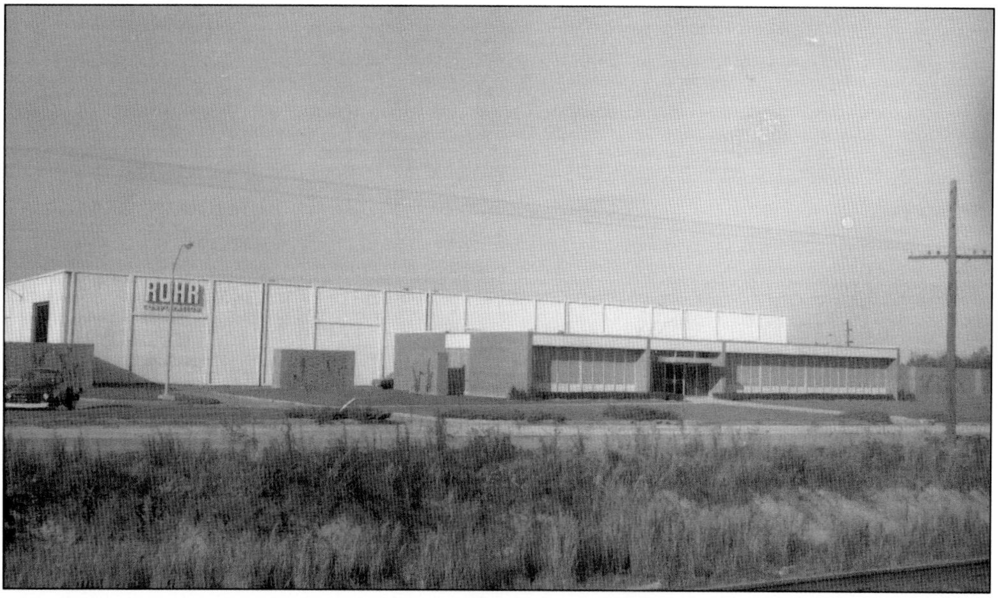

The Rohr Company moved into this building at the Barrow County Airport in 1957. It was later used to manufacture rapid rail cars for the San Francisco commuter rail lines. Today the complex houses the Thrall Car Manufacturing Company, which builds rolling stock for railroads.

Four

FROM THE SKY

Some of the most important images in the Stell-Kilgore files are aerial photos, because they graphically illustrate the tremendous changes the county has seen during the last half-century. Apparently Stell and Kilgore loved to fly, and were experts at the difficult art of capturing vibrant, clear images from the air.

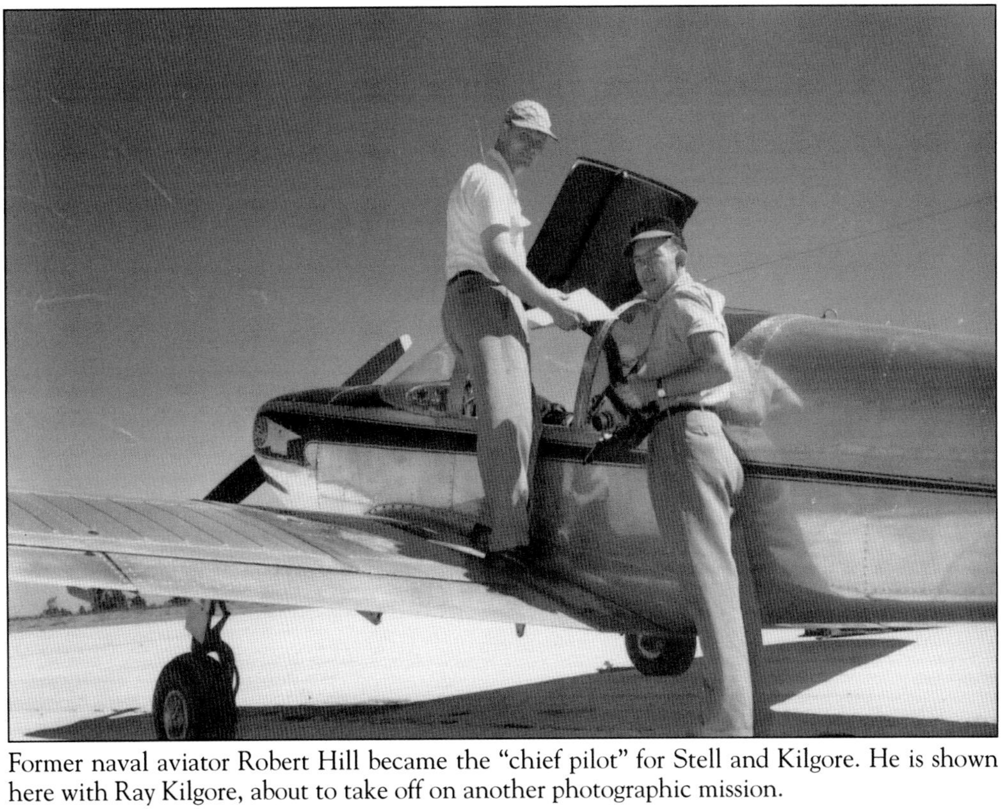

Former naval aviator Robert Hill became the "chief pilot" for Stell and Kilgore. He is shown here with Ray Kilgore, about to take off on another photographic mission.

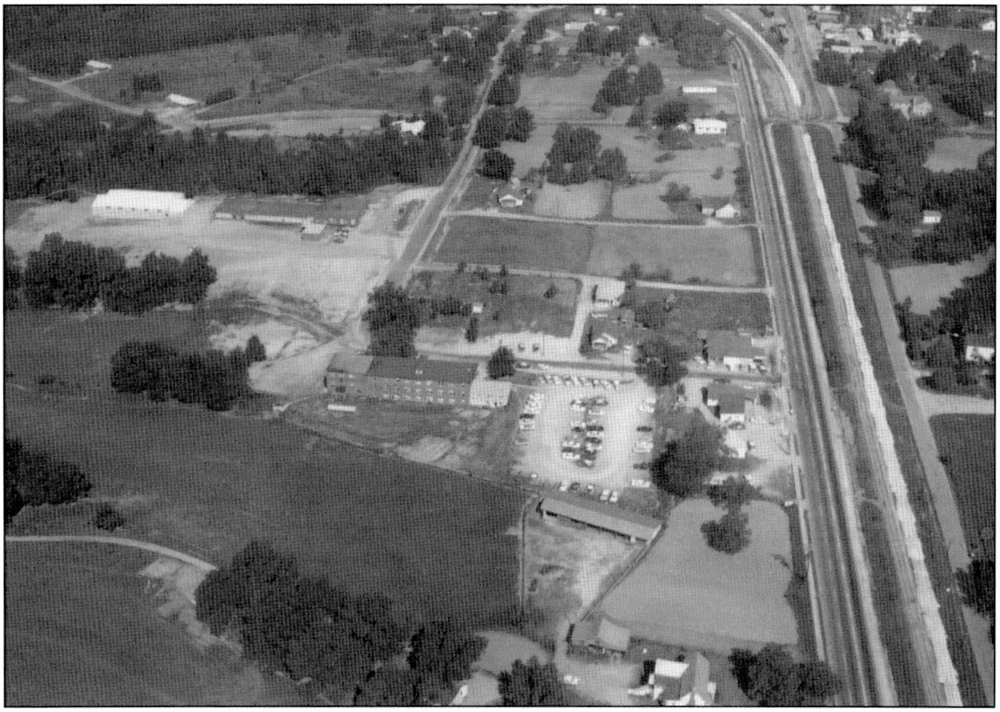

This view is looking west over Auburn in June 1964. Near the center of the picture is the old Auburn School. On the right is Highway 29 and the Seaboard Railway tracks. Downtown Auburn is in the background, upper right. Note that the area on the left of Highway 29 is undeveloped.

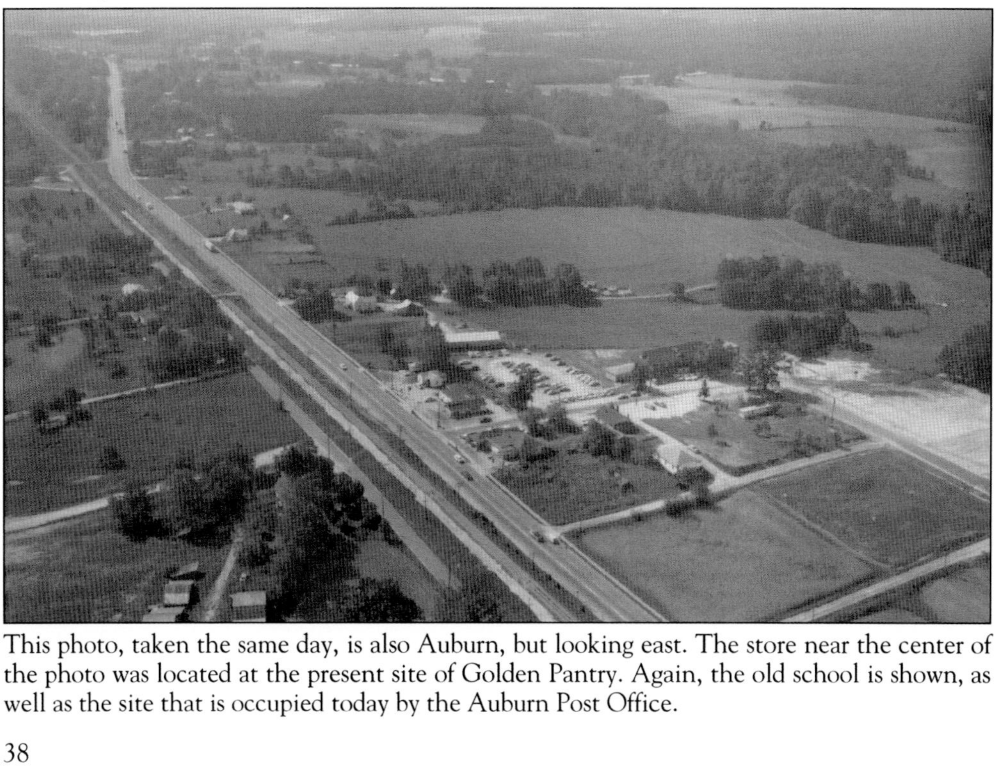

This photo, taken the same day, is also Auburn, but looking east. The store near the center of the photo was located at the present site of Golden Pantry. Again, the old school is shown, as well as the site that is occupied today by the Auburn Post Office.

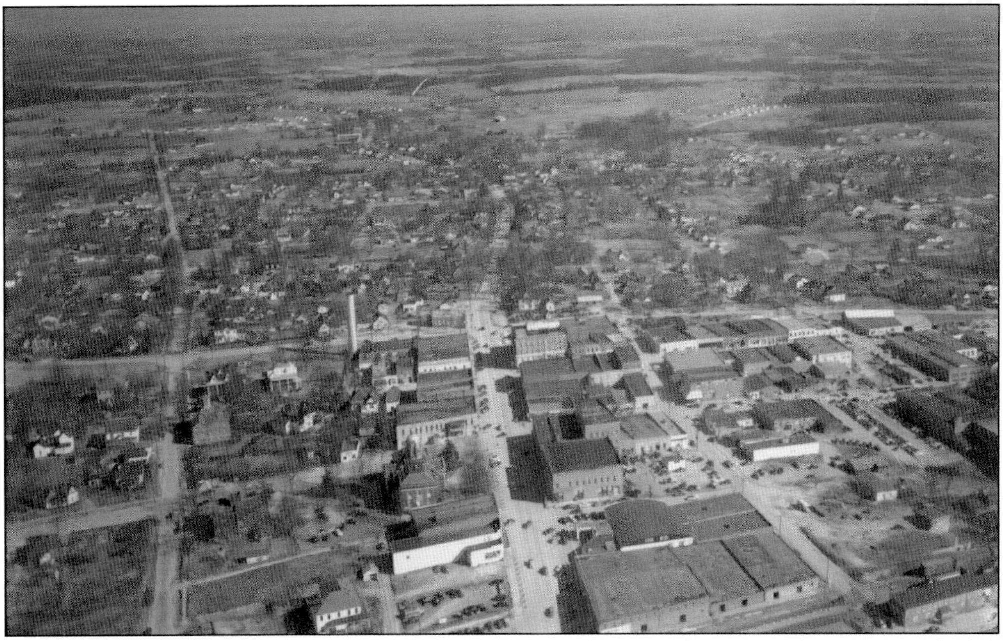

This photo of downtown Winder was made in 1951, looking north, up Broad Street. On the left is the Barrow County Courthouse. The large, tube-shaped structure is a water tank that once stood on Midland Avenue. Just to the right of that is the Winder Post Office, which is now the city hall. The present post office site contains a large white house.

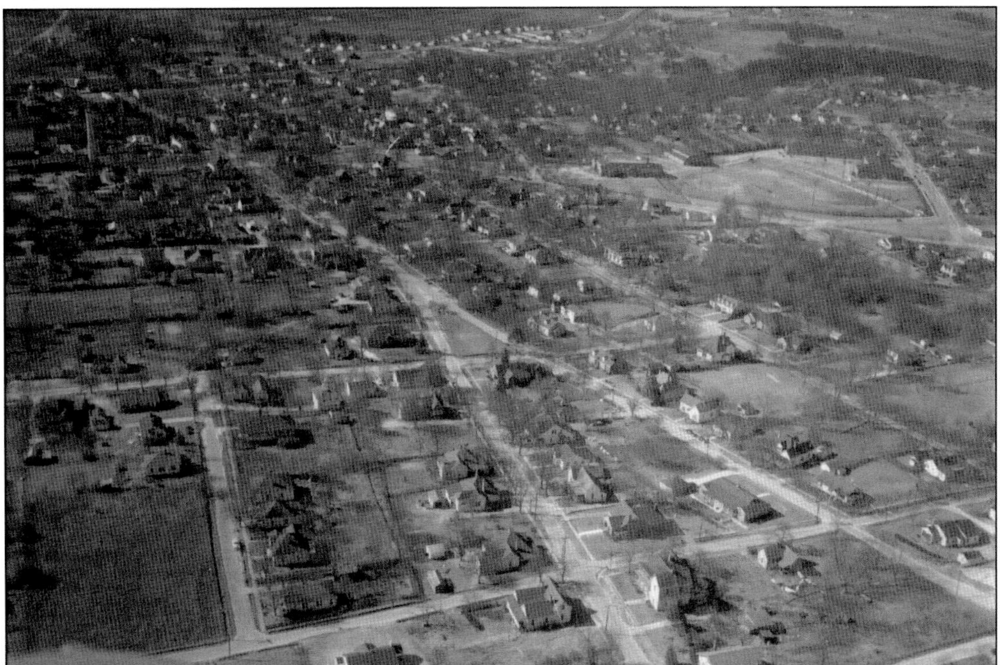

This photo, taken on March 9, 1951, is looking south down Woodlawn Avenue. The triangle-shaped park area and most of the houses shown are still there. The old Winder School and gymnasium are in the upper right of the photo.

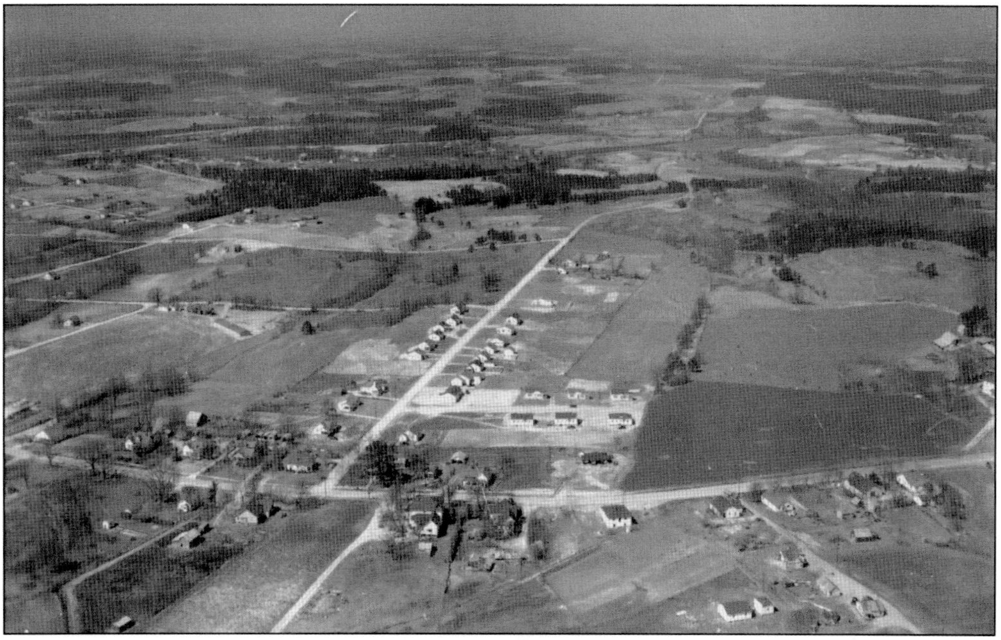

It is difficult to determine what this area is because it has changed so much since 1951. The street going left to right in the photo is North Broad. The street going off into the distance is Buena Vista. The present site of the Winder First United Methodist Church is the field on the right. Note that the street in the bottom of the photo is not paved.

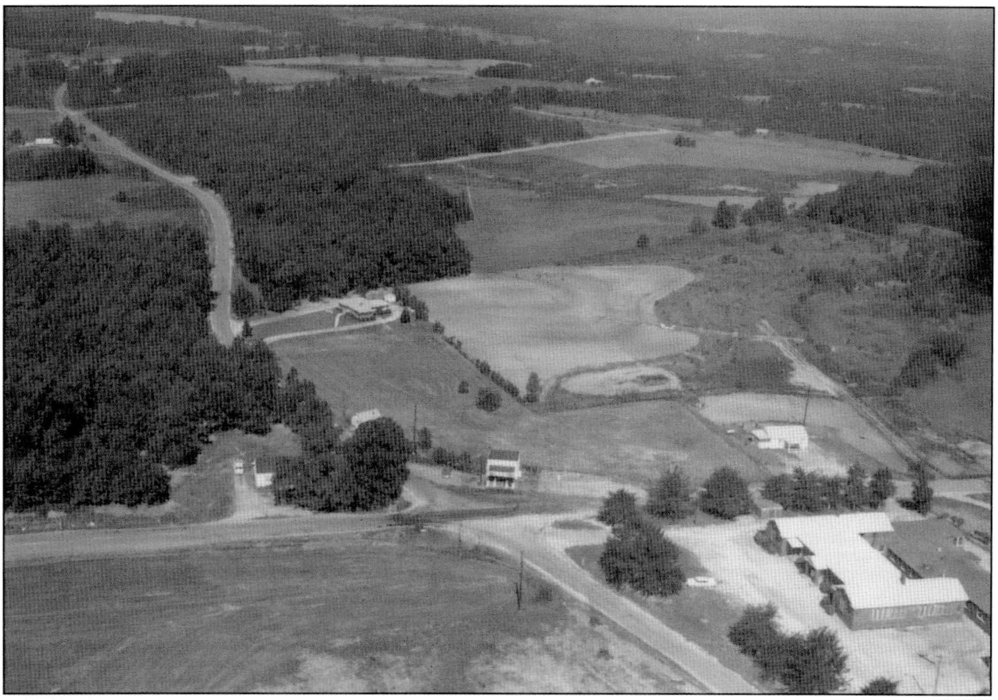

This photo, made in June 1964, shows County Line School at the lower right, and the store that was then operated by Brannon Holder. Auburn-County Line Road is visible going off into the distance.

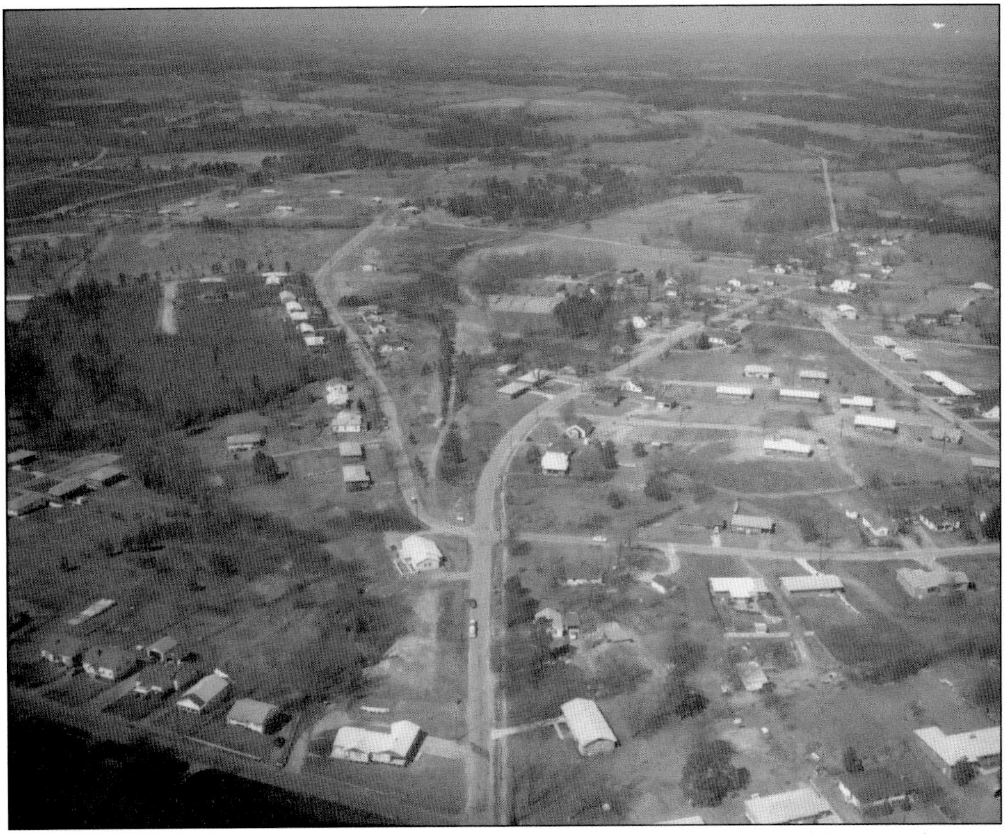

Most folks today do not realize that the area called North Winder is a subdivision that was developed by J.W. Maynard, who had a huge impact on Winder and Barrow County. This photo, made in March 1961, shows the intersection of Midland and Fifth Avenues. The first house in phase one of North Winder is the Geiger home, the first brick home on the left on Fifth Avenue.

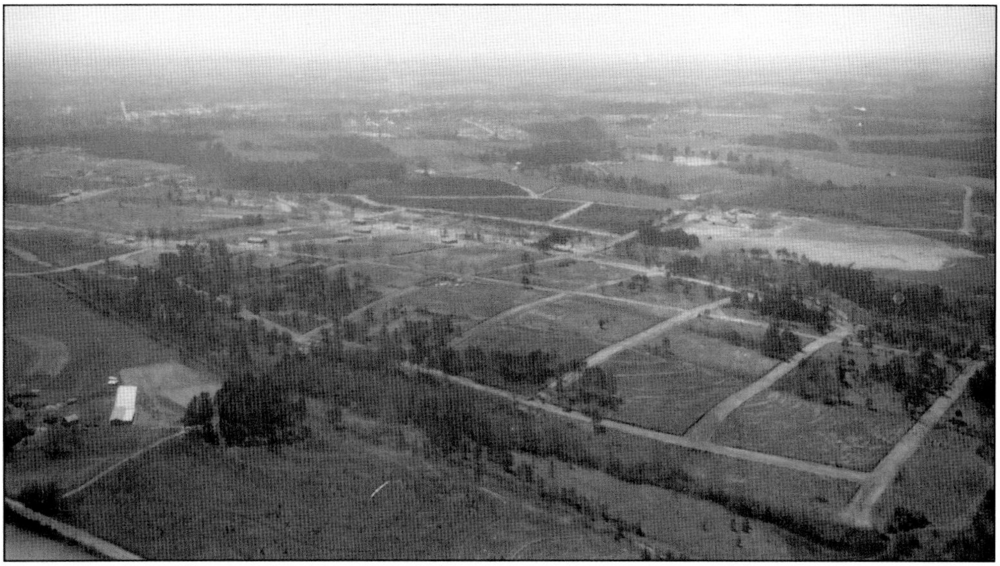

This photo, also made in the spring of 1961, shows the newly cut streets in North Winder. The present location of Winder-Barrow High School is in the middle left of the picture. The subdivision, which ultimately boasted over 1,000 homes, is still the largest subdivision in Barrow County. It was developed in 12 phases over almost 2 decades. H.L. Dunahoo was responsible for the layout and design of the early phases. Upon his death in an automobile accident in 1963, his son, Terry Dunahoo, took over the project. At the time, the younger Dunahoo was a sophomore at Georgia Tech.

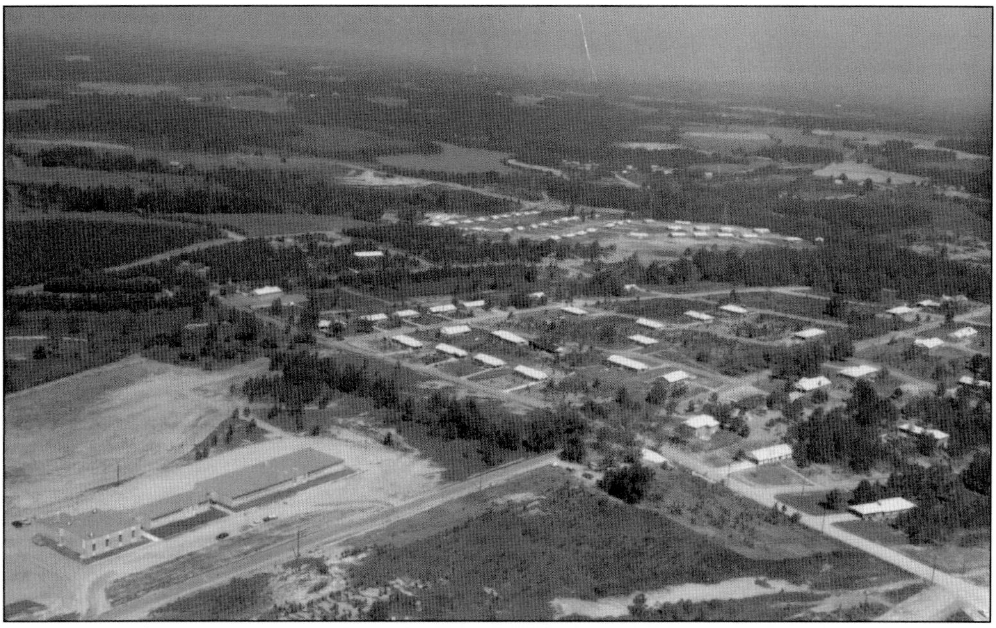

J.W. Maynard was a visionary who did in the 1960s what planners say should be done today. His development included businesses (Holly Hill Mall), multi-family dwellings (apartments behind the mall), and single-family housing. He also reserved a site for Winder-Barrow High School. This view, taken in June 1964, shows the school before the gymnasium or athletic fields were built.

Five

SCHOOL DAYS

Stell and Kilgore served as the "school photographers" in Barrow County for many years. In their files are group photos of almost every class at Winder Grammar School, shots made for school annuals, athletic and social events, as well as photos commissioned by the board of education.

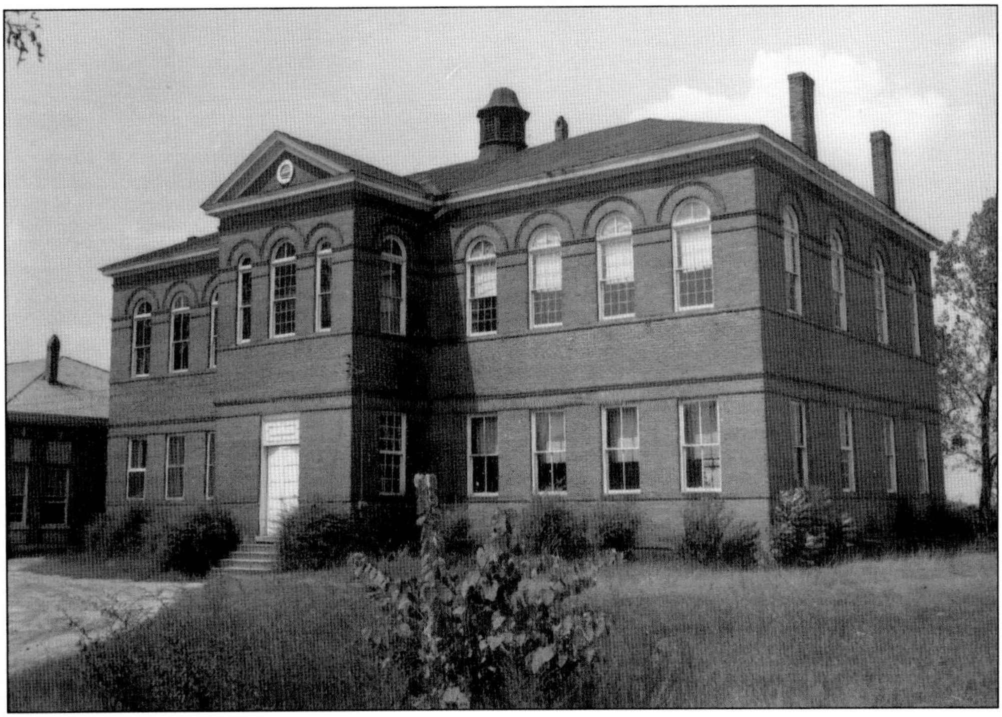

This photo of the old Statham School, taken in August 1953, was one of a series of interior and exterior shots of the building taken for the school board. The photos were made to document the poor condition of the building in an effort to save it; ultimately, it was demolished.

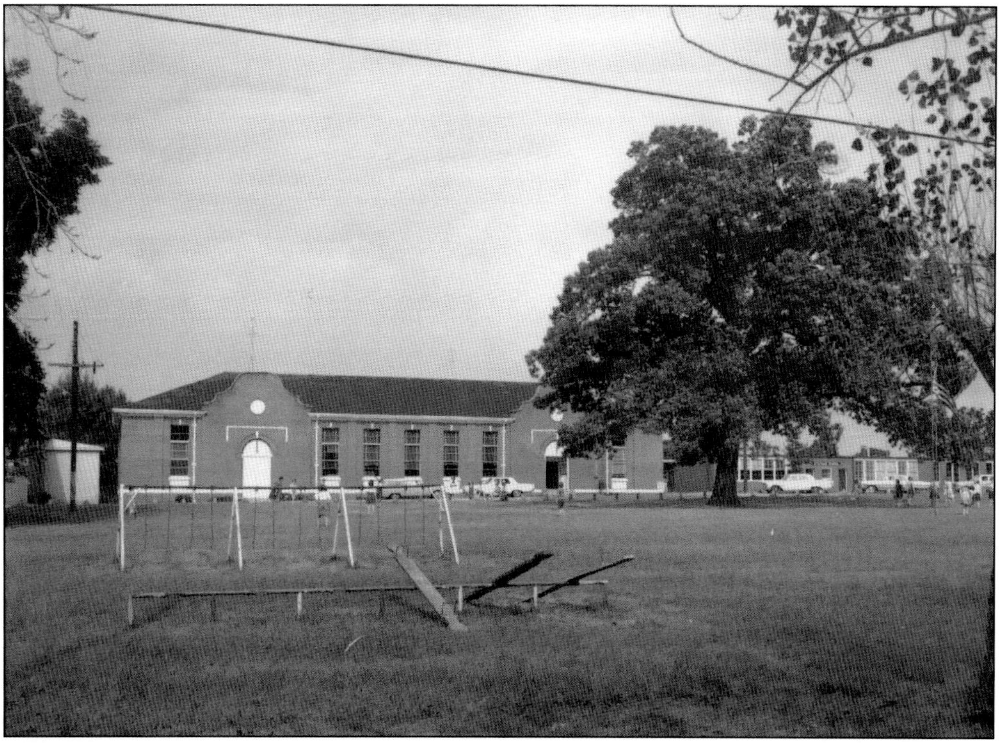

The school board needed photographs of each of the schools in 1966, so Stell and Kilgore made the tour. This photograph is of the Statham School.

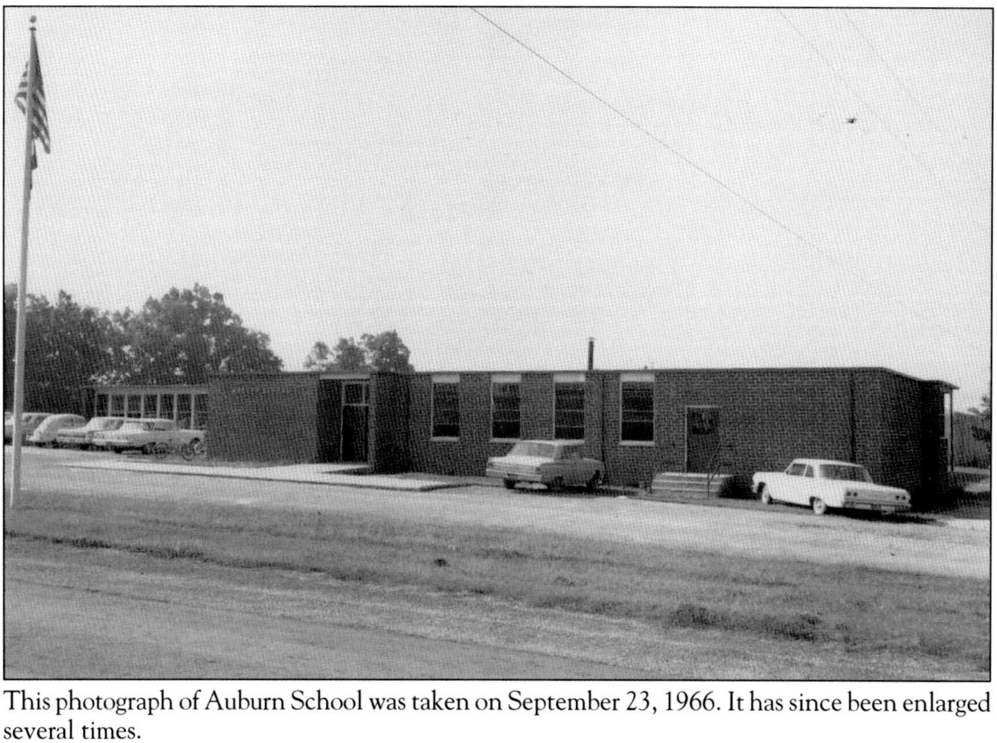

This photograph of Auburn School was taken on September 23, 1966. It has since been enlarged several times.

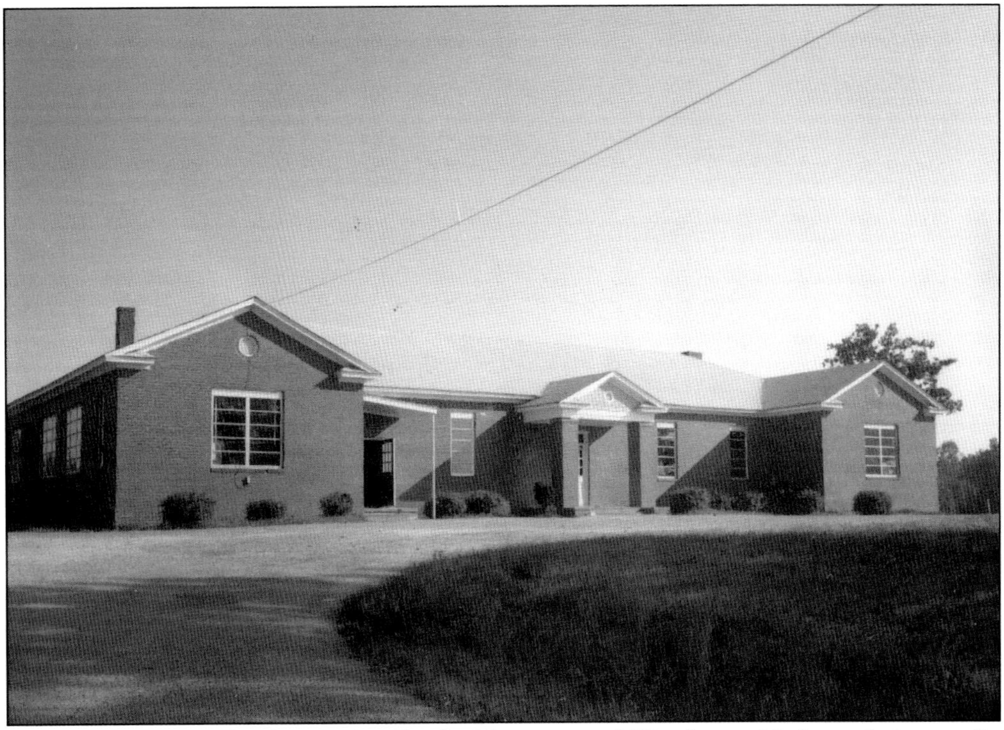

This is Matthews School in 1966. The building, west of Winder on Highway 8, is now St. Matthews Catholic Church.

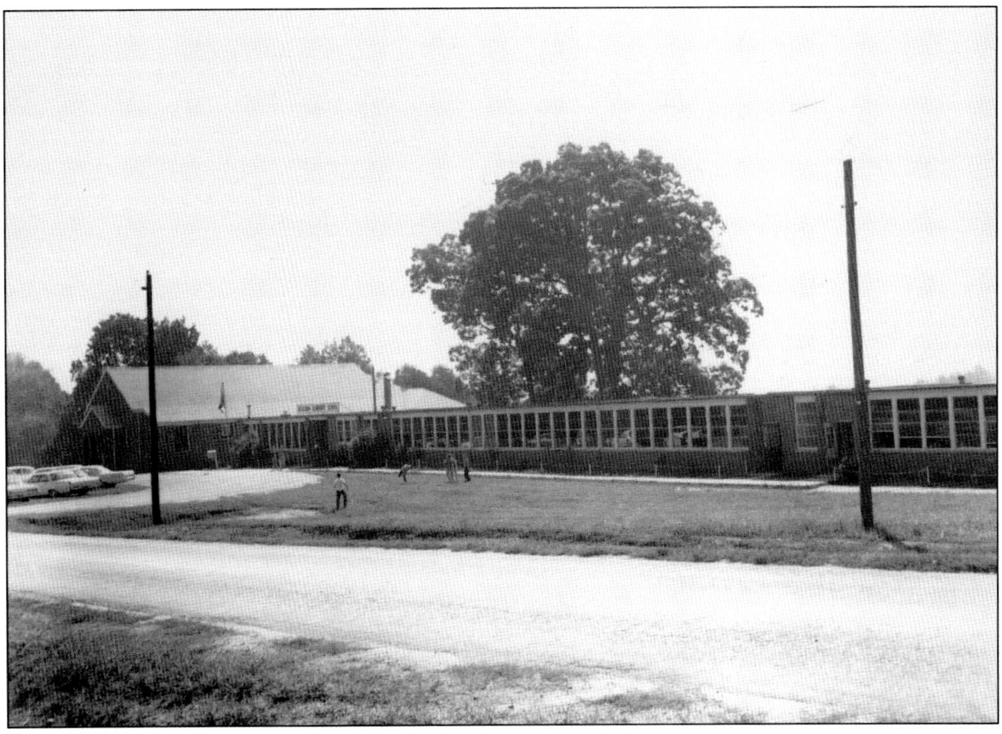

Bethlehem School is pictured as it looked in September 1966.

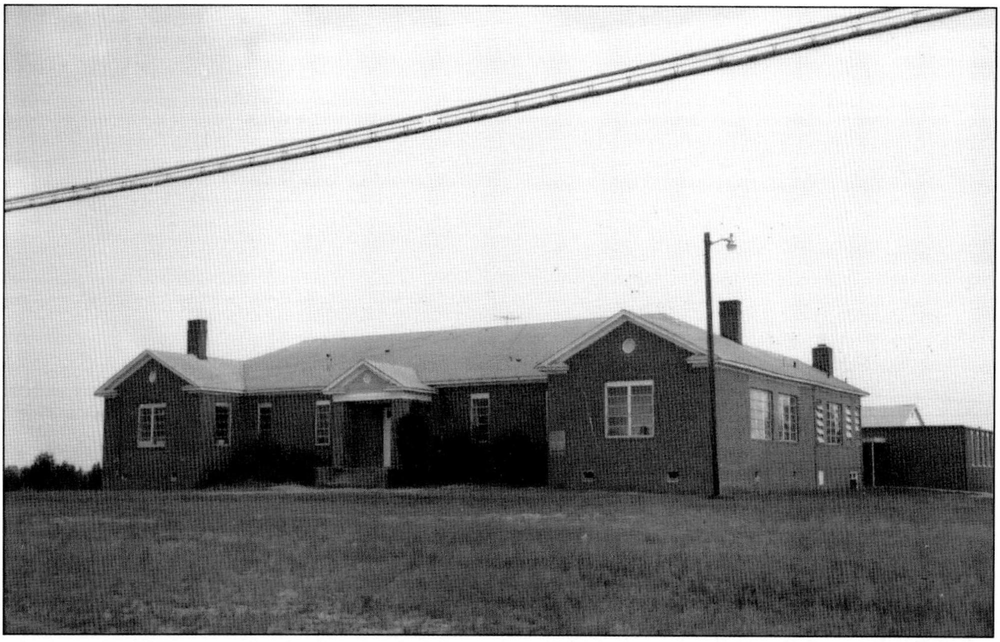

This is a 1966 photo of the Holsenbeck School. The school has since gone through three major renovations and looks nothing like this today.

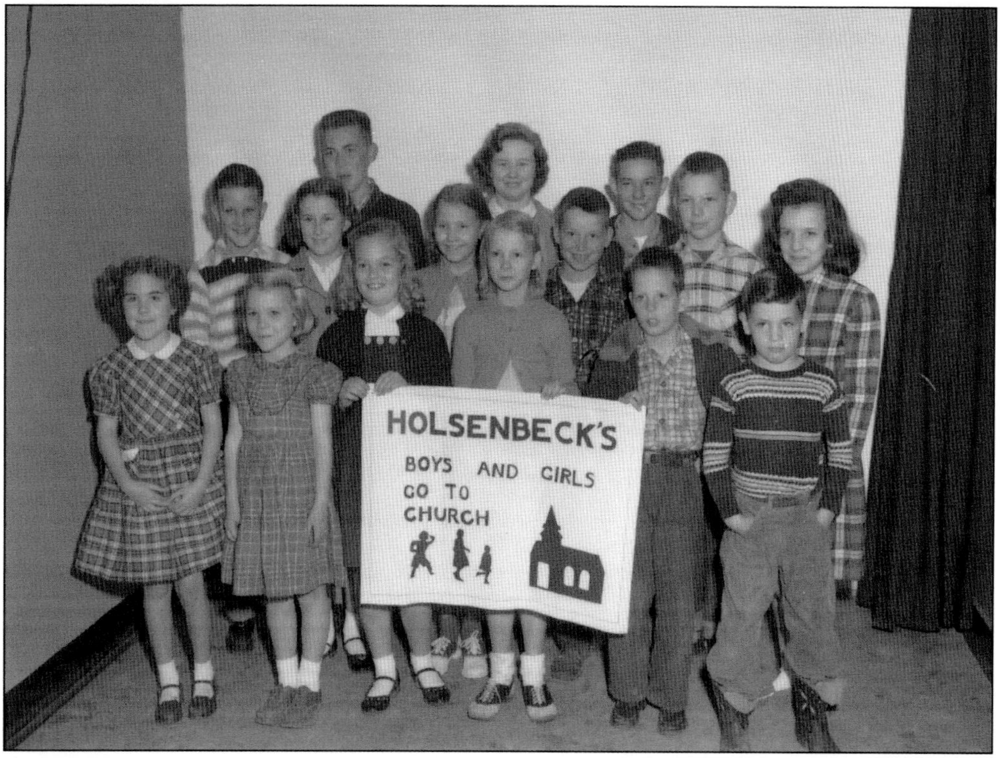

Although it is controversial today, religion played an important role in the schools in the 1950s. This photo of Holsenbeck students shows that they were proud of their church attendance, but they also prayed in class. Linda House Canup is in the center, helping hold up the sign.

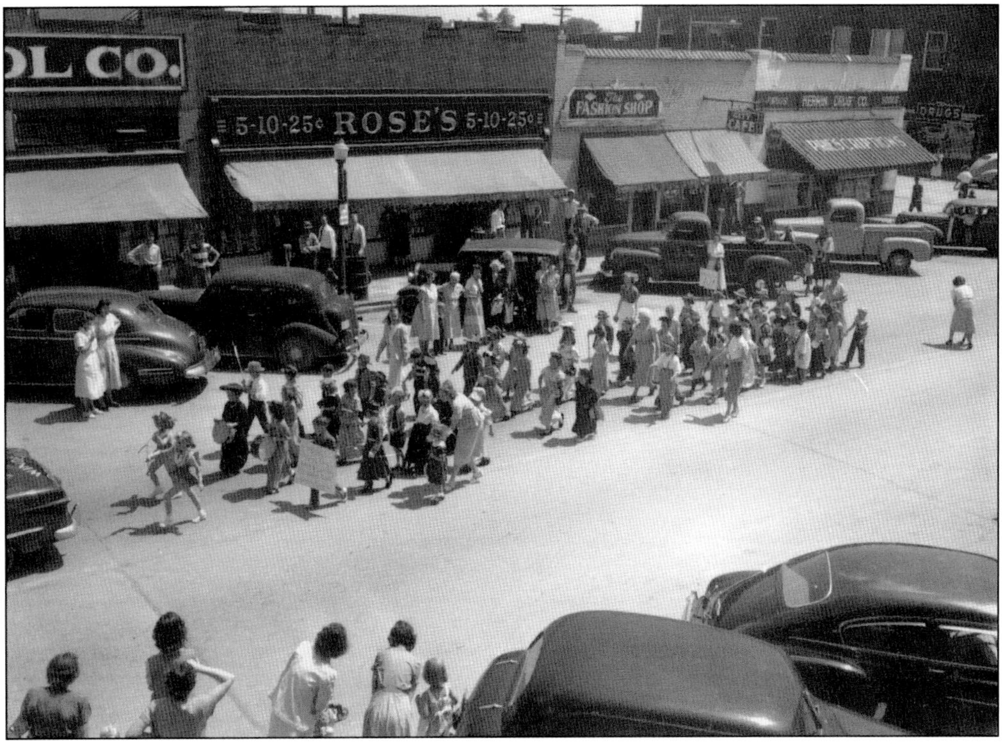

Winder Grammar School's first grade class was a proud one in 1953. They paraded up Broad Street (above), then posed for a class photo (below) on May 23 to celebrate their promotion to the second grade.

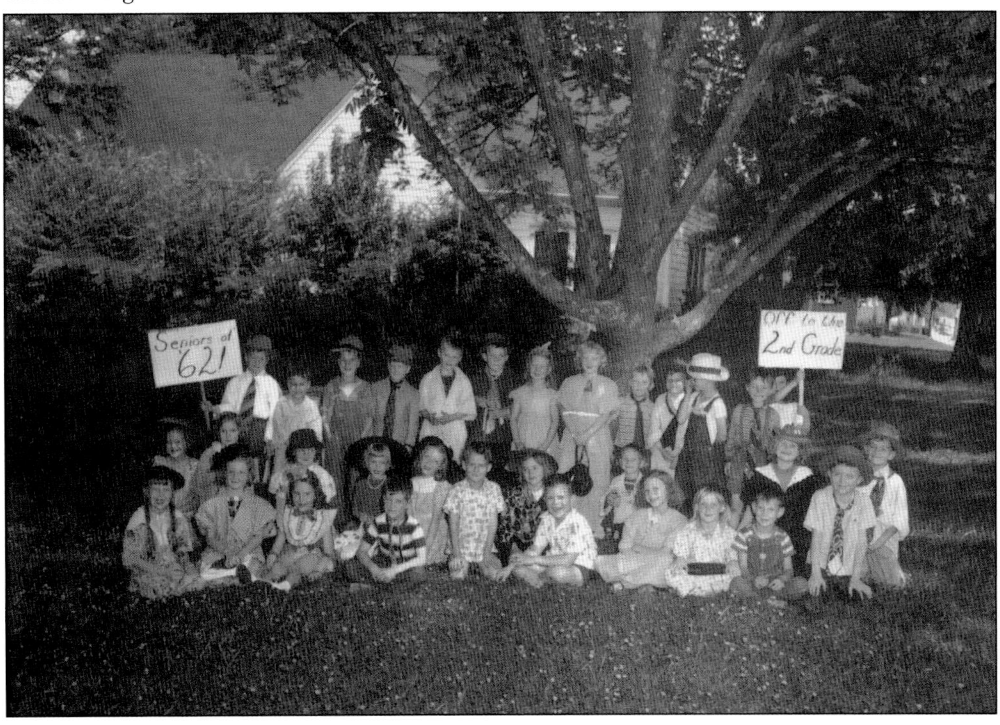

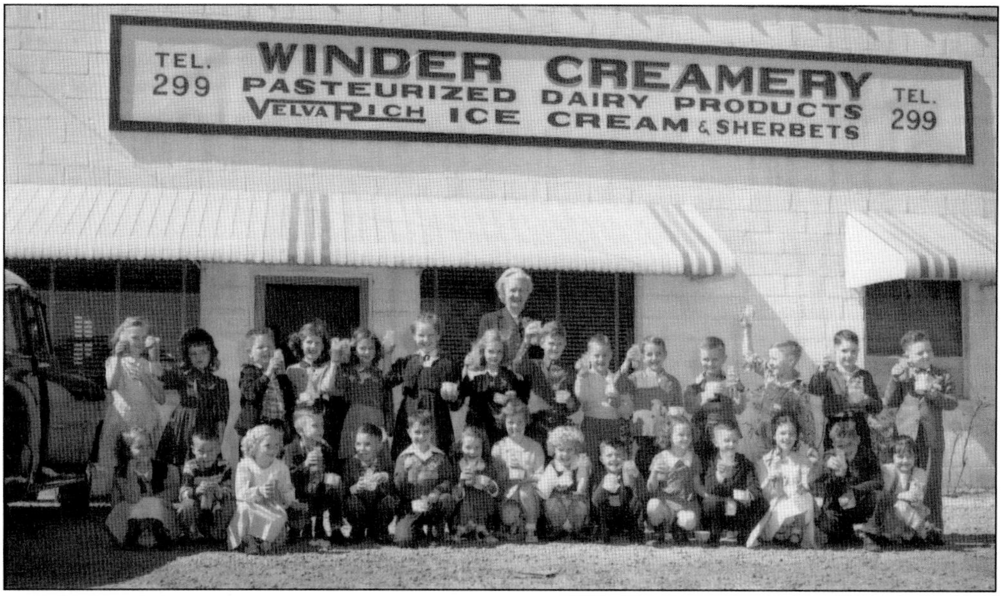

This Winder Grammar School first grade class was treated to a trip to Winder Creamery and ice cream in 1952. From left to right are the following: (kneeling) unidentified, unidentified, unidentified, Bob Ingram, Harry Brown, Steve Griffith, unidentified, Millie Darby, Sandra Lee, Jimmy Cooper, unidentified, Bill Healan, Becky Jackson, Jimmy Manders, and Francis Boone; (standing) unidentified, Judy Grizzle, Cam Hardigree, unidentified, unidentified, unidentified, Jean Howard, Wally Hostetter, unidentified, Jerry Ferguson, Myron Garrett, Emory Casper, Larry Holland, and Wade Jackson. The teacher is Mrs. Bishop.

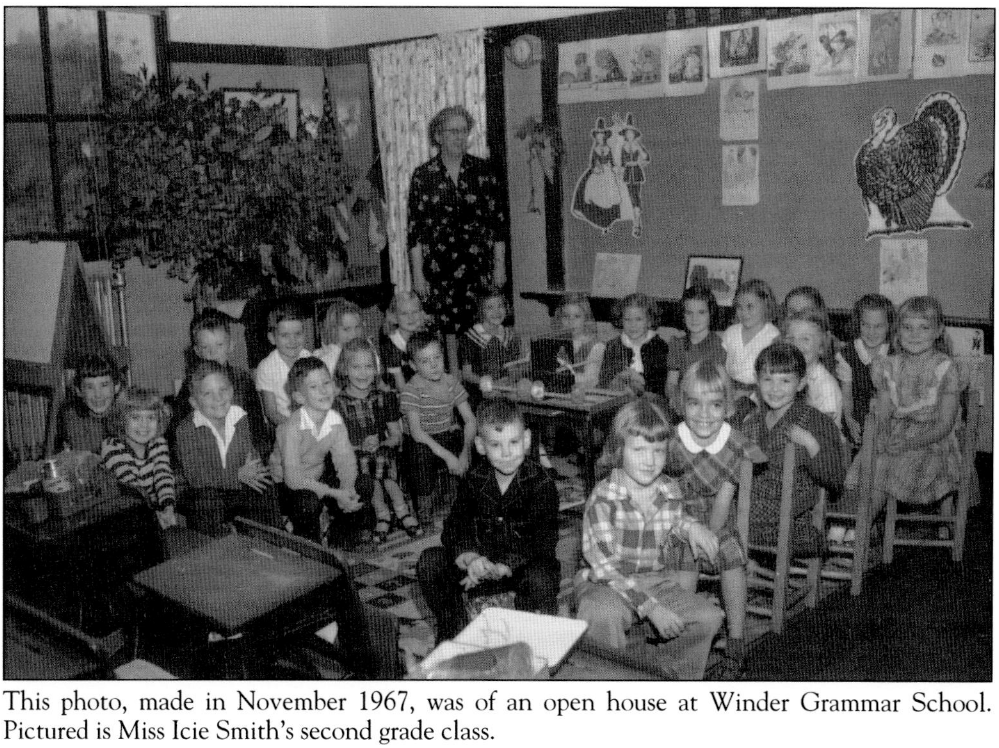

This photo, made in November 1967, was of an open house at Winder Grammar School. Pictured is Miss Icie Smith's second grade class.

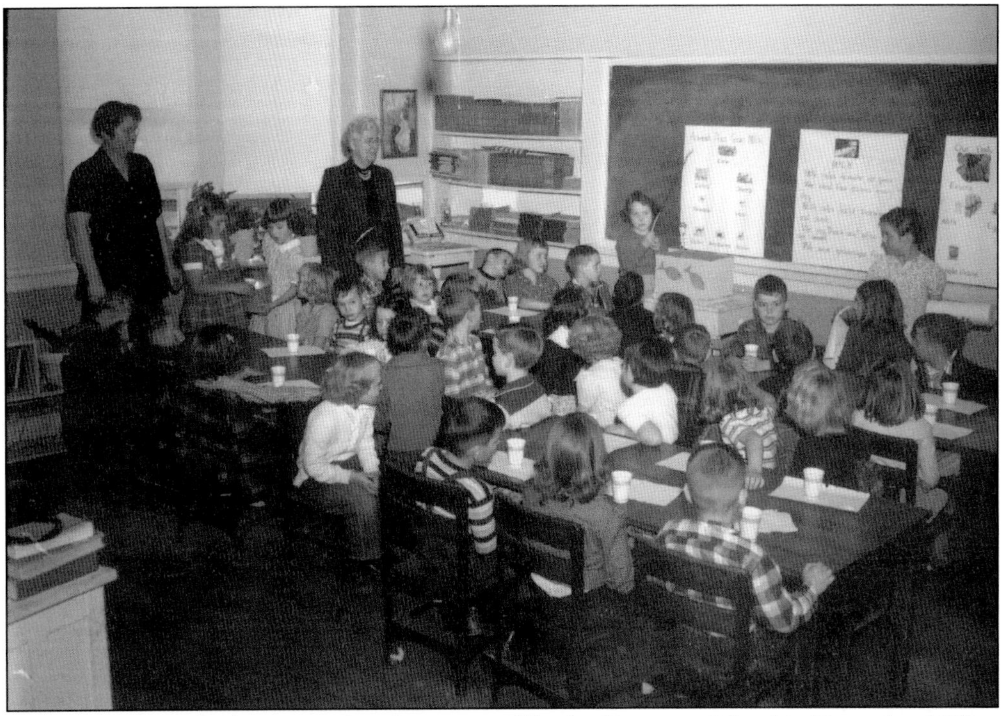

The county nurse paid a visit to this classroom at Winder Grammar School in November 1952.

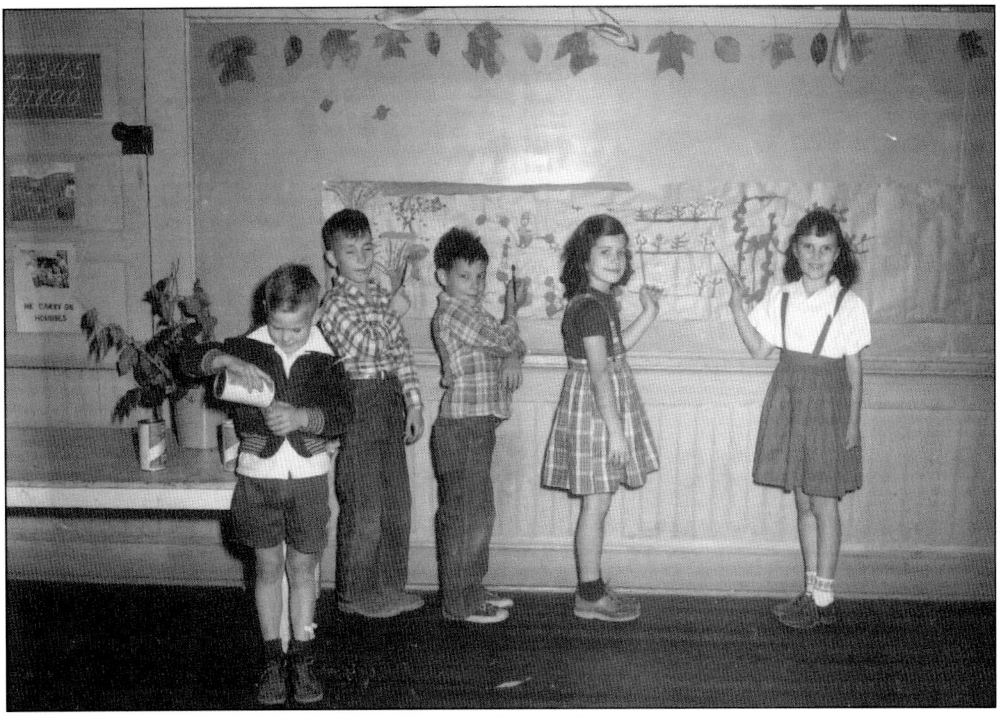

Matthews School students are pictured in October 1952. It is not clear what they are doing, but they sure do look cute doing it. From left to right are Jimmy Ouzts, Larry McElroy, Gene Parker, Jackie Wilkins, and Shirley Carter.

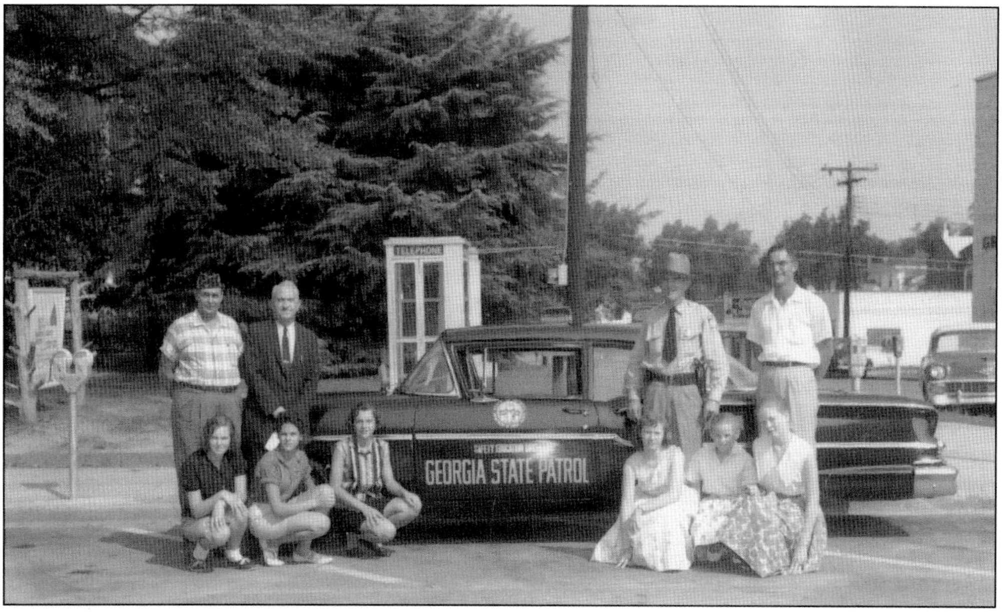

Veterans of Foreign Wars Post 1187 sponsored a trip for these six young women to Camp Safety Patrol in 1958. The students are not identified. The men, from left to right, are Robert Weatherford, Superintendent of Schools P.T. Barrett, an unidentified state patrolman, and Pete Doster.

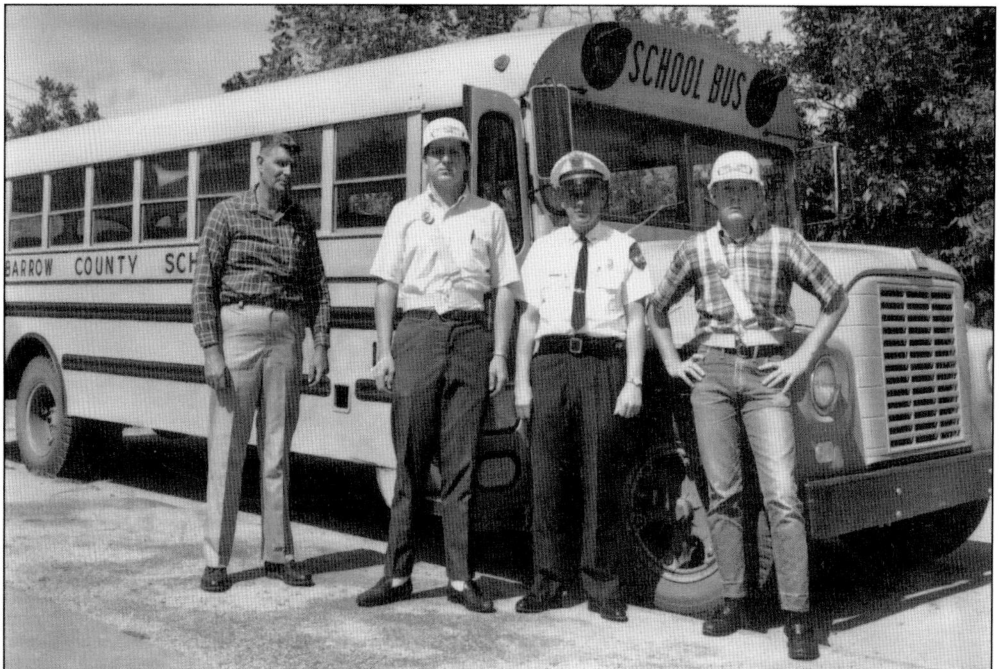

In the 1950s and 1960s the school patrol played an important role in the safety of students. Among other things, these high school students rode on the buses and helped small students safely cross streets and highways. Brady Cooper is at the far left and Winder police chief Gerald Thomas is third from the left. The photo was made in September 1966.

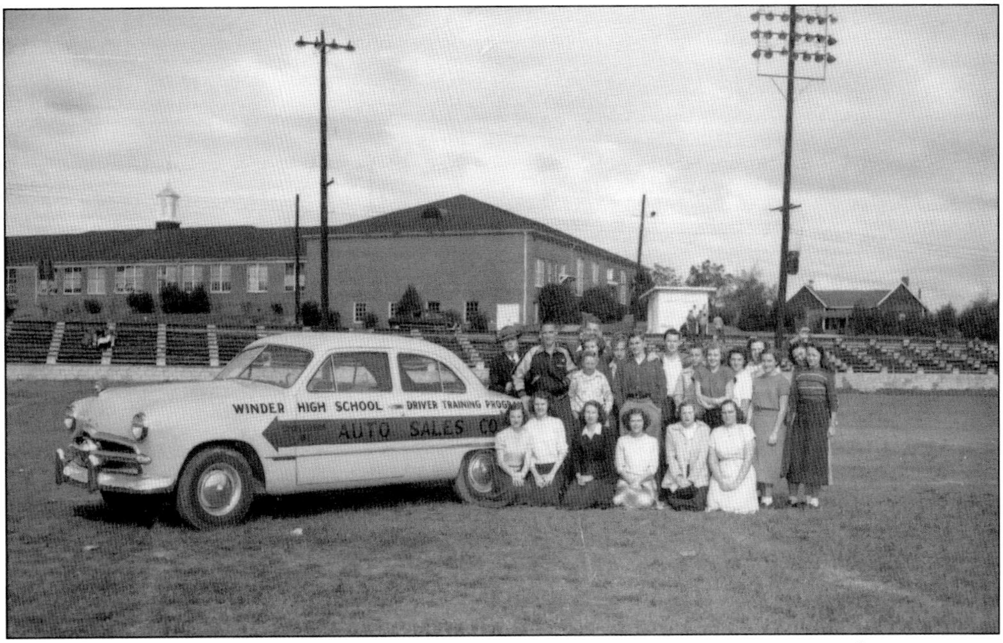

In 1949, Winder High School was among 100 schools in the state to inaugurate a driver training program. Ford dealer Graham Wright of the Auto Sales Co. furnished this new car. Among the students shown are Carolyn McElhannon, Lucille Wood, Aaron Manders, Jean Perry, Grady Morris, Joe Carter, Roy Maynard Jr., Pat Aldridge, and Jackie Hinesley.

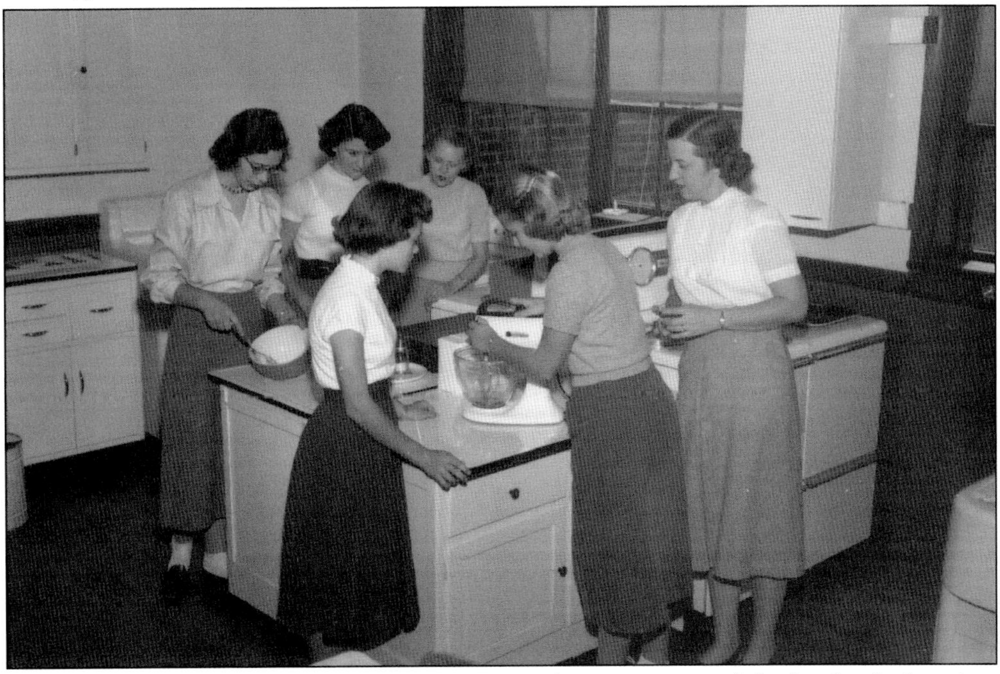

In 1952, home economics was an important part of a young woman's high school education. Nearest to the camera, from left to right, are unidentified, Patsy Hall, and home economics department head Kathryn Kitchens. In the back row, from left to right, are Johnnie Grizzle, Nancy Harrison, and Mrs. Provo, home economics teacher.

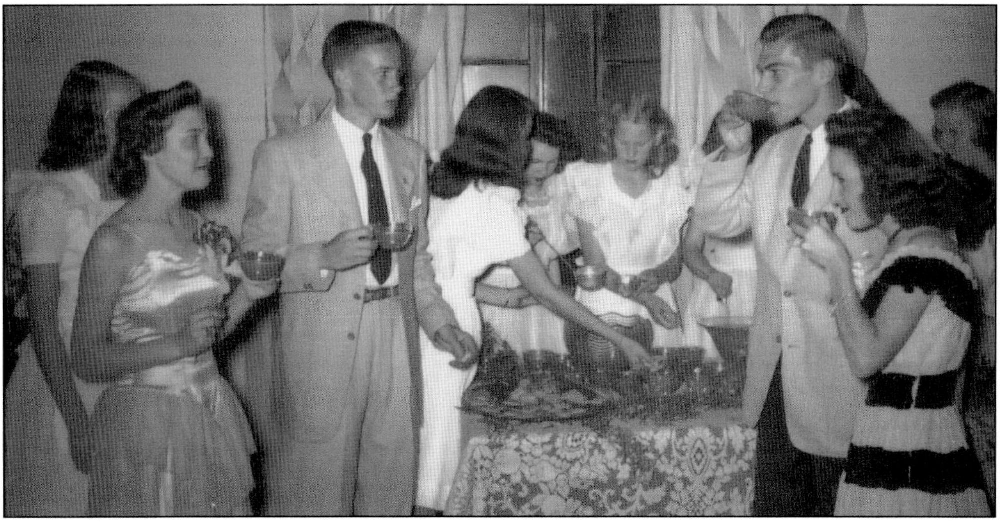

Not long after the photo studio opened, Stell and Kilgore were already capturing scenes of school life. This is the Winder High School Junior-Senior Dance in 1946. The couple at left is Marie Youngblood and Ernest Graham Jr. The couple at right is Lady Mell Arnold and John Randolph.

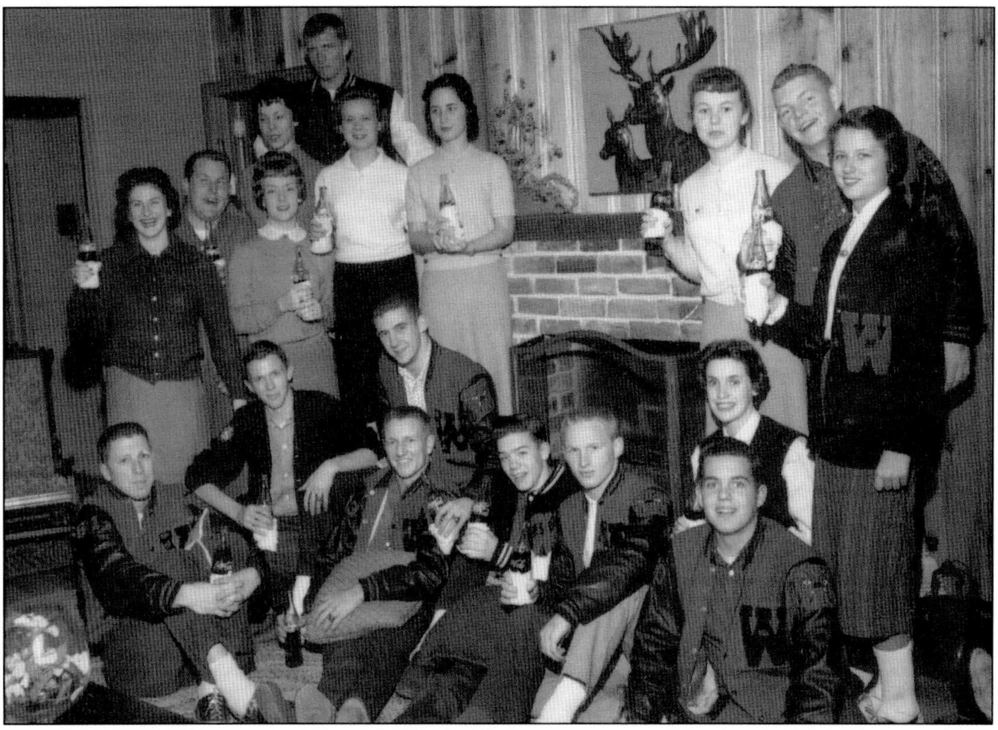

What may look like a Coca-Cola advertisement is actually a gathering of the students elected to "Who's Who" by the Winder High School Class of 1960. They are, from left to right, as follows: (seated) Gordon Blackwell, Bryan Perkins, Jack Ferguson, Dwayne Jackson, Haase Arnold Jr., Ronnie Saunders, Frank Giles, and Sally Russell; (standing) Nancy Harrison, Kinky Roberts, Jane Allison, Pat Taylor, Jan Bentley, Martha Doster, Sonya Wall, Mary Ridgeway, Jody Harrison, and Evelyn Blount.

Winder High School's first band director, W.H. Robison, didn't ride this mower in parades. It was probably a gift to him from a grateful community.

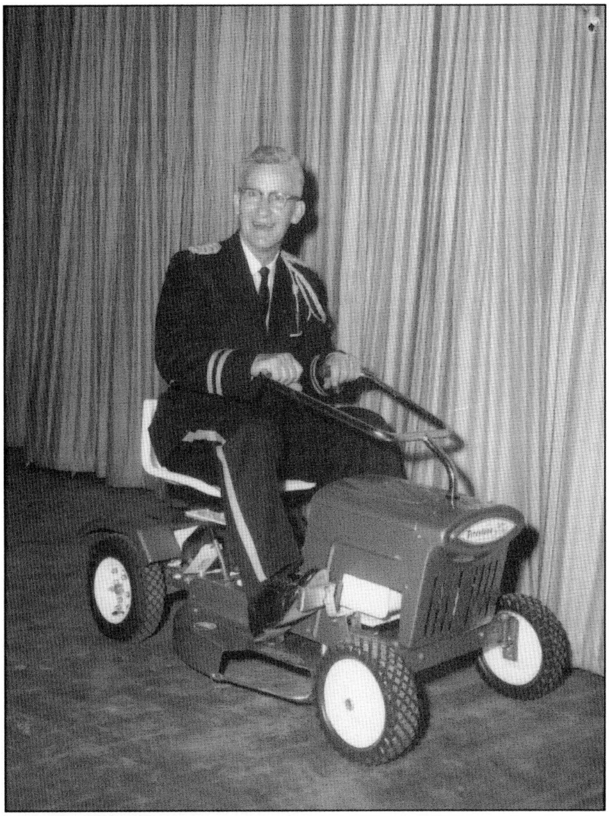

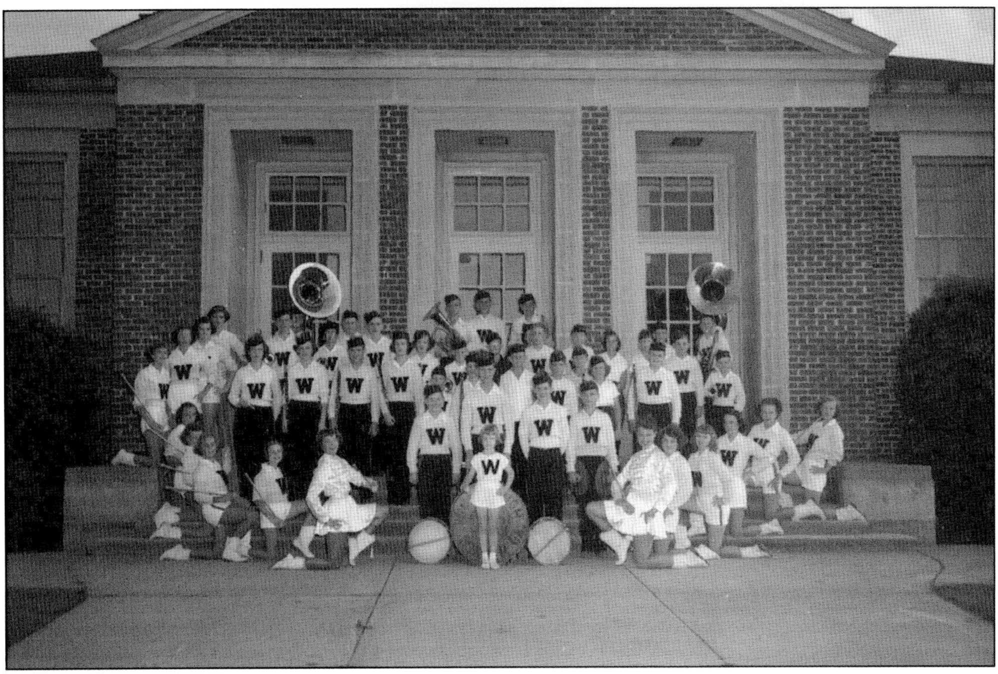

At one time Winder High had a "drum and bugle corp," but this is its first real band, organized in 1950.

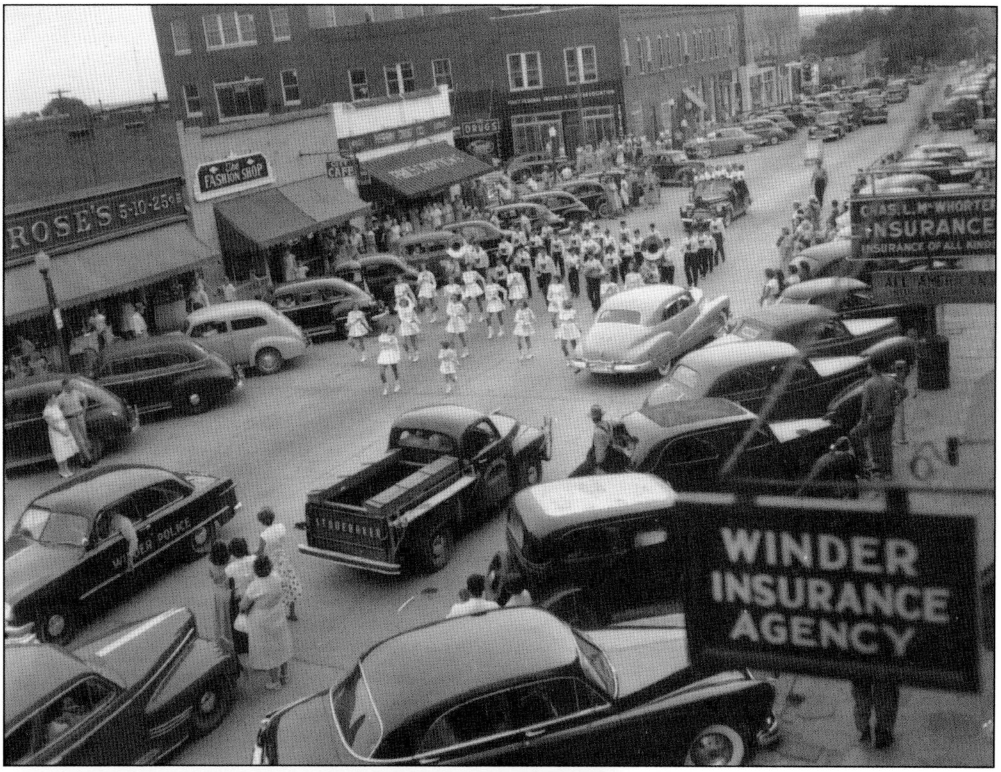

Winder's first band is pictured in its first parade on September 11, 1950.

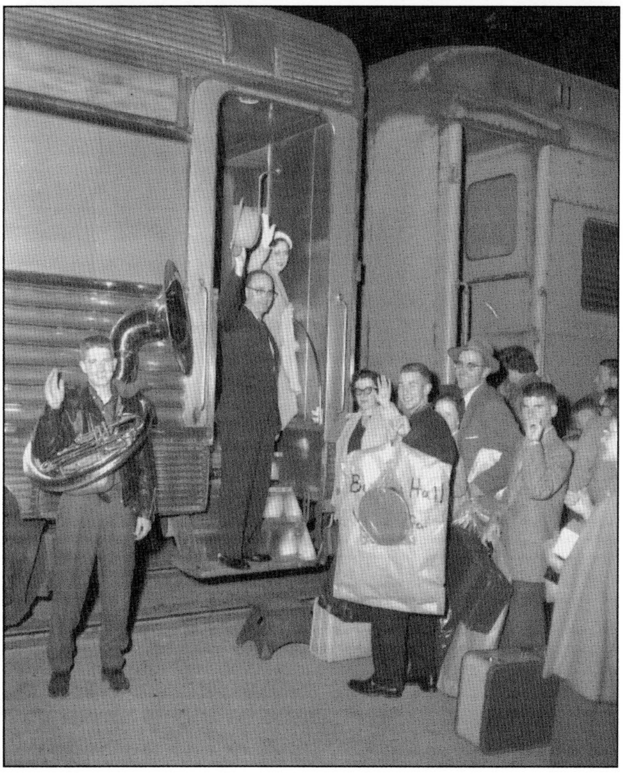

Winder mayor John Kelley and his wife, Jo, board a train bound for Washington D.C. with the Winder High School Band. Others shown include Billy Whitley (far left), Angeline Kelley (waving, with glasses), and James Ouzts (hat and glasses). Billy Hall is standing between Angeline Kelley and Billy Hall.

Six

The Sporting Life

Stell and Kilgore had a great fondness for sports and wonderful ability to capture the action on film. From little league to semi-professional, their files contain hundreds of team and game photographs.

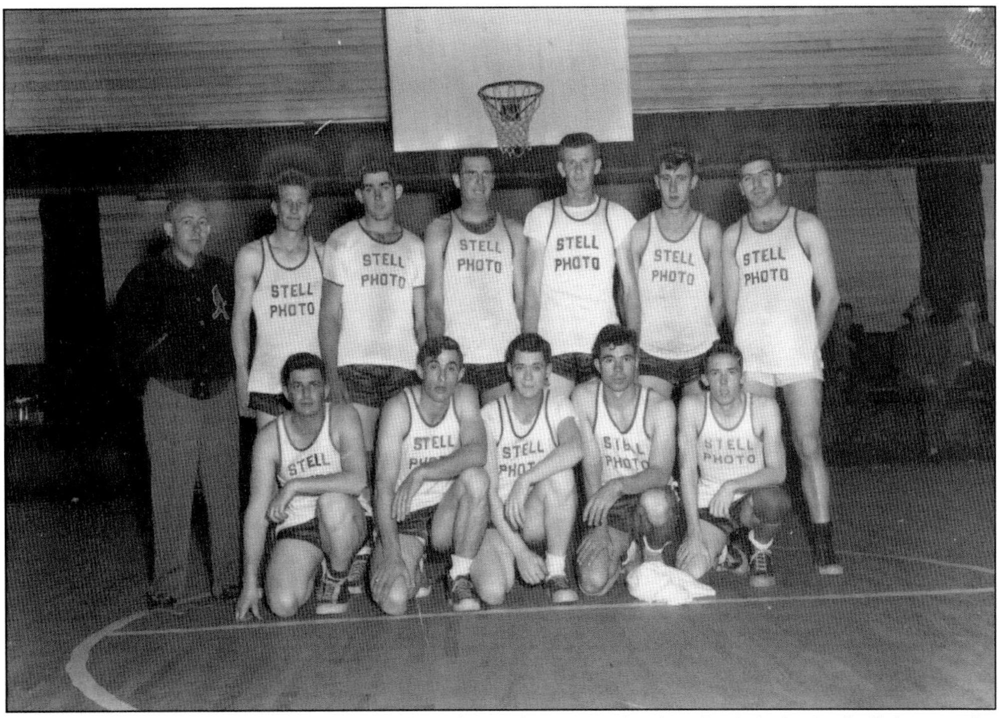

Stell and Kilgore sponsored a team, the Shutterbugs, in the local adult basketball league for many years. Members of the 1955 team were, from left to right, as follows: (front row) Alvin Williams, Joe Allen, Homer Sikes, Billy White, and Jim Forrester; (back row) Coach Ray Kilgore, ? Sellers, Bobby Smith, Hollis Britt, John Fincher, Alan Pentecost, and ? Henderson.

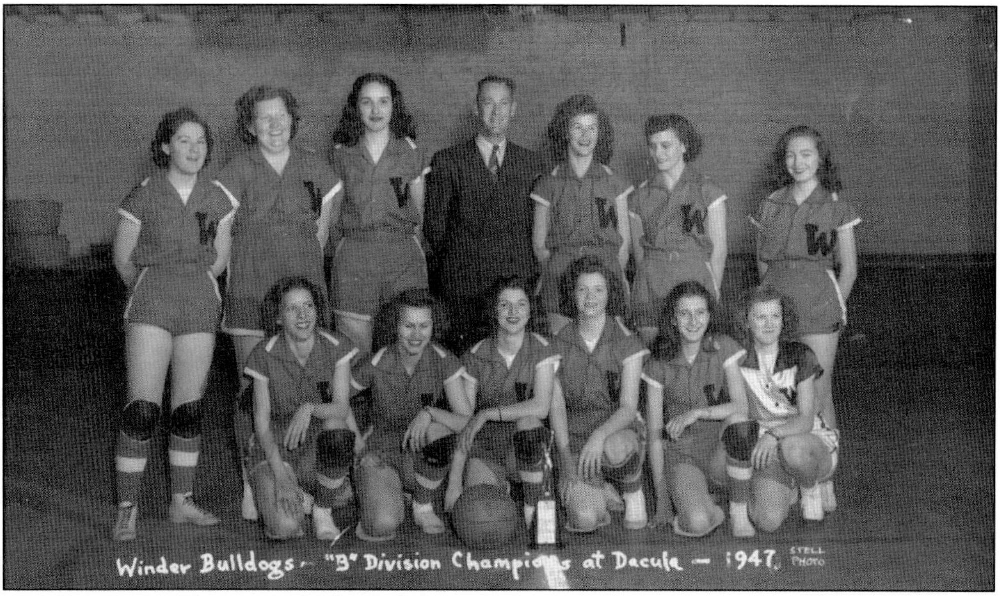

The Winder Bulldogs girls' basketball team was crowned "B" Division Champions in 1947. From left to right are as follows: (kneeling) Bobbie Wiley, Eloise Wages, Phoebe Cook, ? Elrod, Joyce Elliott, and Johnny Steed; (standing) Delores Magness, Edna Hogan, Irene Blackstock, Coach Harry L. Garland, Lou Hendrix, Frances Wheeler, and Martha Jean Fox.

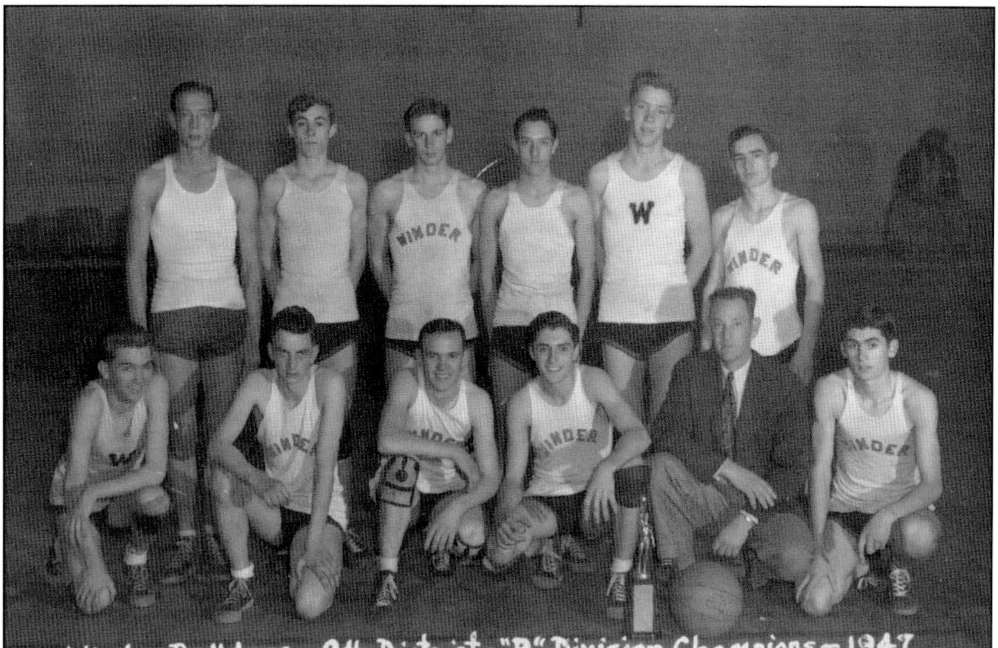

Basketball in Barrow County experienced a very good year in 1947. The Winder Bulldogs were 9th District "B" Division Champions. Pictured from left to right are the following: (front row) Harry Holder, Jack Williams, Jack Dillard, Julian Price, Coach Harry L. Garland, and Louis Lovin; (back row) Bill Kilgore, Joe Allen, Ernest G. Graham, E.C. Carson, Dewell Jones, and Henry M. Oakley.

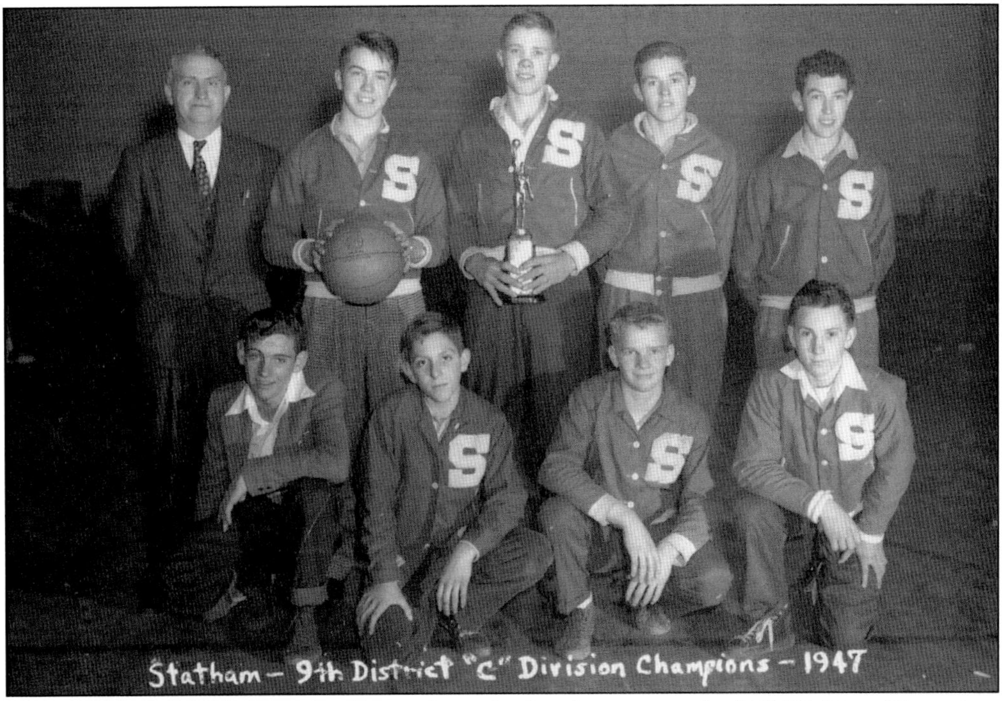

Things were no different in Statham, where the boys' team was the "C" Division Champion. From left to right are as follows: (kneeling) Johnny Lyle, Bill Barrett, Bobby Young, and Stanley Pentecost; (standing) Mr. Paul T. Barrett, Benny Bowman, John R. Pentecost, Lester Austin, and Jack Coker.

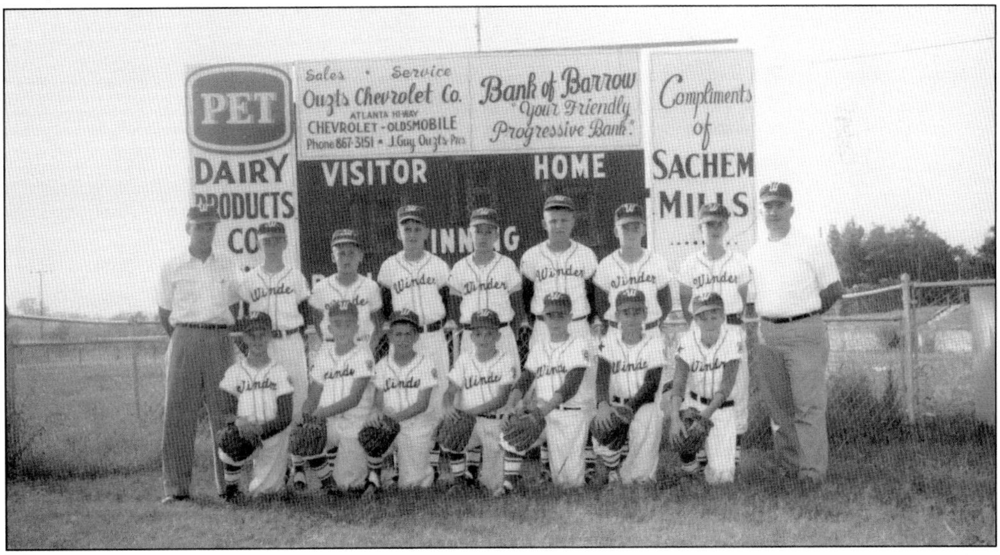

Winder's Little League All Stars finished second in the state tournament in 1964. Team member Ricky Peppers believes they could have won the game in Elberton, but says "they wouldn't pitch to Mike Walden all day." From left to right are as follows: (kneeling) Ricky Peppers, Roland Shepley, Kerry Kilgore, Dwight Wall, Wayne Parker, Wayne Delay, and Larry Cook; (standing) Coach B.L. Shepley, Ronnie Magness, Olin Wilson, David Ridgeway, Victor Savage, Mike Walden, Jerry Clack, Clifton Shedd, and Coach Billy Shedd.

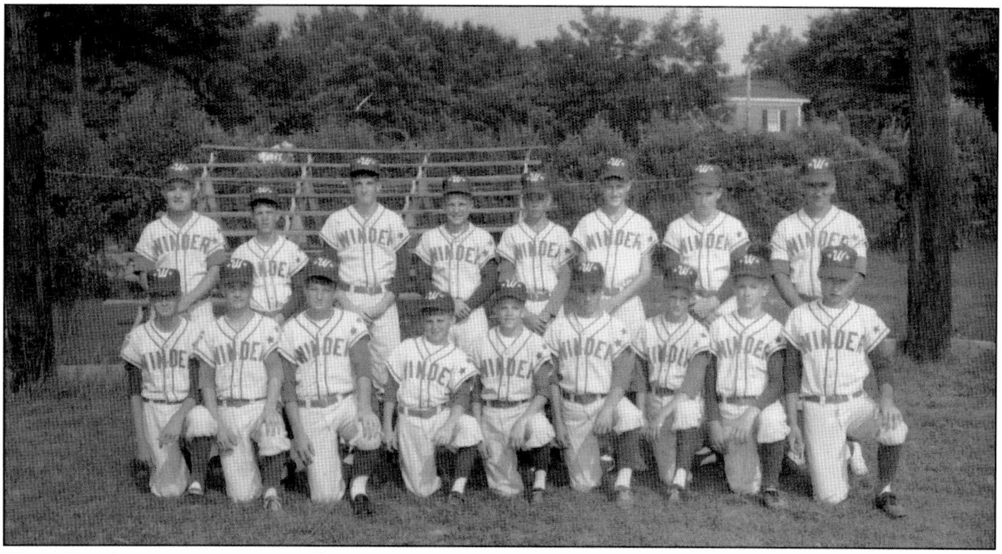

The Winder Pony League All-Star Team had a run at the state tournament in 1965. In a double-elimination tournament they beat Monroe in the first game in Gainesville, but lost the tournament to them in the second game. Members of the team, from left to right, were as follows: (front row) Cary Lipscomb, Steve Bowen, Jerry Clack, Johnny Wages, Mike Rice, Wade Smith, Al Jackson, Ronnie Shepley, and John Hamilton; (back row) Coach Simuel Doster, Gary Grizzle, Sammy Hunter, Mike Walden, Victor Savage, Ronnie Brasfield, Johnny Sosebee, and Coach Victor Lord.

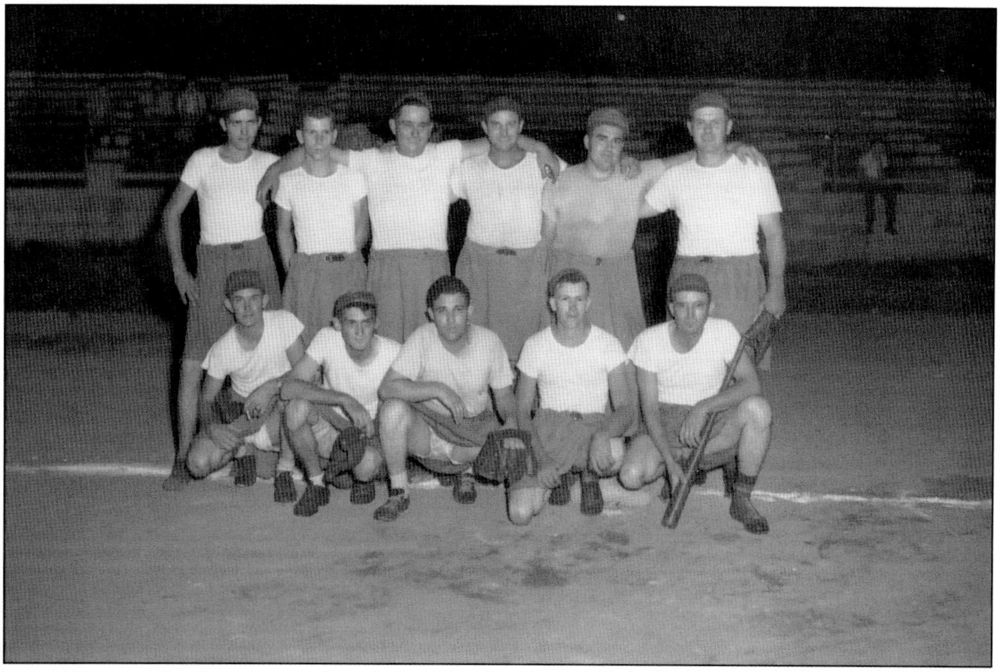

The Whistleville Red Skirts played the Winder Lions Club, also wearing skirts, in a charity baseball game on August 25, 1949. None of the players could be identified, and we were unable to find the score of the game. It is obvious, however, that they knew little or nothing about wearing skirts.

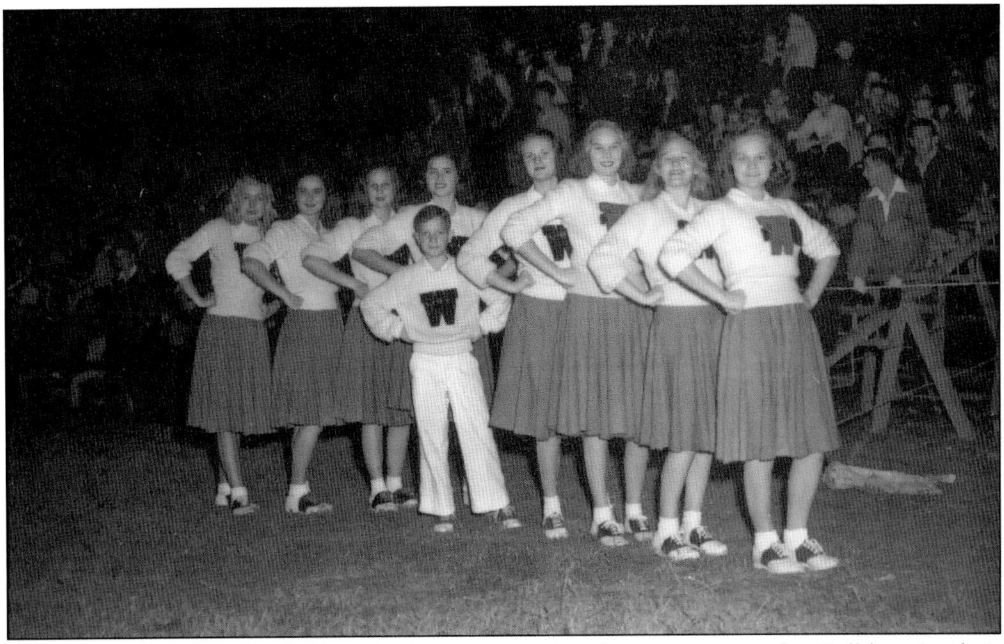

The Winder High School Cheerleaders were on hand to encourage the Bulldogs in their football game against Elberton in 1947. From left to right are Nan House, Carolyn McElhannon, Lillie Dell Edgar, Barbara Wayne, Lucille Wood, Joanna McElroy, Maggie Waddel, and Betty Freeman. The young man pictured is Bobby House.

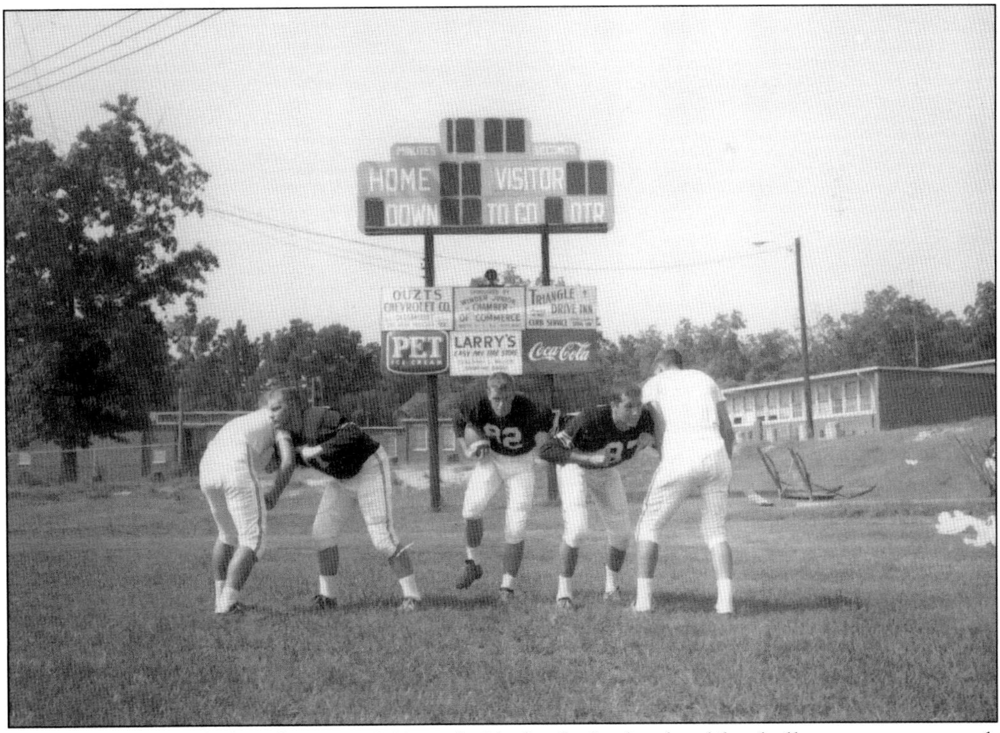

Stell or Kilgore took this photo in 1964, probably for the high school football program or annual. The players facing the camera are John Briscoe, Chris Zodrow, and Doug Ivey.

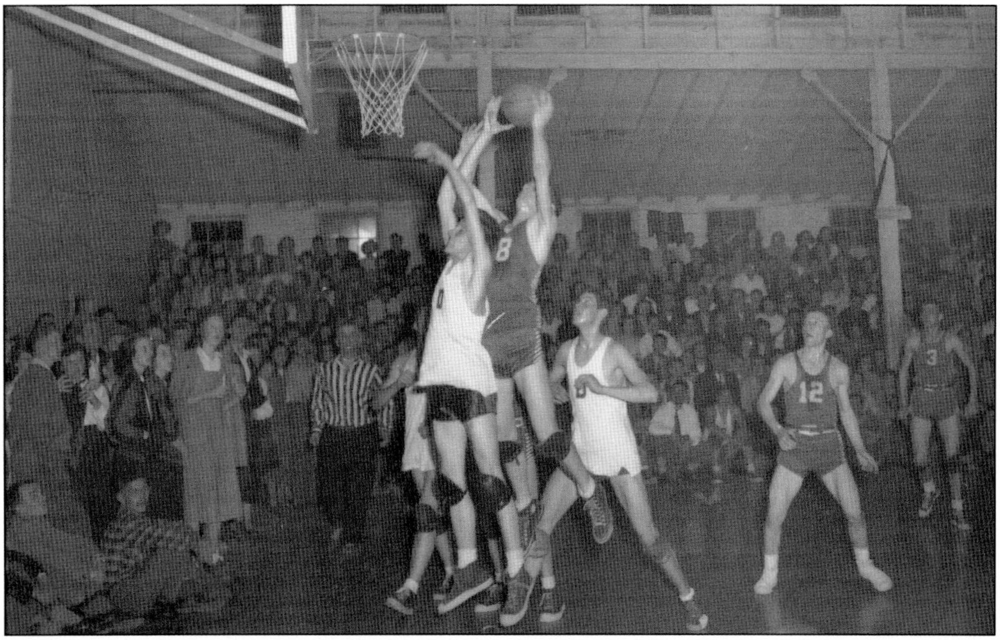

Stell and Kilgore took many action shots during basketball, baseball, and football games. This photo was made at a tournament in the old gymnasium in Winder in February 1950. The Statham High School players in dark shirts are Johnny Lyle (8), Billy Crowe (12), and Robert Peppers (3).

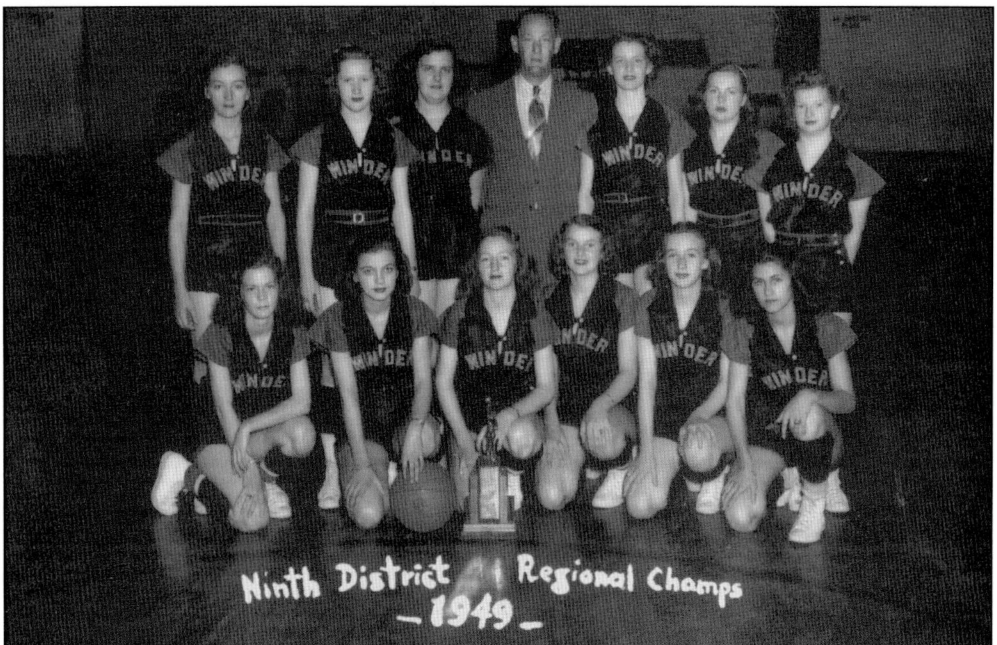

The Winder High School girls were Ninth District Regional Champions in 1949. From left to right are as follows: (kneeling) Sadie Woodall, Jeanette Doster, Betty Sue Carter, Jeanette Cronic, Betty Giles, and Joanne Ivey; (standing) Bobby Jean Carter, Mary Belle Allen, Fay Williams, Coach H.L. Garland, Charlotte Simpson, Joanne Letson, and Betty Garner.

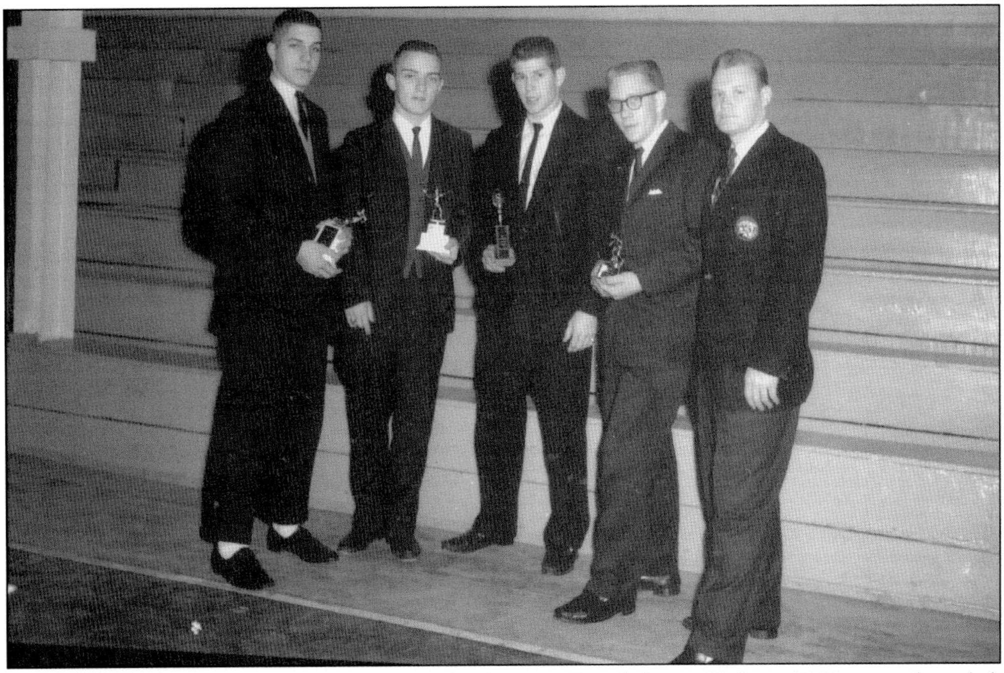

Among the athletes honored by the Winder-Barrow Touchdown Club in 1962 were, from left to right, Tony Lay, Simuel Doster, Sonny Morris, and Bobby Wiley. On the right is Coach Charlie Horne.

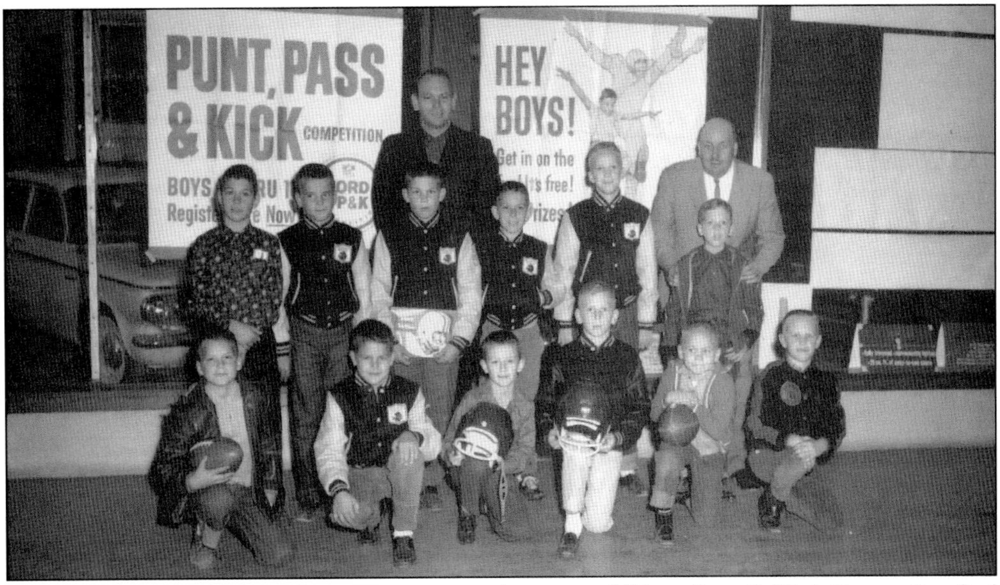

For many years Ford Motor Company sponsored a national "Pass, Punt & Kick Contest" to find the boys who could best do those three things. The 1962 winners received jackets, while the second and third place finishers received a football or a helmet. From left to right are as follows: (kneeling) Jimmy Gilstrap, Steve Burrell, Charles Bentley Jr., Eddie Mitchell, Mike Graves, and Chip Rutledge; (standing) Wade Smith, Tim Reynolds, Tom Collins, Mark Mitchell, Johnny Gilstrap, and Tommy Rhodes. The adults are Ford dealer Herb Nix (left) and J.C. Cook, city recreation director.

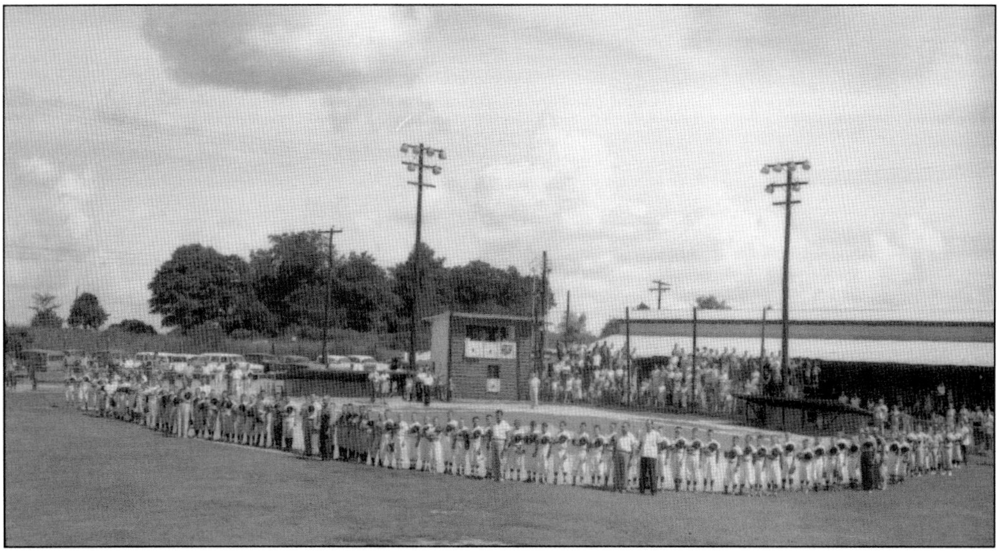

Little league baseball was very popular in 1959, as evidenced by this photo of the season's end ceremonies at the Winder Lions Club field on July 27. Youth baseball in Barrow County is even bigger today, sanctioned by the Dixie Youth League.

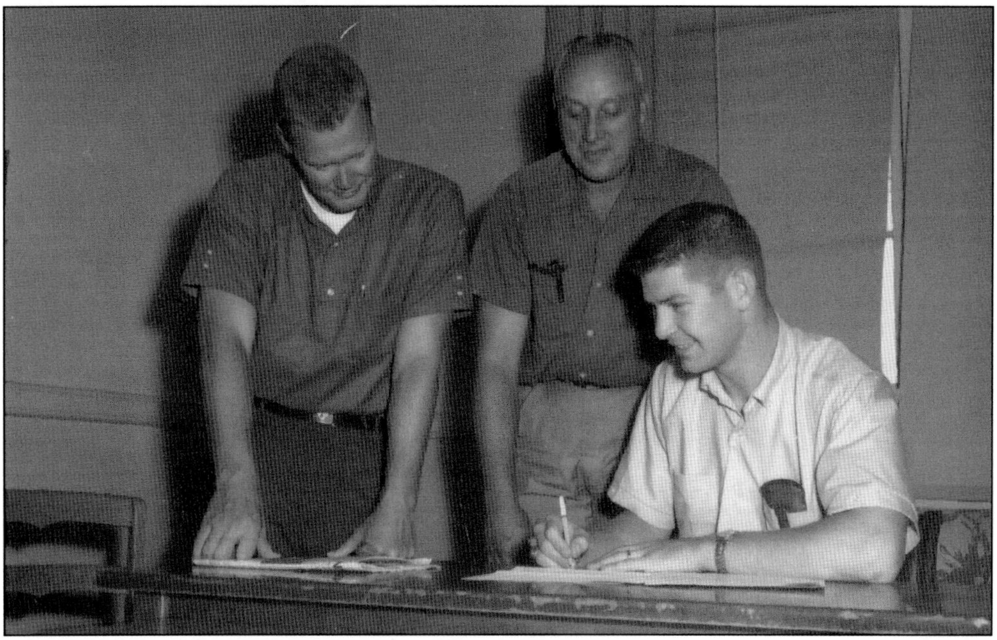

Coach Charlie Horne (left) looks on as James L. "Sonny" Morris signs a professional baseball contract with the Cleveland Indians in June 1962. Representing the Indians was Bill Herrin (center). Morris received a $10,000 bonus from the Indians, and was later picked up on waivers and paid a $25,000 bonus by the Chicago White Sox. Other local men who played professional baseball include "Doodle" McDonald, who was signed by St. Louis, and Lamar Murphy (photo on p. 17). Murphy made it to the major leagues with the New York Yankees and roomed with Chuck Conners. After his baseball career, Conners became a television and movie star. Long-time Winder city councilman Billy Sheridan would probably have signed professionally, but he developed serious vision problems while attending Florida State on a baseball scholarship.

Seven

Separate, not Equal

Stell and Kilgore photographed almost every aspect of life in Barrow at one time or another, including the African-American community. Their files contain hundreds of photographs of black citizens taken during the 1940s, 1950s, and 1960s, when segregation was a fact of life in the South. We believe their files will prove to be invaluable in studying African-American history in this county.

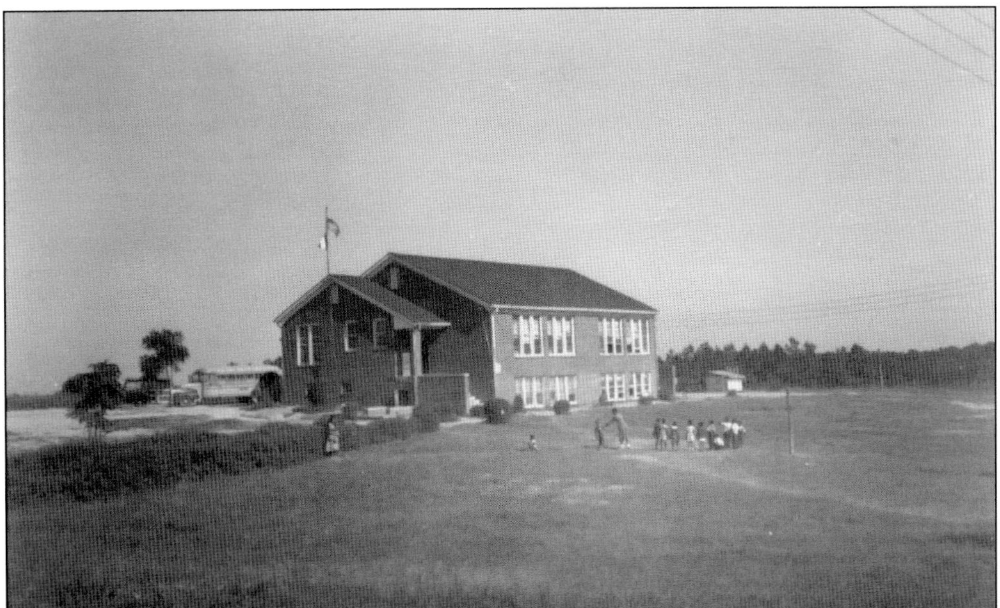

Glenwood School housed all the ten grades that made up the African-American school system when this photo was taken in 1952. Students who wanted to finish all 11 grades and receive a diploma had to drive to Athens for their senior year. Unfortunately, most couldn't do that. The school had outdoor toilets and no gymnasium.

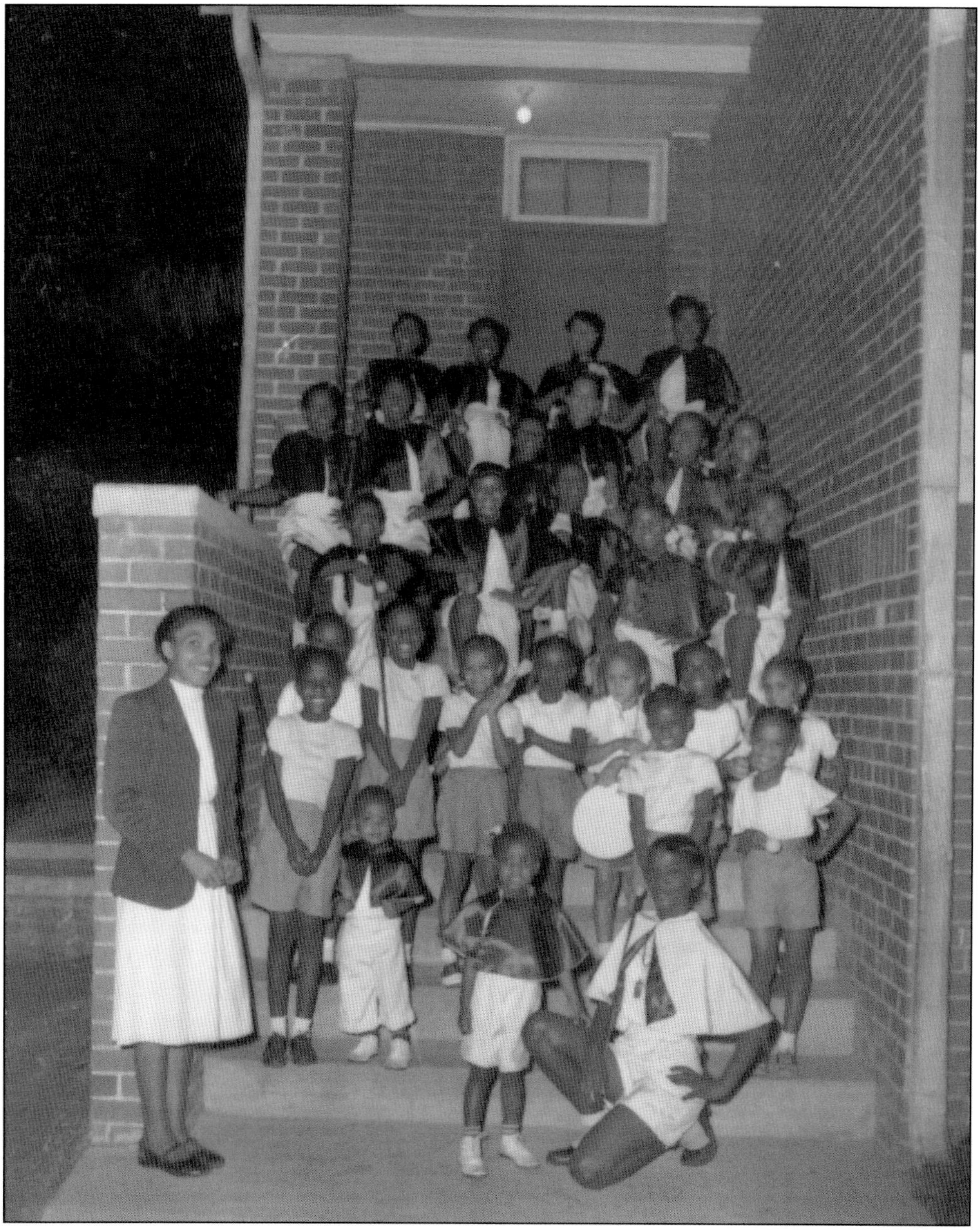

When Mary and LaFar Sims arrived in Winder, just out of college, they immediately began their tireless efforts to make a difference in the African-American community. One of Mary Sims' first efforts was the organization of a school band. The fact that they had no musical instruments was obviously a challenge, but one she met by having them blow through combs with tissue paper. The only instrument shown in this photo is the toy drum held by Rachel Roberts (now Mrs. Robert Wimberly), bought by her father at Roses' Dime Store. Mrs. Sims is shown standing at left. Some of the children shown include Mary Ann Teasley, Susie Teasley, Betty Sims, Grace Caldwell, Marjorie Roberts, Joanne Riley, Jeanette Riley, LaNoir Sims, Maria Sims, Catherine Pattmon, Anne Roberts, Vickie Ansley, Neva Joyce Mayweather, Catherine Wingfield, and Shirley Caldwell.

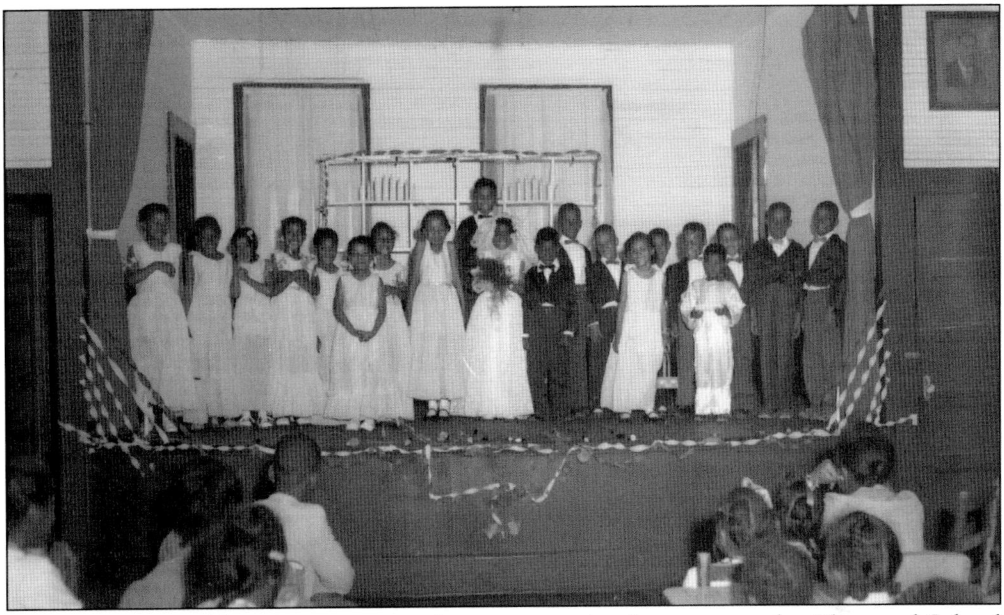

"Tom Thumb Weddings" were among the more popular shows put on by Glenwood School students. This one was photographed on April 4, 1955, and shows, from left to right, unidentified, Carolyn Price, Patricia Moon, Mary Jane Barnes, Mary Sue Riley, Joanne Jackson, Patricia Carter, Cheryl McCluskey, unidentified, Maria Sims (the bride), unidentified, Douglas Smith, William Strickland, Crystal Morrow, Alfred Finch, unidentified, unidentified, Phillip Wells, Jimmy Johnson, and J.W. Grissom.

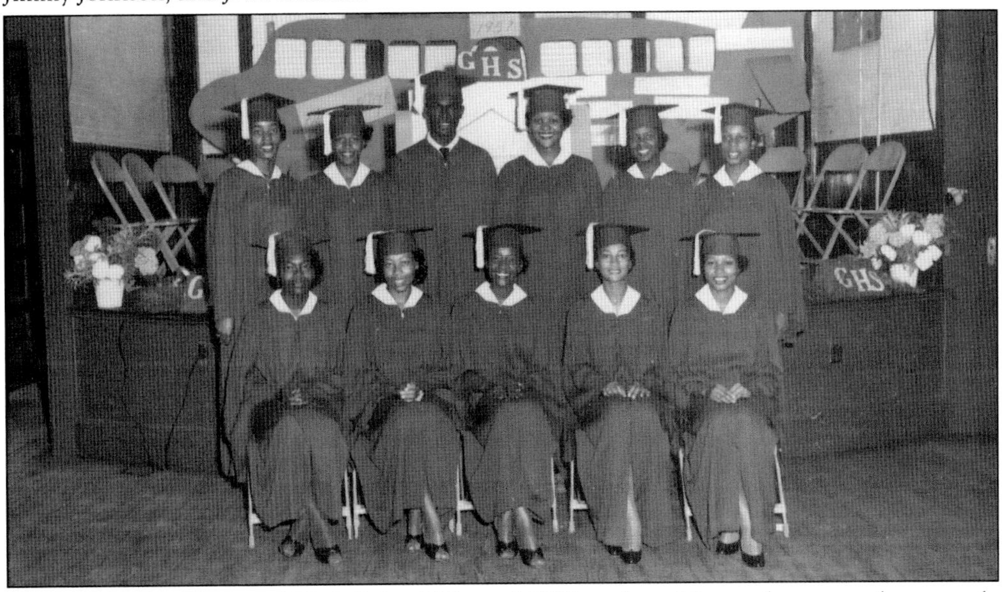

By the time the Glenwood High School Class of 1957 graduated it was down to only one male member. "We girls wouldn't let him quit," said Ella Ruth Price. The class consisted of the following, from left to right: (front row) Mona Hale Jackson, Betty Bush Lewis, May Frances Moon Lay, Ella Ruth Price, and Junette Ansley Tibbs; (back row) Vergie Sutton Kilgore, Wyetta Lay, Robert Bernard Hale, Pearlie Sims Thurmond, Maudean Riley Maxey, and Gennette Green Jones.

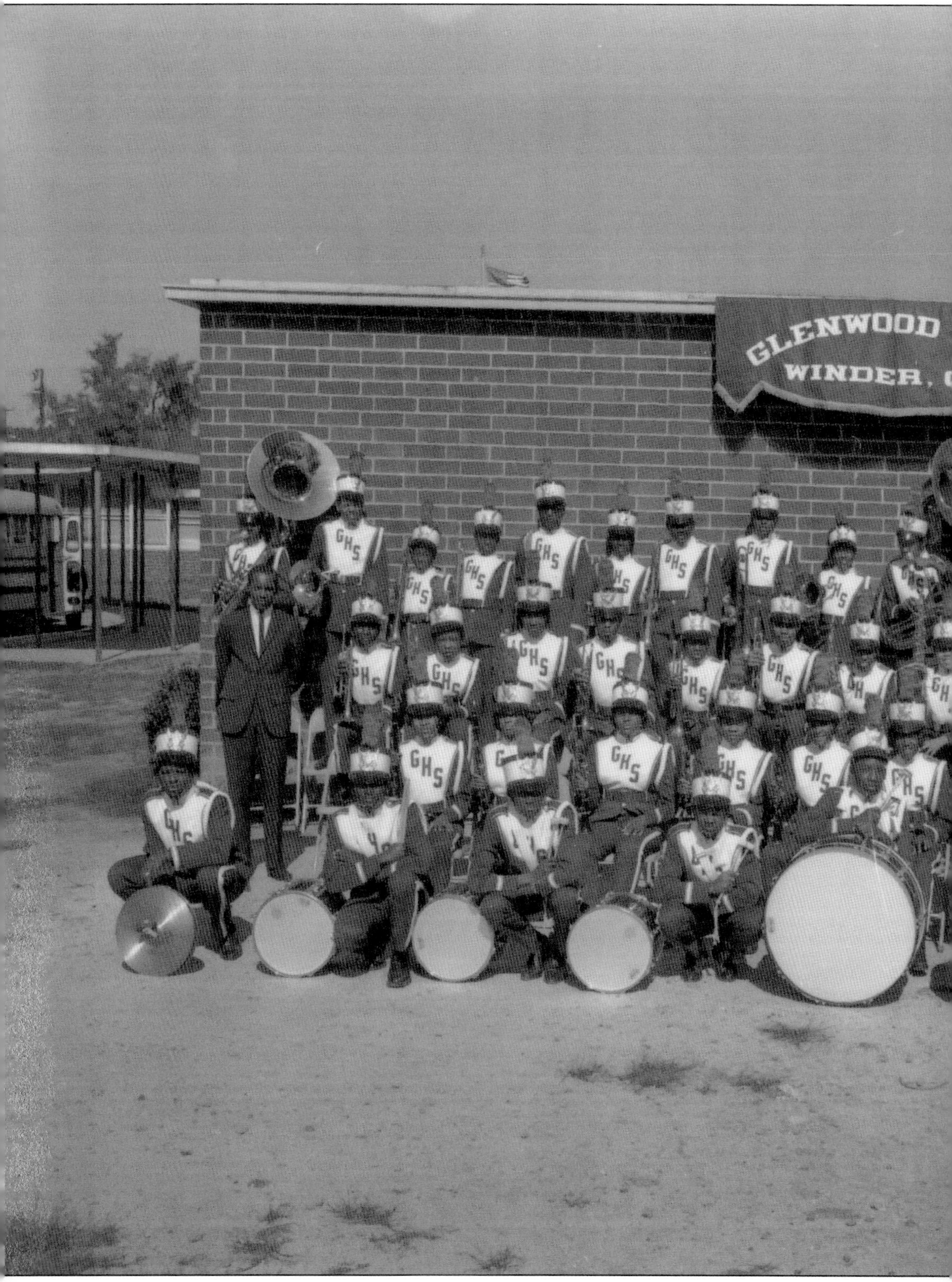
GLENWOOD
WINDER,

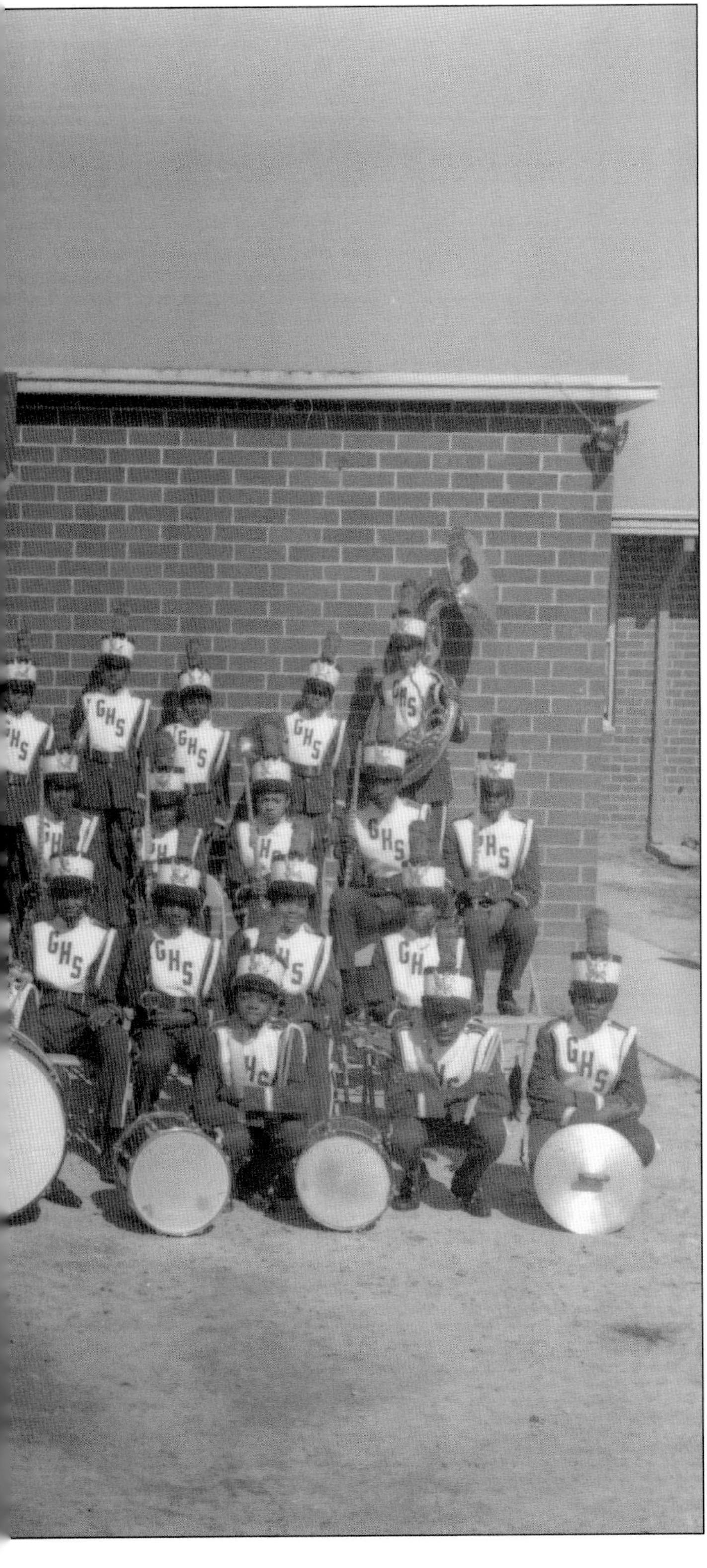

By 1966, Glenwood School had a full-fledged band—and a very good one—under the leadership of band director Wilson M. Bostic.

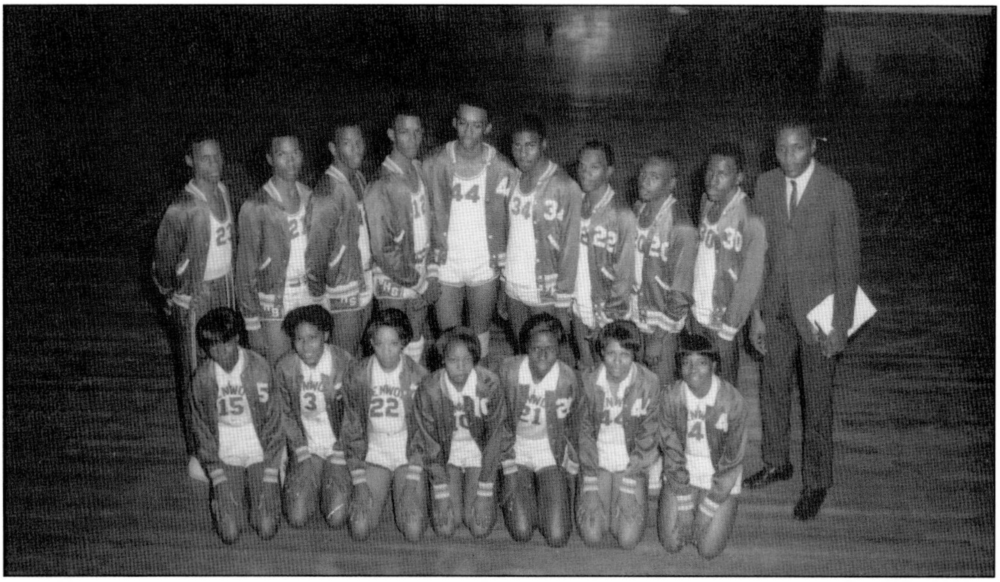

Bob Wimberly (back row, far right) coached the 1968 Glenwood High School basketball teams. Members of the girls team, from left to right, are Dorothy Berry, Helen Yarbrough, Jo Evelyn Jackson, Myrna Camp, Elaine Hillman, Neva Mayweather, and Lois Hayes. The boys, from left to right, are David Hunter, James Rogers, Doyle Dotson, Samuel Harris, Jimmy Johnson, John Morrow, Charles Jackson, Walter Harris, and Larry Griggs. Wimberly later served for many years as a principal in the integrated school system.

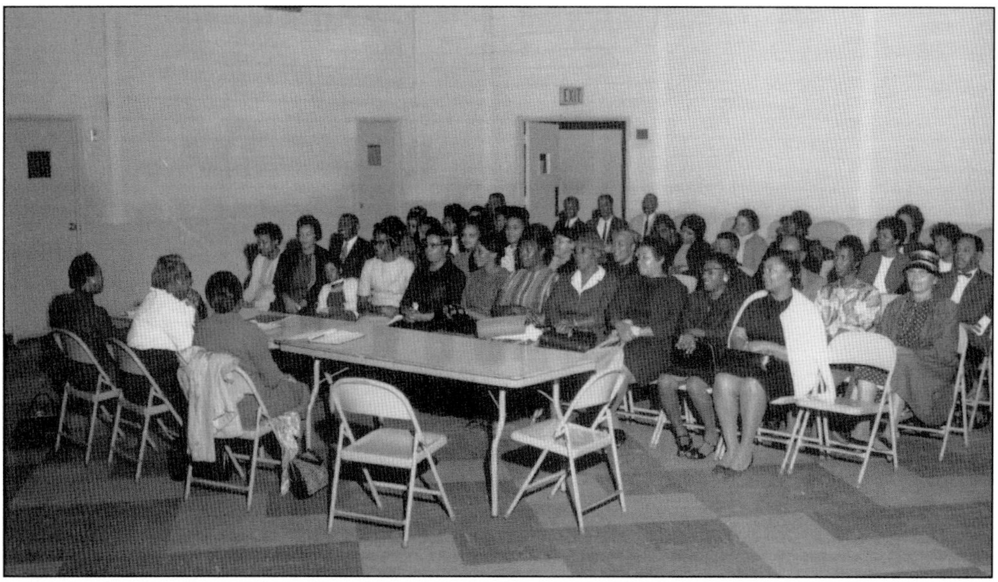

Glenwood School was blessed with an active Parent-Teacher Association (PTA) that stood ready to help the school meet its needs. Mamie Barnes, Robert Borders, and Nelese Hutchins were among the organization's presidents. At this November 1966 meeting, Josephine Jackson is in the middle facing the audience. Those in attendance included Elise Brown, Louise Smith, Curlie Roberts, Lamar Thompson, Rosa Burton, Maggie Winfrey, Katrina Johnson, Mary Barksdale, Claudine Ansley, Winnie Lee Russell, Robbie Teasley, Frances Ellington, and her daughter Nora.

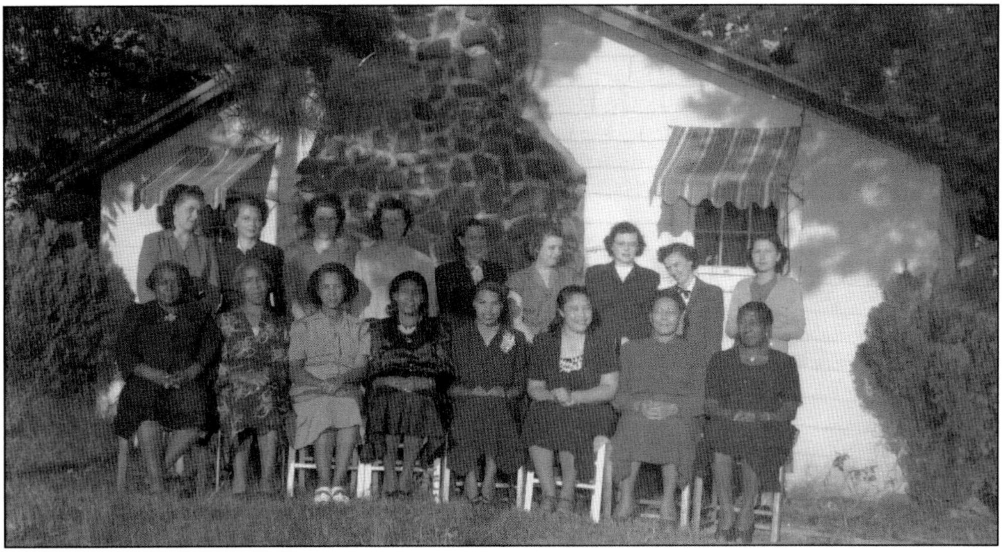

This photo, taken in October 1950, is an indication of the positive interracial relations in Barrow County during this difficult time. The Nosegay Garden Club, made up of all white members, organized the Gladiola Garden Club for African Americans and held several joint meetings. This photo was made at such a meeting in 1950. From left to right are as follows: (seated) Cora Campbell, Mamie Barnes, Mary Morrow, Ieuca Barnes, Mary Sims, Margaret Daniel, Curlie Roberts, and Stella Barnes; (standing) Mary Nell Colson, unidentified, Elizabeth Browh, Tootsie Lay, Nell Perry, Lois Cronic, Reba Hill, Hazel Cook, and Thelma Cooper. The meeting was held at the home of Mr. and Mrs. James Lay.

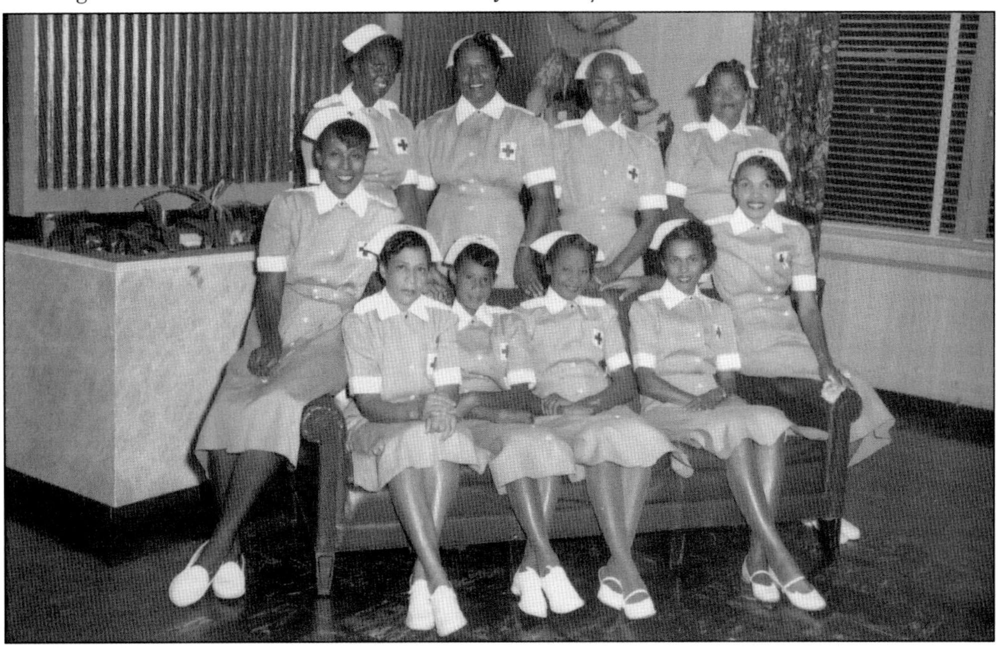

Another of Mary Sims' community projects was the organization of an African-American volunteer hospital auxiliary. From left to right are as follows: (seated) Reba Jones, Willie Mae Bell, Ruenette Johnson, Anna Ellington, Hazel Kilgore, and Mary Sims; (standing) Marie Kilgore, Belle McClusky, Mamie Barnes, and Goldie Thompson.

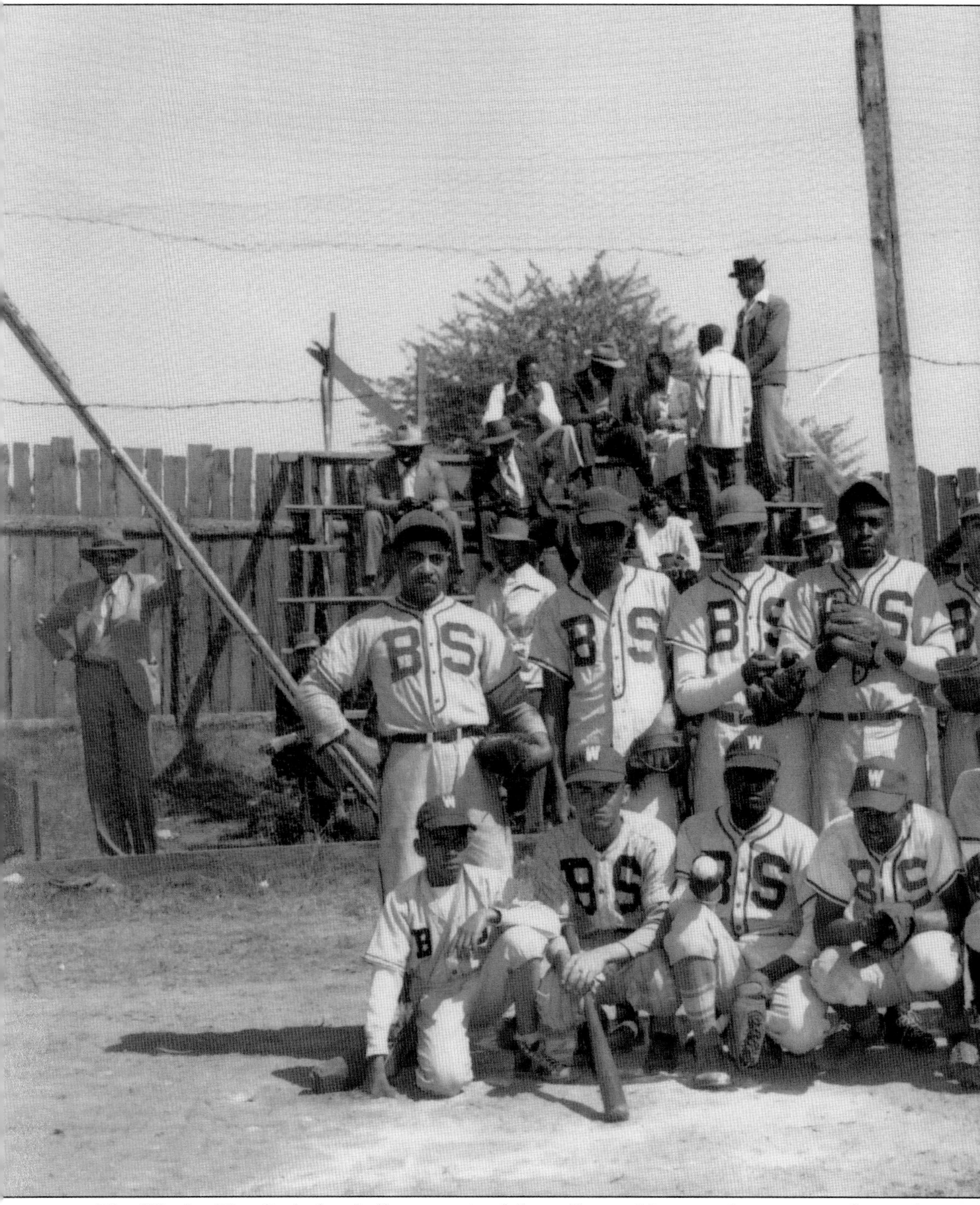

The Winder Blue Socks baseball team existed for well over 20 years, playing teams from other area towns and mill teams as far away as South Carolina. The 1949 team was composed of the following, from left to right: (front row) David Barnes, bat boy; James Johnson, outfield; John Price Jr., pitcher; Walter Hosch, third base; Robert F. Barnes, center field; Allen Griffeth, shortstop and second base; "Paten," the umpire; J.T. Shields, center field; and Horace Wells,

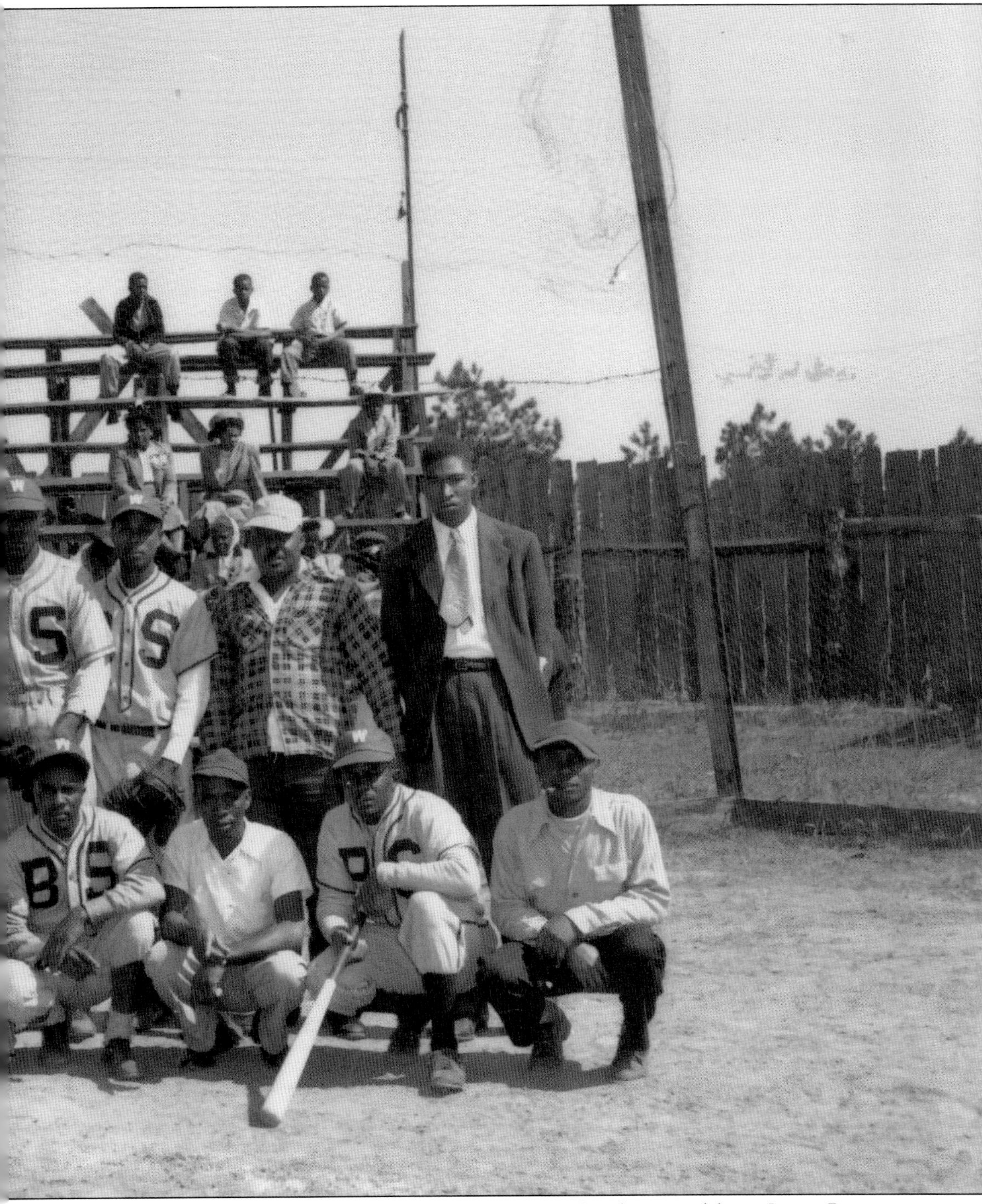

manager; (back row) Judson I. Jordan, catcher; Lucas S. Smith, second base; James Barnes, shortstop; Thomas P. Ross, pitcher; Edward Wade Ross, first base, Jessie Thompson, relief pitcher; Herbert Hunter, right field; Jim Robinson, shortstop; and Alfred Barnes, treasurer and business manager. Were they serious about their game? Study the facial expressions, then look at the field they are on. They built it themselves, on Highway 11, just outside Winder.

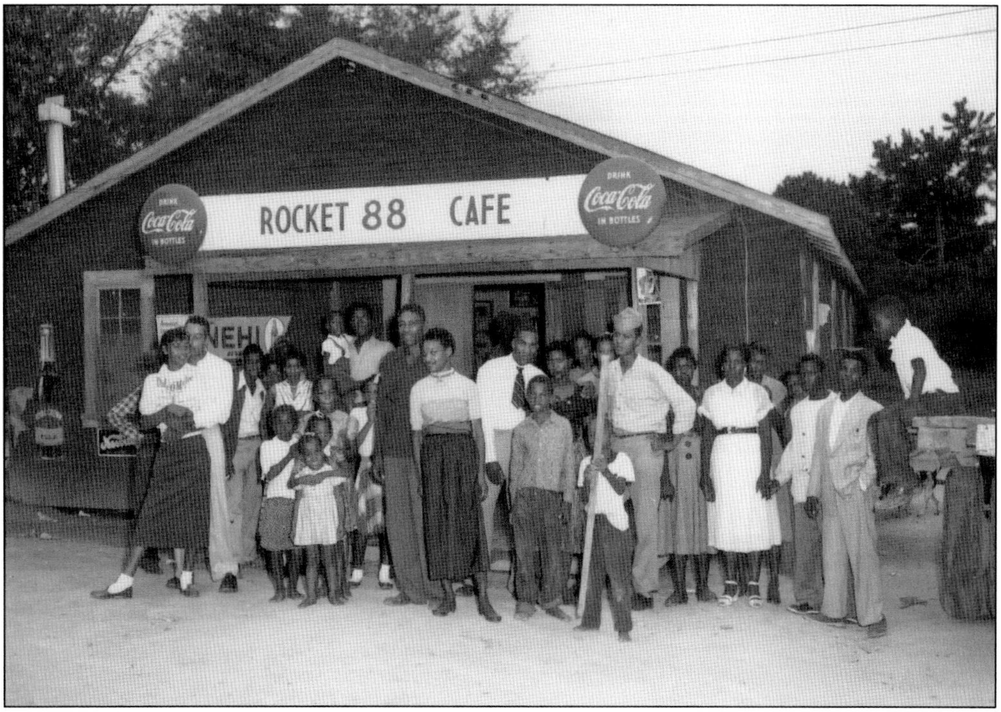

The Rocket 88 Café was a popular gathering place in Glenwood in 1953. According to the photo files it belonged to "Coot" Lee.

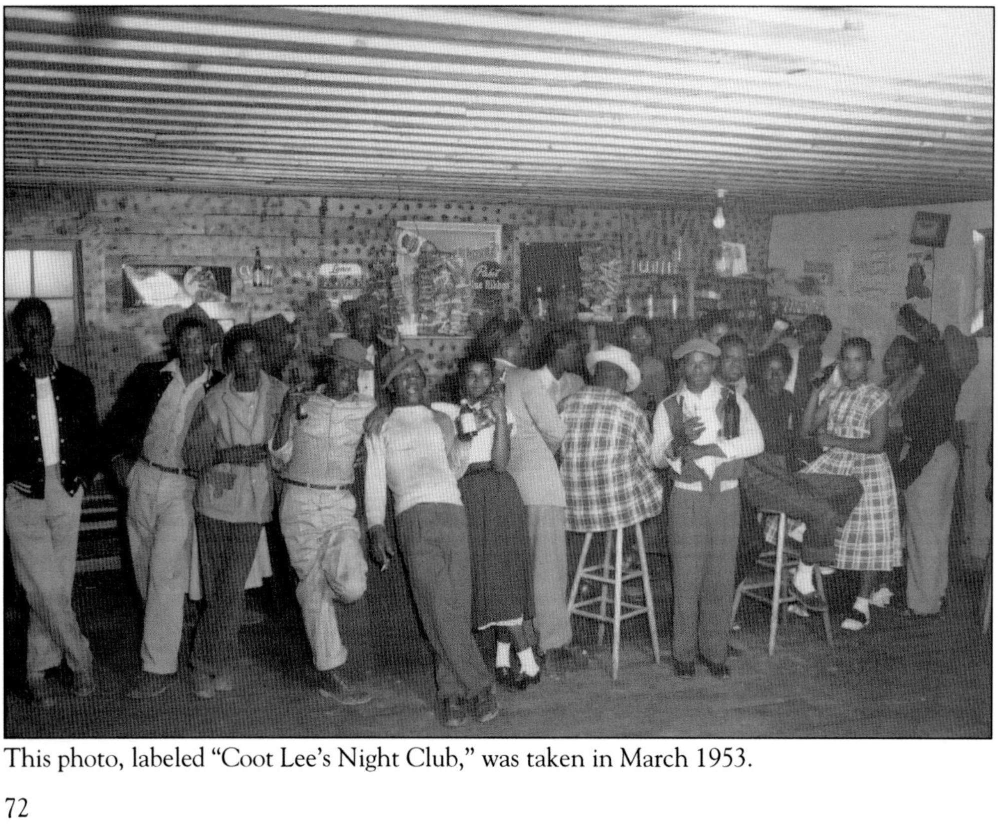

This photo, labeled "Coot Lee's Night Club," was taken in March 1953.

Eight

COTTON TO CHICKENS

Cotton was still king when the studio opened in Winder, but Stell and Kilgore would compile a photographic record of huge changes in agriculture during the next four decades. They were often called upon to photograph chicken operations, prize cattle and hogs, as well as some other forms of agriculture that were tried but didn't catch on.

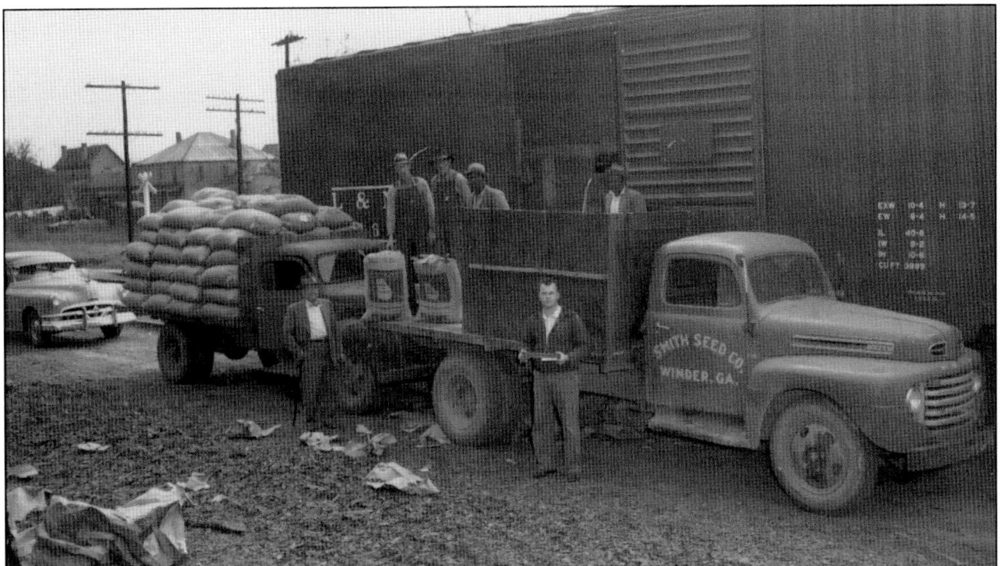

Barrow County was still a thriving cotton-growing area in the early 1950s, and P.R. "Bobby" Smith was a major figure. His Smith Seed & Gin Company marketed certified planting seed throughout the world. This shipment being loaded onto boxcars was headed for Syria. Smith is standing near the truck. Smith operated a cottonseed delinting plant, a cotton gin, and a cotton warehouse. The family grew cotton until 1977, and was the last family to grow cotton on a large scale in Barrow County. Smith served as an assistant secretary of agriculture during President Jimmy Carter's administration.

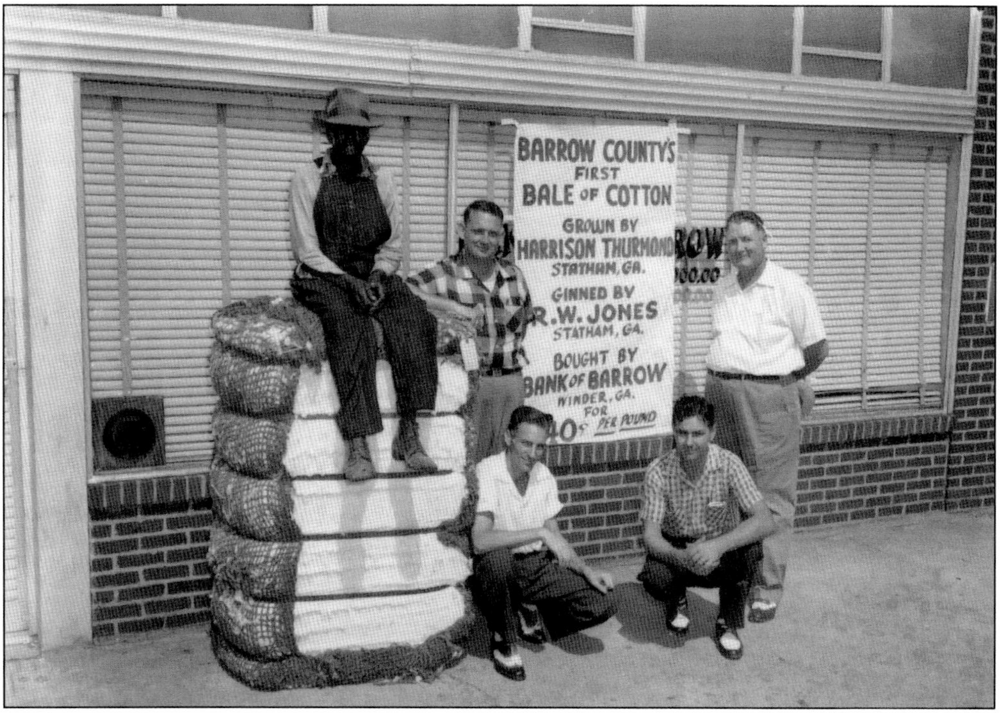

Local banks traditionally bought the first bale of cotton grown in Barrow County each year. In 1951 The Bank of Barrow purchased the first bale in 1951. From left to right are Harrison Thurmond, Joe Collins, Fred Hutchins, W.B. "Doc" Chandler, and R.W. Jones.

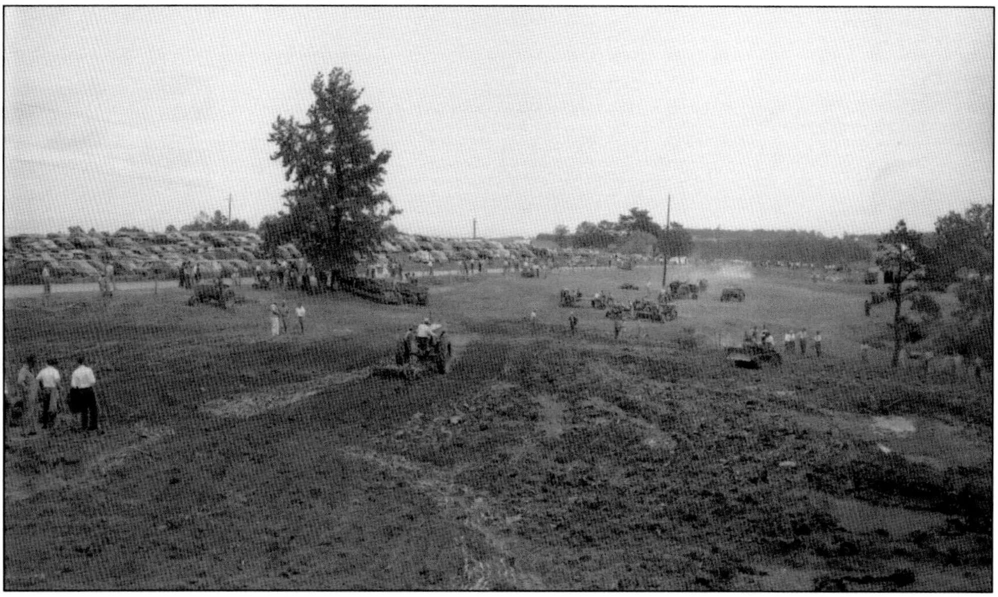

By the late 1940s, cotton farming, poor farming practices, and erosion had turned much of Barrow County's farmland into useless dirt; however, a huge demonstration on May 12, 1948, started a change for the better. In one day, the 186-acre Carlyle-Blakey farm was transformed by a huge force of men and machines into a soil-conserving model farm. The event, covered by national news media, was sponsored by the U.S. Soil Conservation Service.

Harold Harrison did more than any one person to transform agriculture in Barrow County. He provided farmers with a way to make a living without cotton. After working his way through the University of Georgia and graduating in 1941, he entered military service and served in the European Theater as a platoon leader and company commander. Upon his discharge at the end of World War II, he became interested in the then-infant poultry industry.

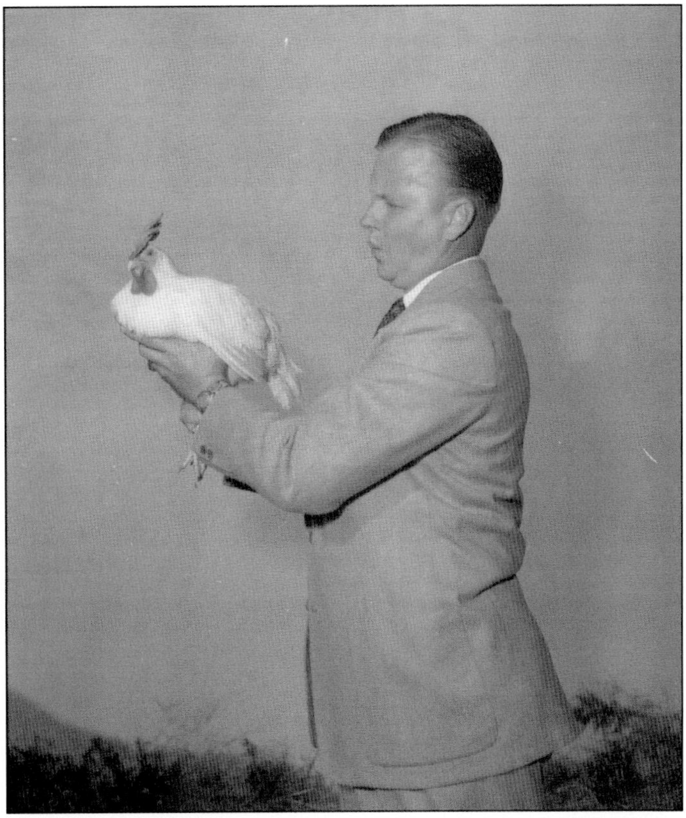

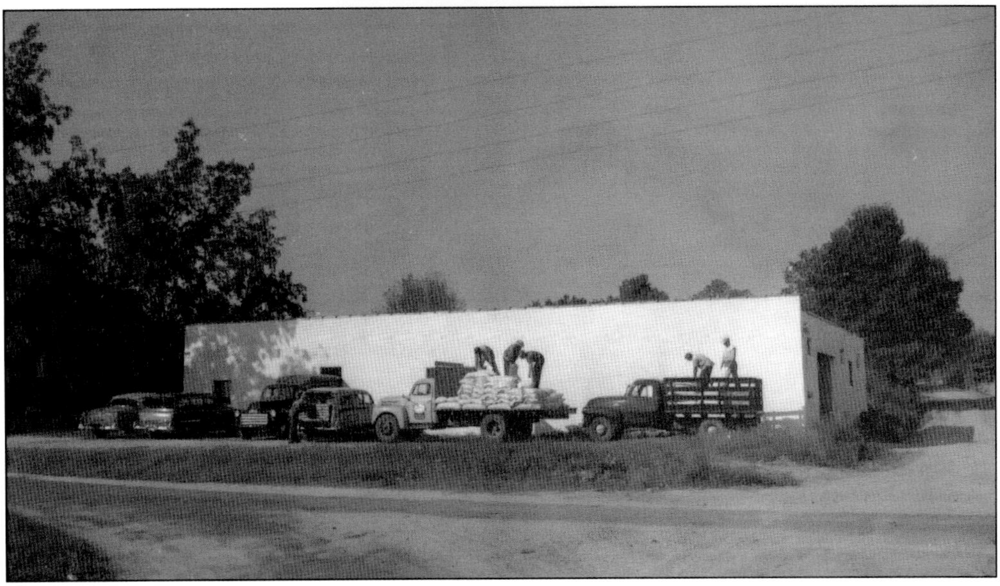

This hatchery building, shown in a 1953 photo, was the first structure in what would become an integrated poultry operation in Bethlehem and Winder. At the time, Harrison was selling most of his chicks to area feed dealers, but by 1954, the broiler market was depressed and he could not sell them. At that point he started contracting with farmers to grow his chickens to market weight.

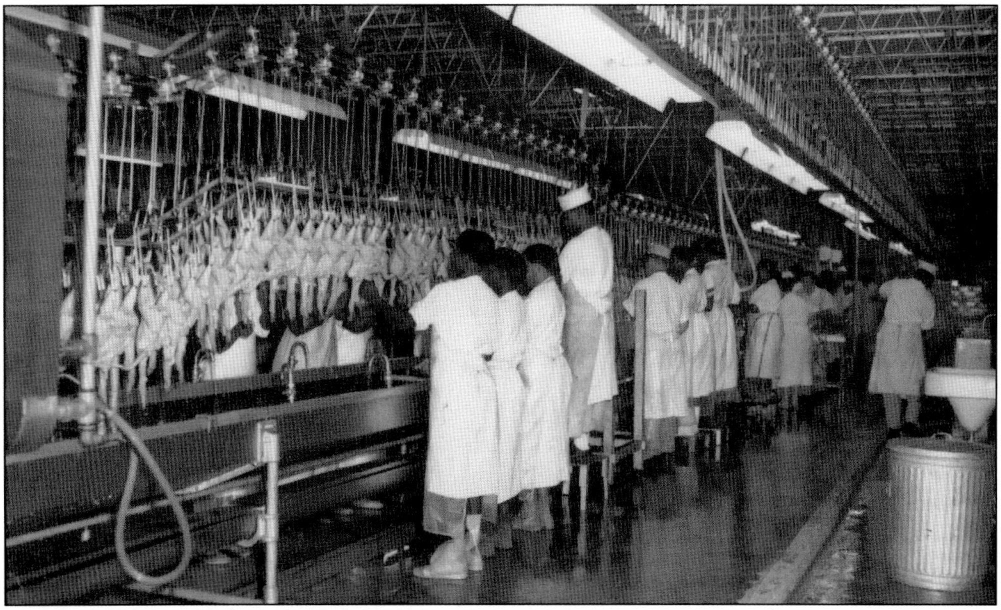

In 1958, Harrison built this processing plant in Bethlehem and started dressing broilers in 1959. In 1966 he became completely integrated with the construction of a fully-automated feed mill in Winder. Today, Harrison Poultry Company is one of Barrow County's largest employers. They hatch, grow, and process about 800,000 broilers per week. The company has approximately 200 contract growers. Total grower payments and payroll average about $24 million per year.

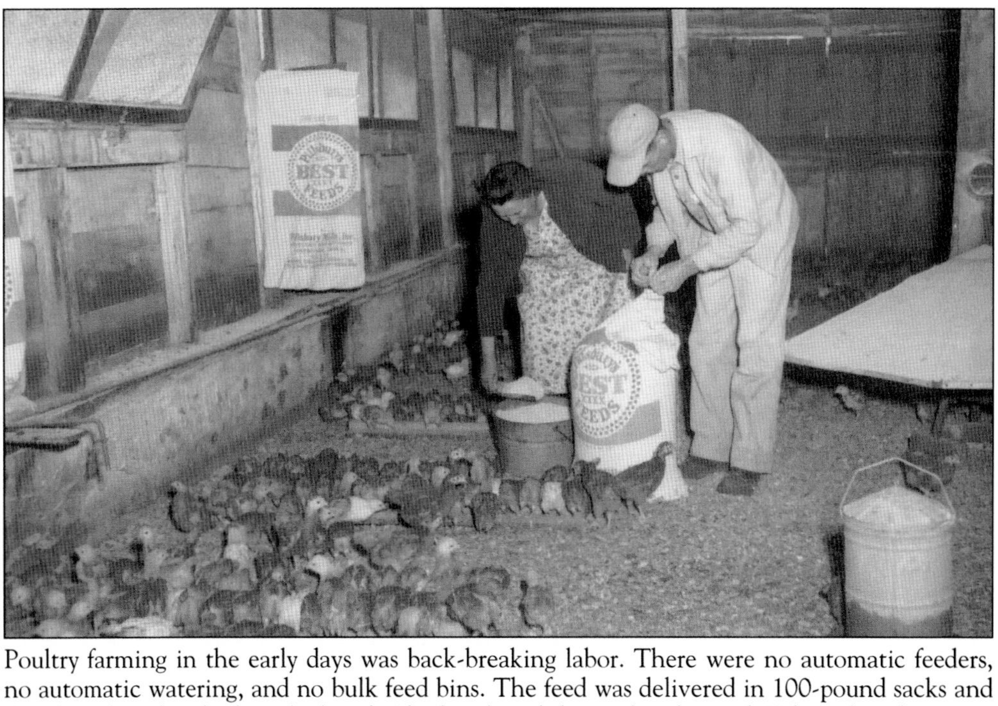

Poultry farming in the early days was back-breaking labor. There were no automatic feeders, no automatic watering, and no bulk feed bins. The feed was delivered in 100-pound sacks and distributed to the chickens by hand. Chicken breeds have also changed. When this photo was made at the E.C. Perkins farm in 1951, the Rhode Island Red was the breed of choice.

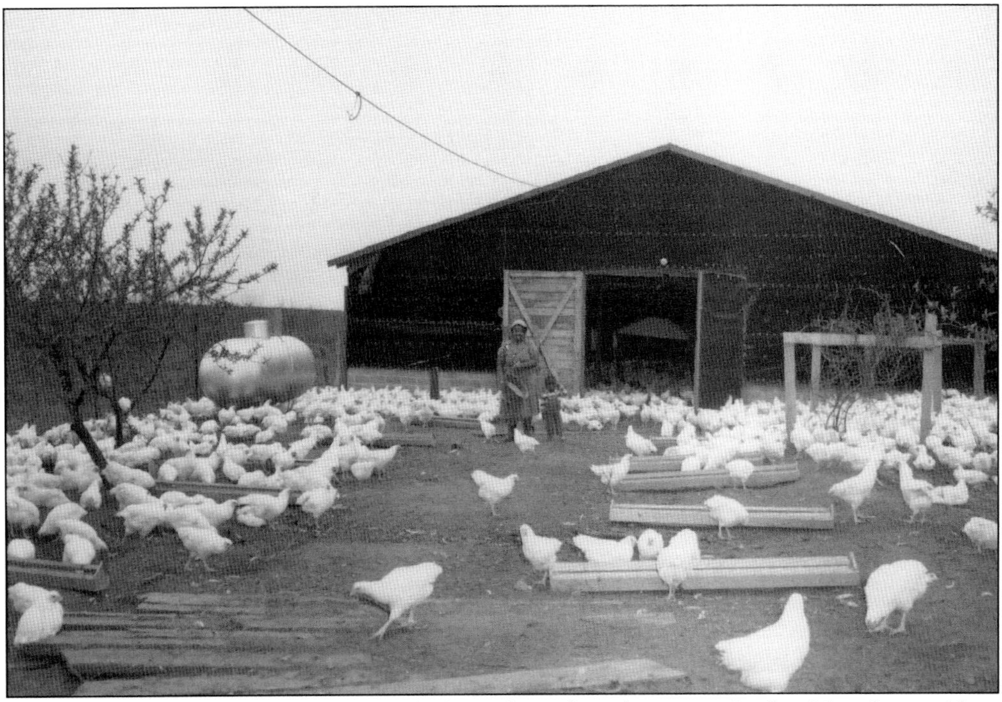
This photo, made in March 1955, is of a layer farm, furnishing eggs for local hatcheries. Note that the hens are able to move inside or out at will.

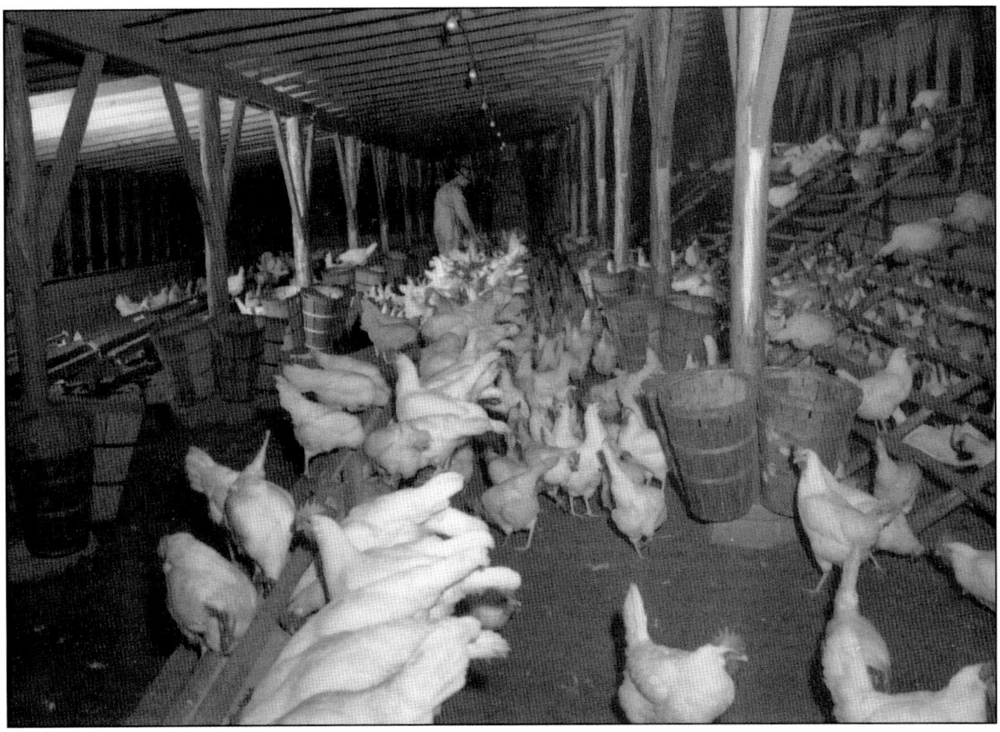
This is a photo of a Harrison Poultry hatching egg operation. Note the baskets for gathering eggs and the hen roosts on the right.

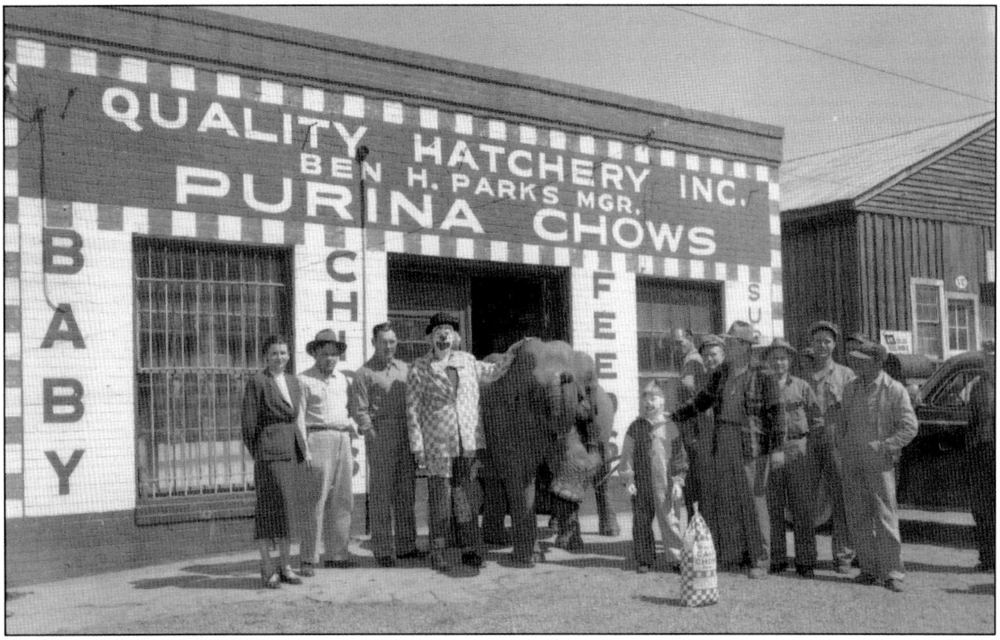

Quality Hatchery was also a force in the early days of the chicken industry in Barrow County. This photo, made in March 1950, was of a promotion the business sponsored in conjunction with the Strand Theater to promote the movie *Song of India*. Office Manager Kathleen McClure is the woman at left. The third person from the left is manager Ben Parks.

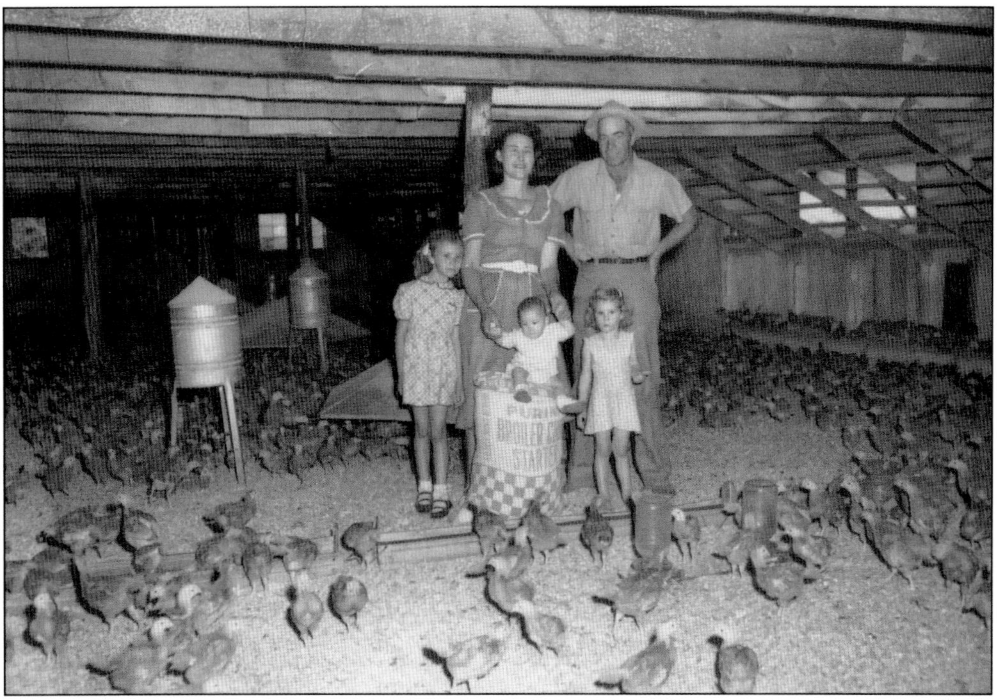

Ida Mae and Clarence Mooney were growing chickens for Quality Hatchery when this photo was made in September 1953. They are shown with their children, Janice, Randy, and Gail. Their farm was on Highway 82 near Old Pentecost Church.

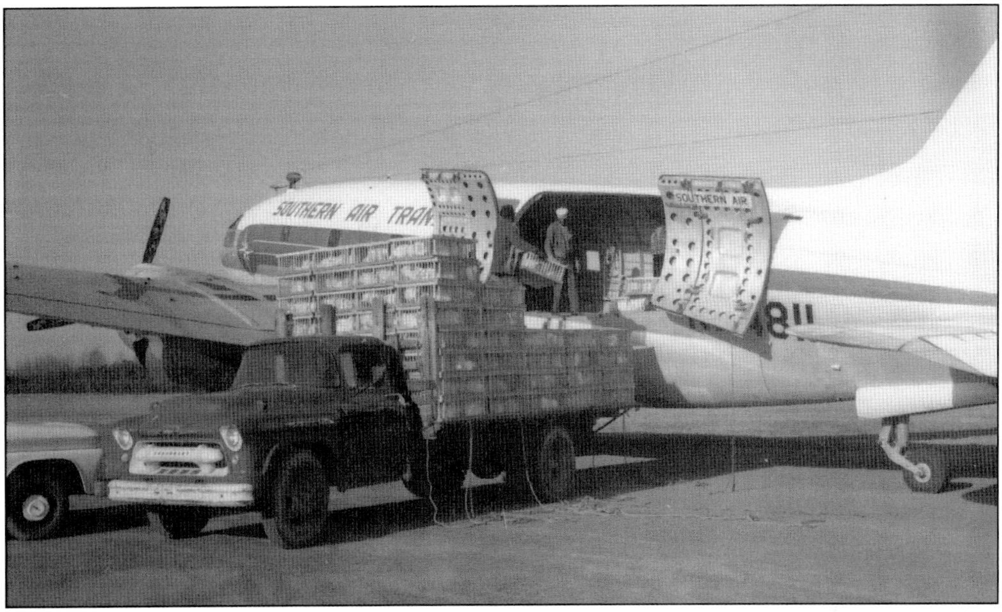

Barrow's poultry industry took to the skies in early 1964 when R.W. Thompson Breeders of Hoschton initiated the first air transport of poultry from the Winder-Barrow Airport. More than 118,000 pounds of breeder stock poultry were shipped to the Caribbean to replace chickens that had been lost in a hurricane. Southern Air Transport of Miami handled the shipment.

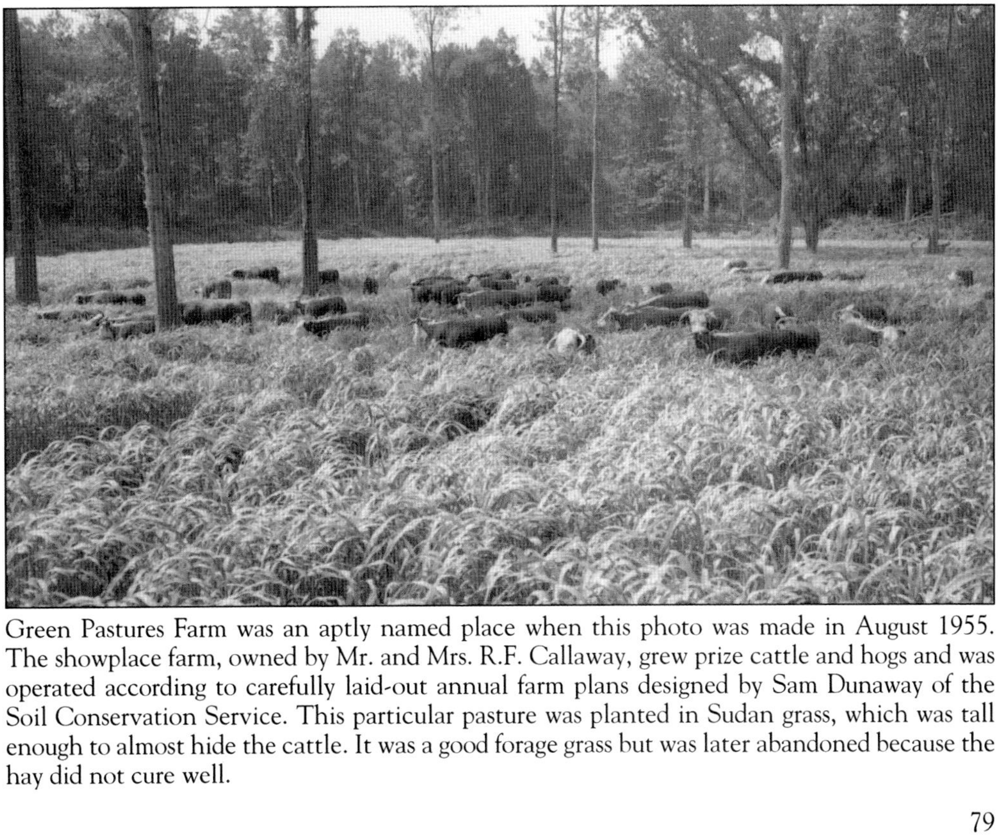

Green Pastures Farm was an aptly named place when this photo was made in August 1955. The showplace farm, owned by Mr. and Mrs. R.F. Callaway, grew prize cattle and hogs and was operated according to carefully laid-out annual farm plans designed by Sam Dunaway of the Soil Conservation Service. This particular pasture was planted in Sudan grass, which was tall enough to almost hide the cattle. It was a good forage grass but was later abandoned because the hay did not cure well.

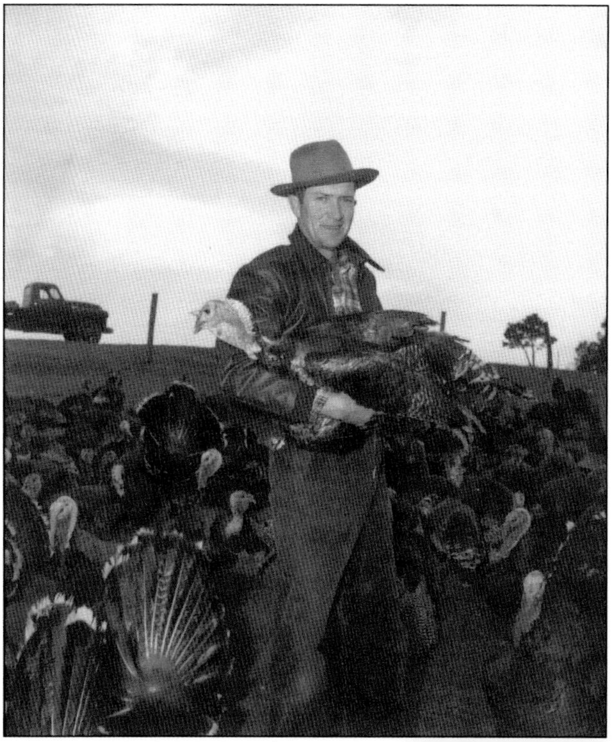

Chickens were not the only poultry industry in Barrow County in the 1950s. Bill Segars had a large turkey operation on his farm near the airport on Highway 82. Segars operated a hatchery and sold turkey chicks to other farmers—including James Carruth and Clarence Mooney—as well as a feed mill. Turkey farming was abandoned because of the difficulty in getting the birds to distant processing plants.

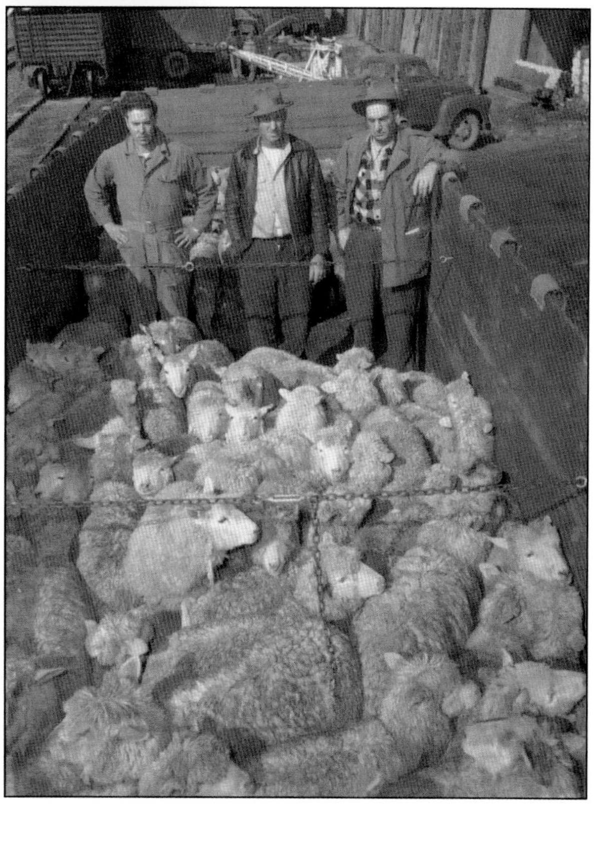

Another short-lived idea in Barrow County was sheep farming. This photo shows, from left to right, sheep farmers Jack Segars and J.B. Lay with County Extension Agent Claude Williams. The difficulties of raising sheep soon became apparent. They had to be rotated from pasture to pasture to keep down parasites, they required a lot of grass, and the shearers had to be brought in from Mexico. Predators were also a problem. Retired Soil Conservation Agent Sam Dunaway recalls that he bought 50 sheep and two rams and kept them two years. When he realized the purchase not a good decision, he advertised them for sale in the *Market Bulletin*, setting the price he wanted. When a man came to look at the sheep, Dunaway said he offered a much lower price. "All the way back to town I kept trying to get my price, but at the same time I was thinking, 'Mister, you just bought yourself some sheep.' "

Nine

FAMILY TIES

From children's parties to family reunions, Stell and Kilgore documented the lives of hundreds of Barrow County families. Their files contain hundreds of photos taken in homes all over the county, including many Christmas Eve and Christmas Day photographs of children with their new toys.

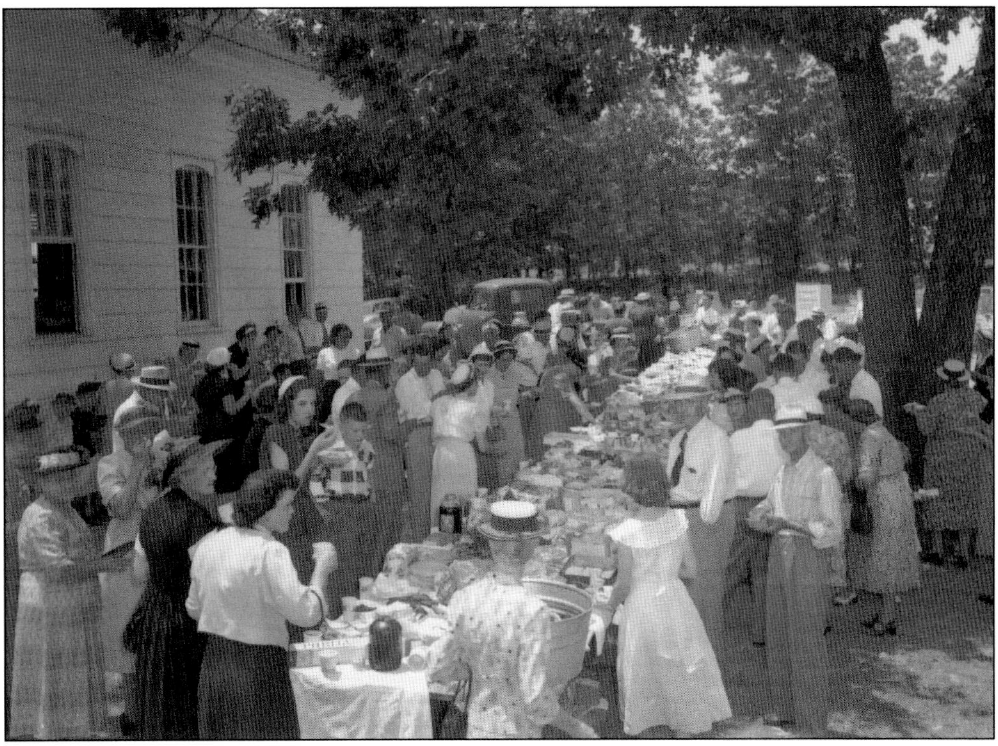

Stell and Kilgore were on hand for homecoming and "dinner on the grounds" at the Corinth United Methodist Church on June 3, 1951.

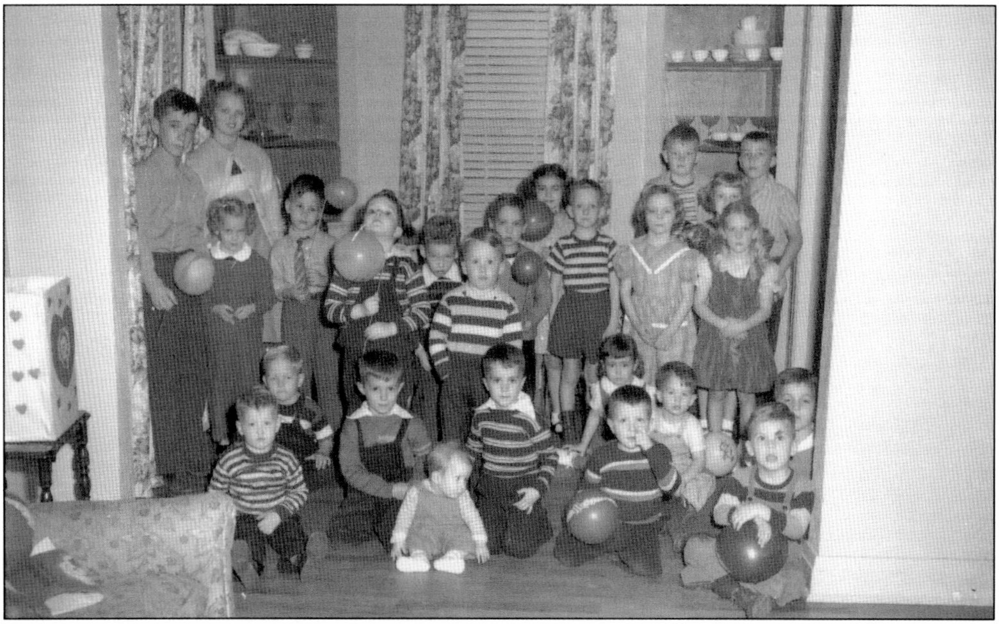

Robert and Reba Hill commissioned Stell and Kilgore to photograph their son Bob's fourth birthday on February 14, 1950. Bob is in the center of the photo looking directly at the camera. His younger brother, Doug, is the infant nearest the camera. Guests included Jimmy Griffith, Steve Griffith, Ludger Lanthier Jr., Richard Henson, Colter McGinnis, Stoy Hogan, Hal Miller, John Robert Robinson, and Jeff Thompson.

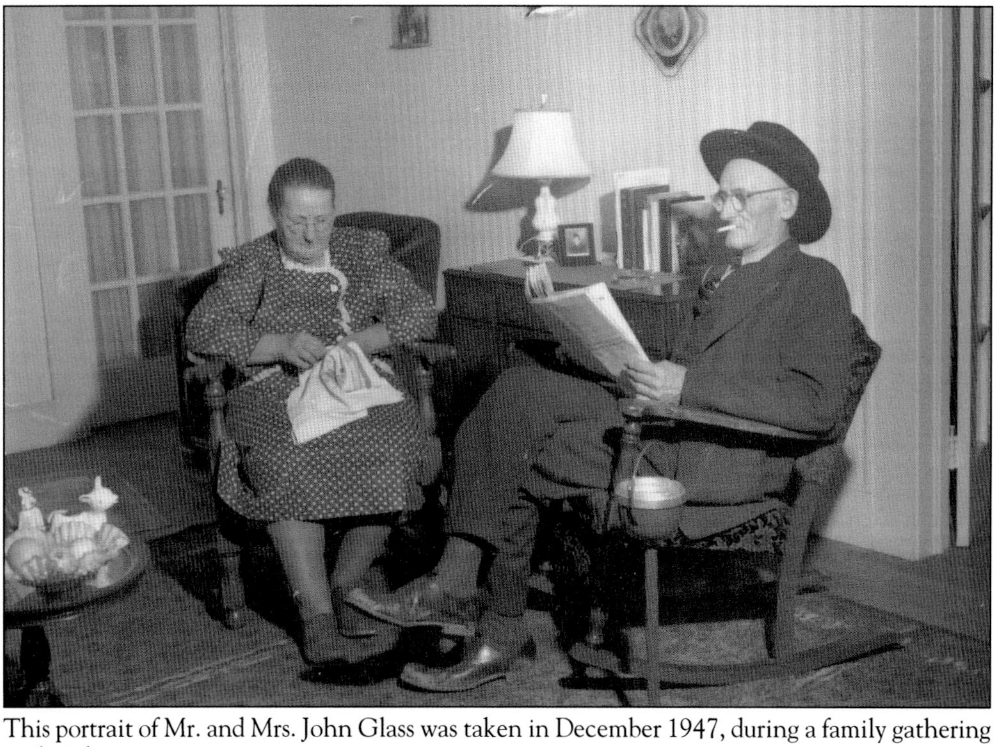

This portrait of Mr. and Mrs. John Glass was taken in December 1947, during a family gathering at their home.

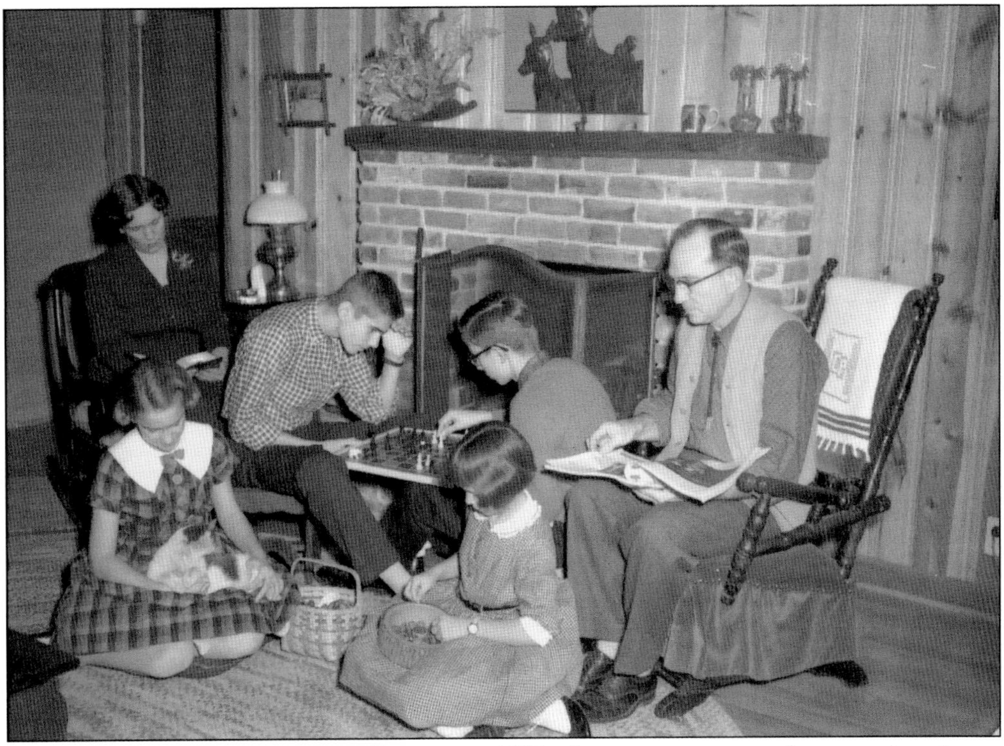

When C. Fred Ingram came to Barrow in 1950, the county got much more than just a vocational/agriculture teacher. It got two leading citizens in "Mr. Fred" and his wife, Charlotte (left), and four fine young people in sons Pepper (left) and Bob, and daughters Beth (left) and Jane. After his retirement from the school system, Fred became the driving force behind the Barrow County Historical Society and is responsible for much of the preservation that has been accomplished.

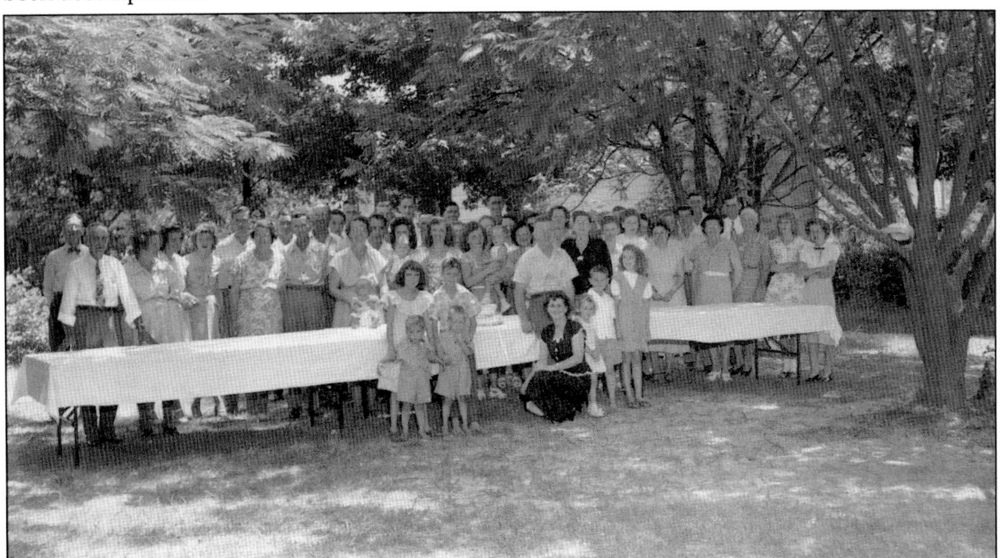

Stell and Kilgore photographed the Hall family reunion in July 1948. Not much is known about this particular photo, but it may have been made in the Harbins area of Gwinnett County.

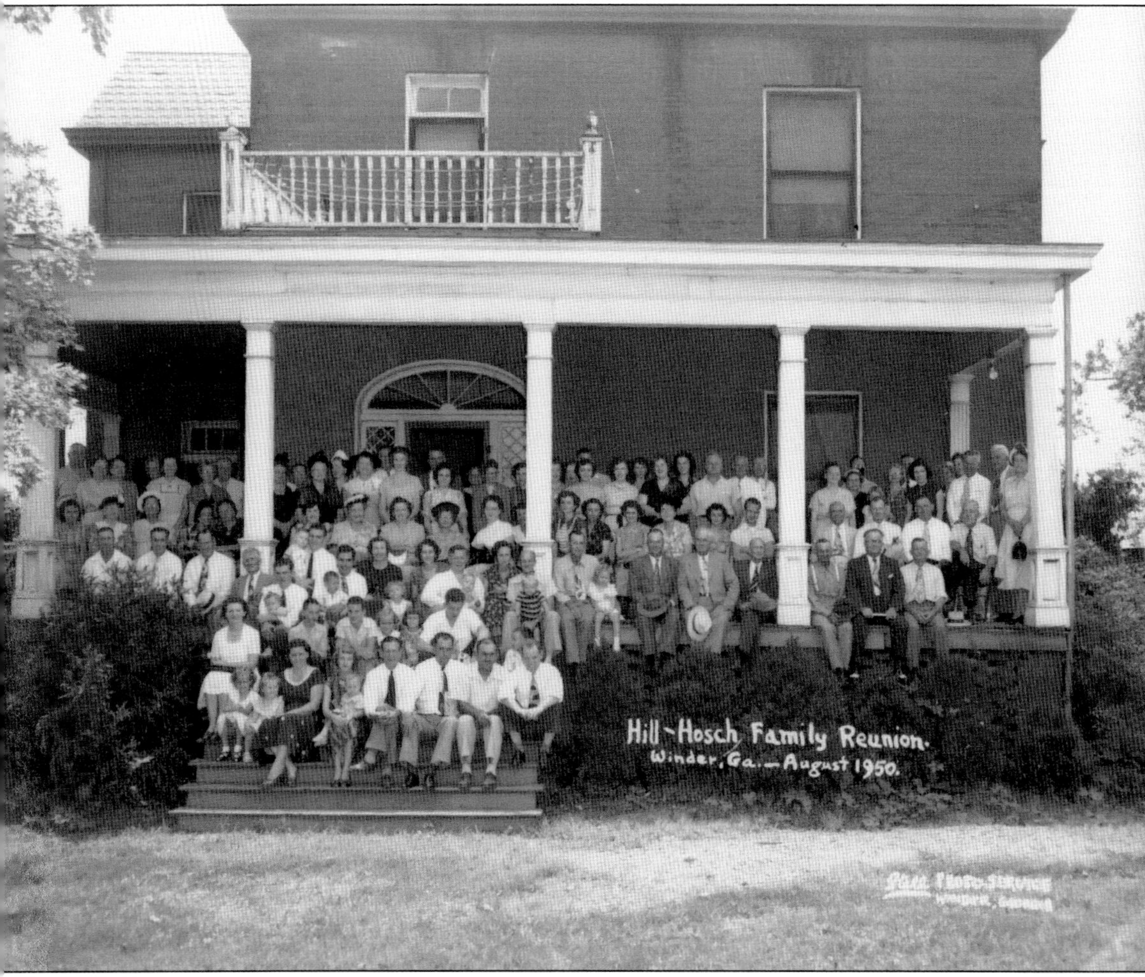

The Hill-Hosch family reunion was held in the first home of the Winder Lions Club in August 1950. The building was located on May Street, across from where the Dairy Queen is located today.

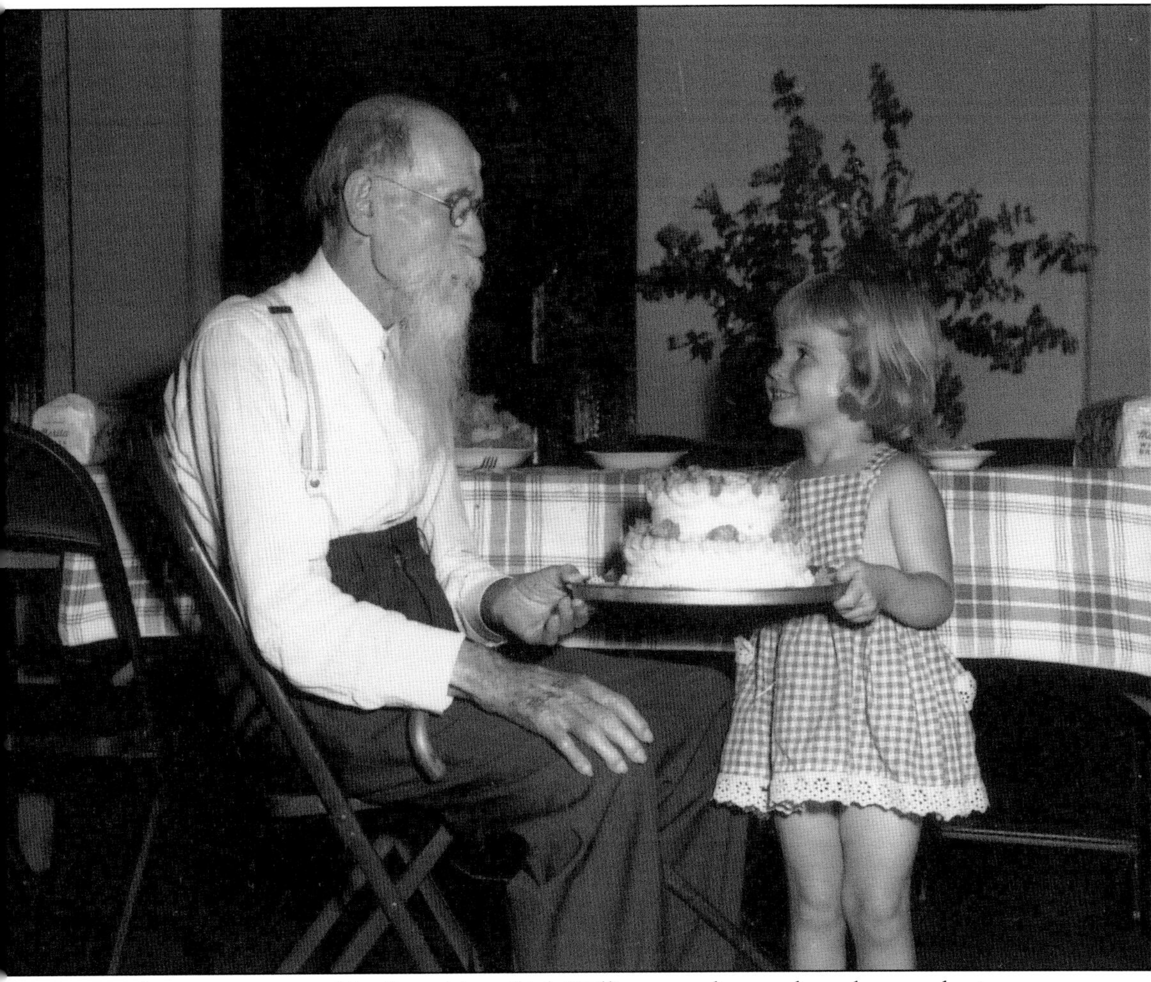

Barrow County pioneer and leading citizen Pink Williams was honored at a huge gathering on his 90th birthday in July 1949. His great-granddaughter Judith Grizzle is shown presenting the birthday cake.

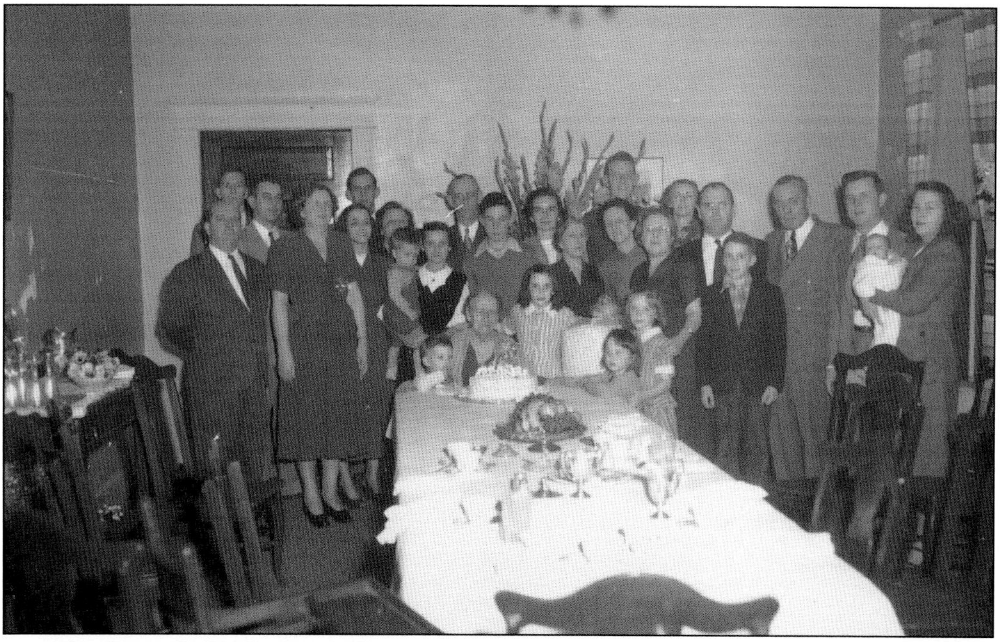

Ina Dillard Russell (Mother Russell), the matriarch of a large and influential family, was honored at a birthday party in February 1950. This remarkable woman was married to Richard Brevard Russell, chief justice of the Georgia Supreme Court, and raised 13 children—including future Georgia governor and U.S. senator Richard Russell.

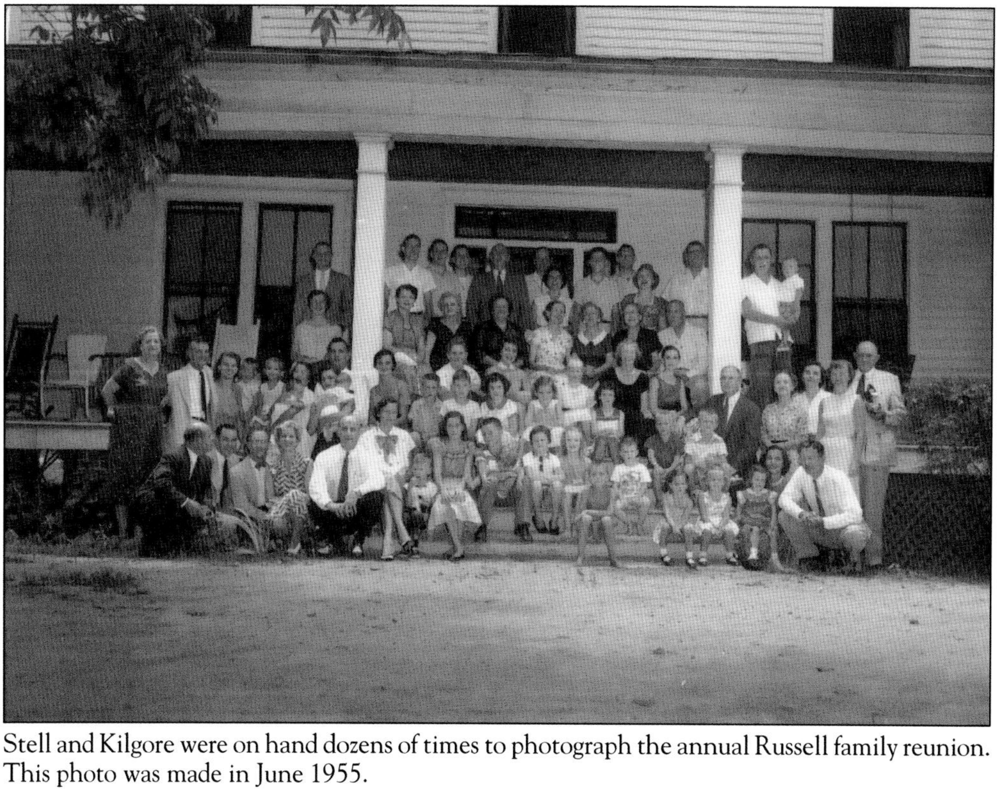

Stell and Kilgore were on hand dozens of times to photograph the annual Russell family reunion. This photo was made in June 1955.

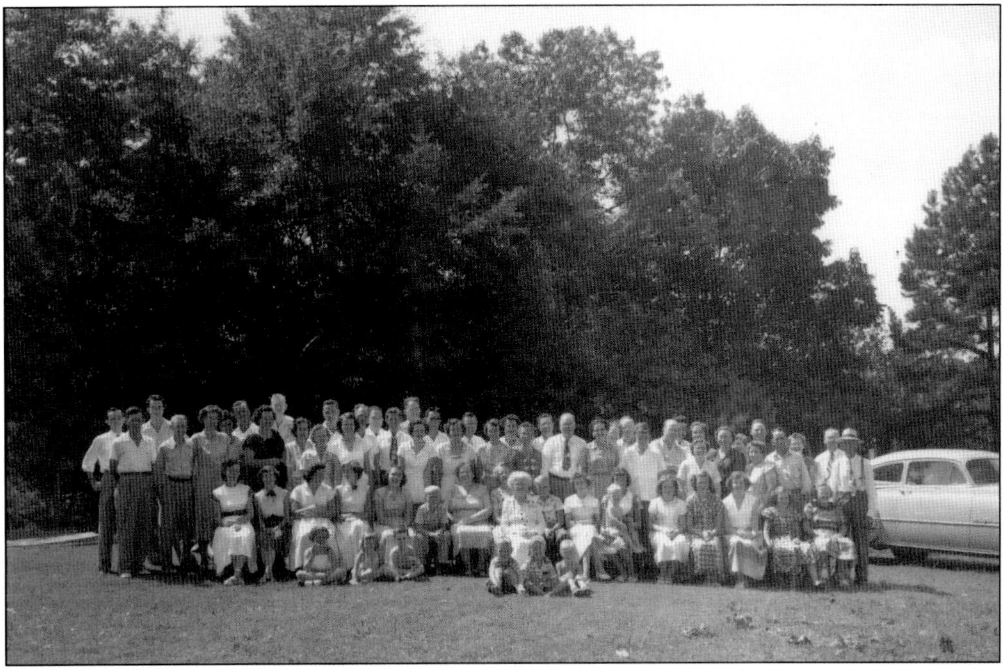

This photograph of the Wilbanks reunion was taken August 20, 1950.

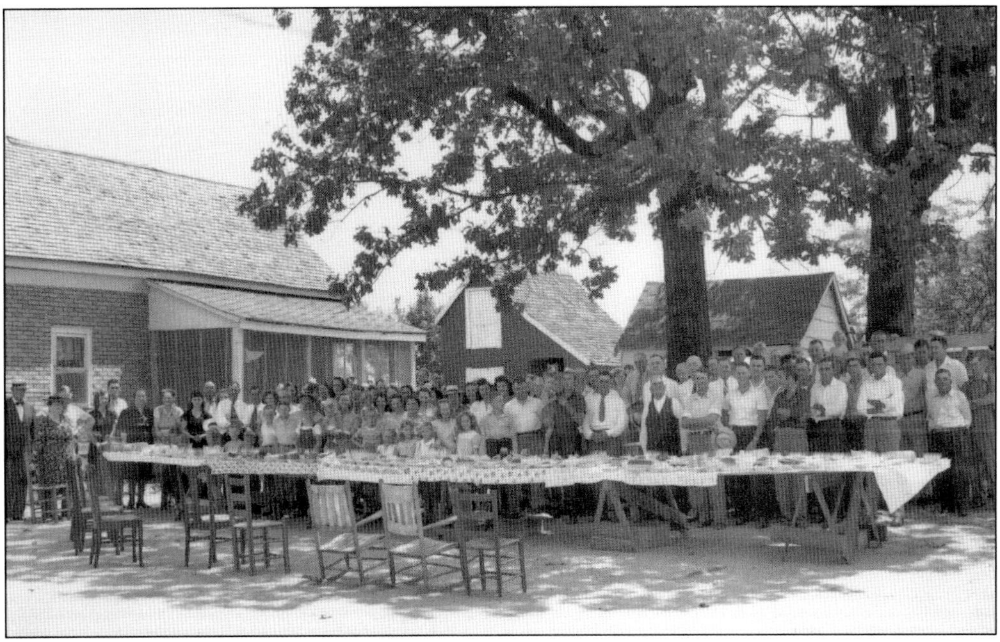

Guyton Teal's annual barbecue was always a big social event in the Bethlehem area. At sundown on the night before, Teal and his children would dig a pit, prepare the coals, and begin barbecuing a 150-to-175-pound hog, and start preparing up to 40 gallons of Brunswick stew. Meanwhile, wife and mother Bessie Florence Teal would be busy in the kitchen preparing fresh vegetables. Guests would also bring covered dishes, so there would be enough food for a small army. His son Bob recalls that Guyton would also invite local politicians, doctors, and businessmen to the event

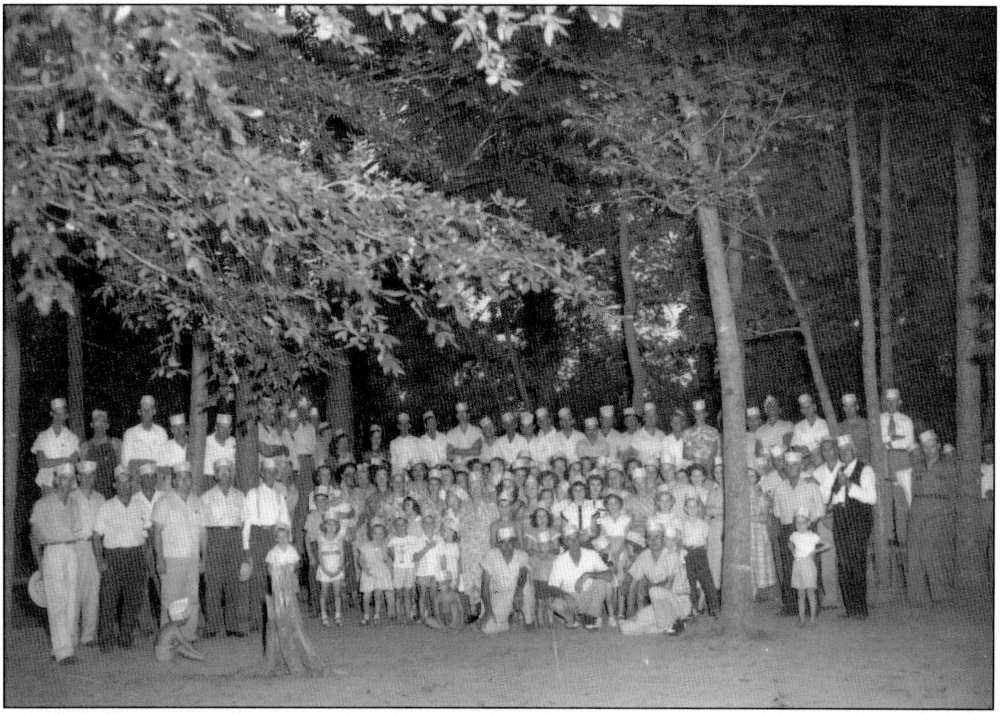

This gathering, hosted by E.C. Perkins, was held at Bellgrade Park, which was just off South Broad Street in Winder. The Bellgrade Manufacturing Company owned the park.

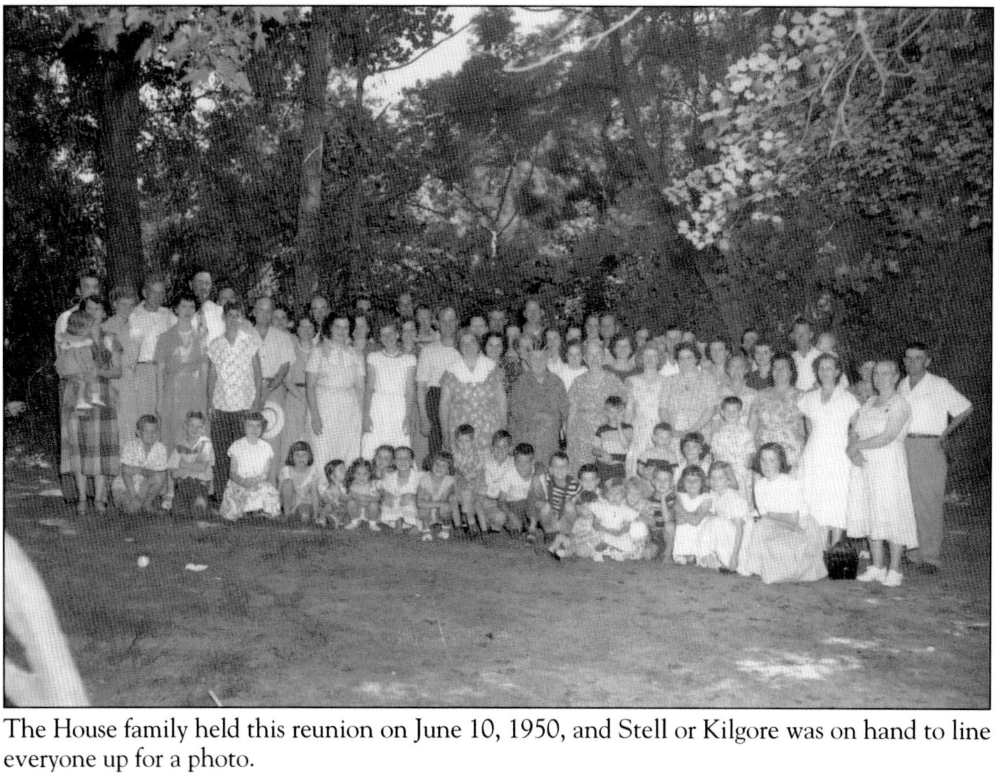

The House family held this reunion on June 10, 1950, and Stell or Kilgore was on hand to line everyone up for a photo.

Ten

FUN AND GAMES

There wasn't much in the way of television, and there were no tapes or video games during this period, but folks in Barrow County didn't lack for things to do for entertainment.

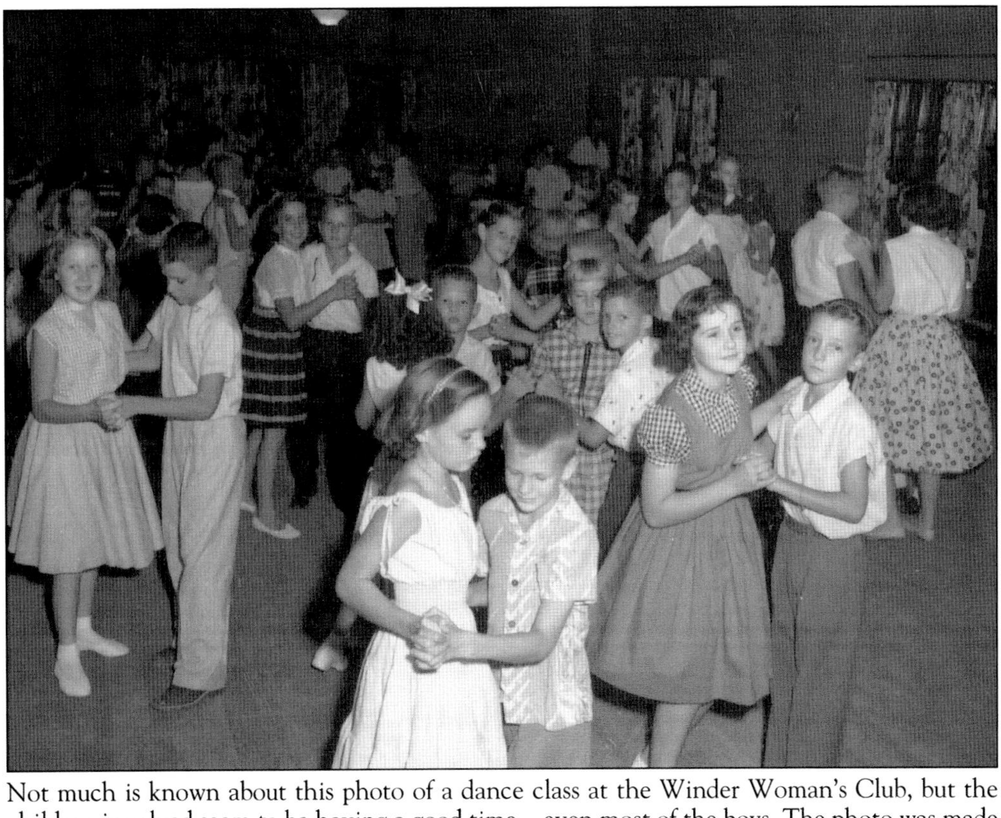

Not much is known about this photo of a dance class at the Winder Woman's Club, but the children involved seem to be having a good time—even most of the boys. The photo was made August 29, 1955.

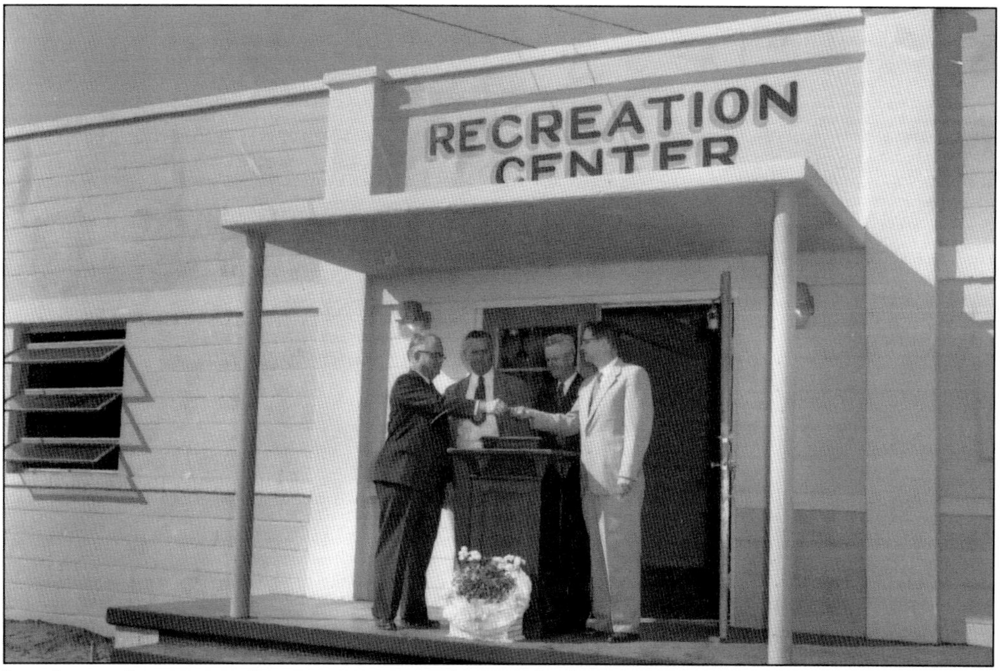

Local manufacturers and community contributions built a recreation center for Winder on land donated by the Jackson family. Shown at the presentation, from left to right, are Paul Hosch, School Superintendent D.F. Osborne, School Board Chairman Bill Blount, and Winder mayor Guy Ouzts. The building on Midland Avenue was later used as the county library and is now the school system's alternative education center.

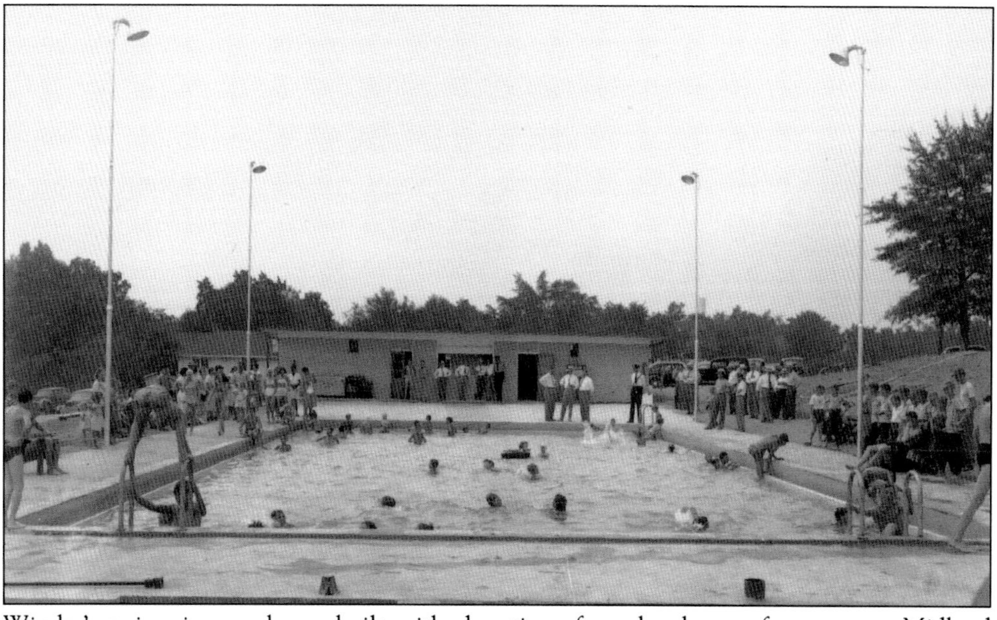

Winder's swimming pool was built with donations from local manufacturers on Midland Avenue, also on land donated by the Jackson family. This photo, taken in August 1948, would give today's insurance industry nightmares. It was filled, and open, but the fence had not yet been built.

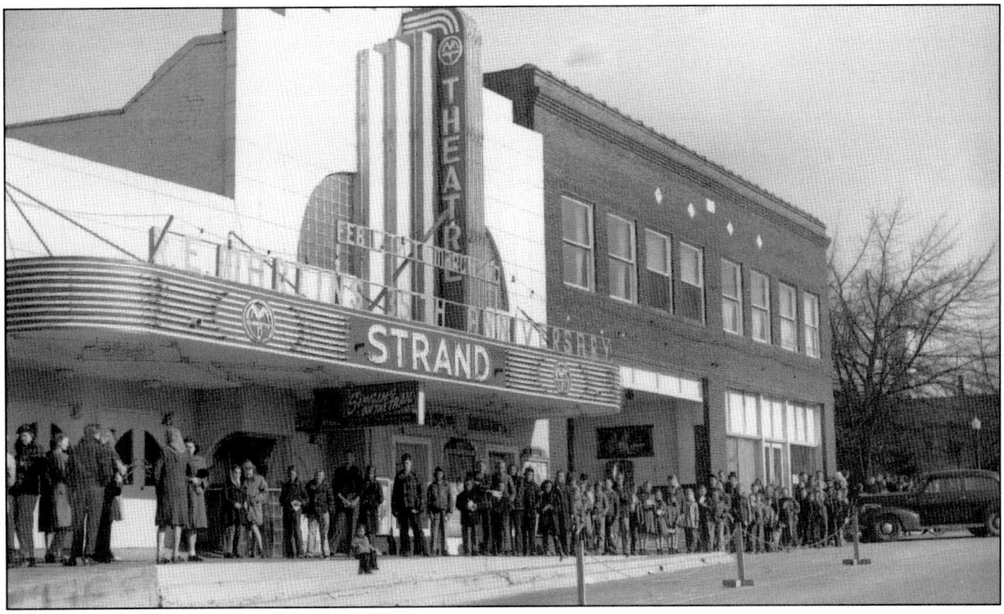

The Strand Theater was "entertainment headquarters" in the 1940s and 1950s. It was located on North Broad Street, on the site now occupied by the courthouse addition. This photo was made in April 1947. At one time there was a second theater in Winder, also on North Broad, next to The Peoples Bank.

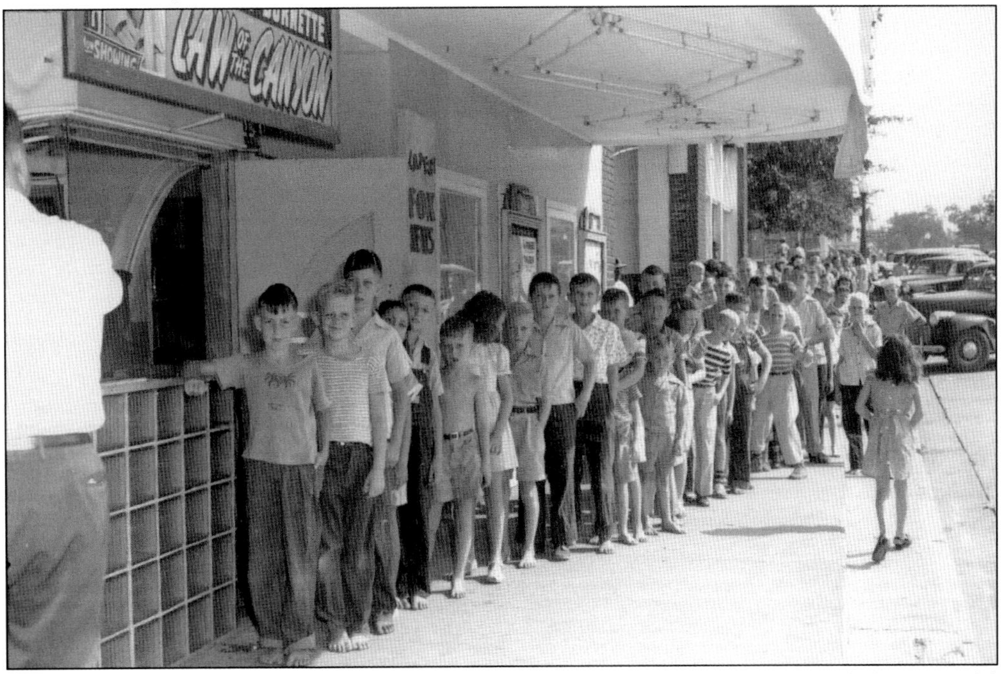

The Strand attracted huge crowds of kids for Saturday matinees. One particularly successful promotion allowed children to get in free if they brought three Merita Bread wrappers. Shown from left to right are Jimmy Mote, Kenneth Thornton, Douglas Mote, Martha Allen, Donald Allen, Bill Sharpton, Delores Simmons, Eddie Booth, Kermit Booth Jr., Billy Ray Weils, Ottis Smith, Louie Smith, Jimmie Hardegree, and Billie Hardegree. The others are unidentified.

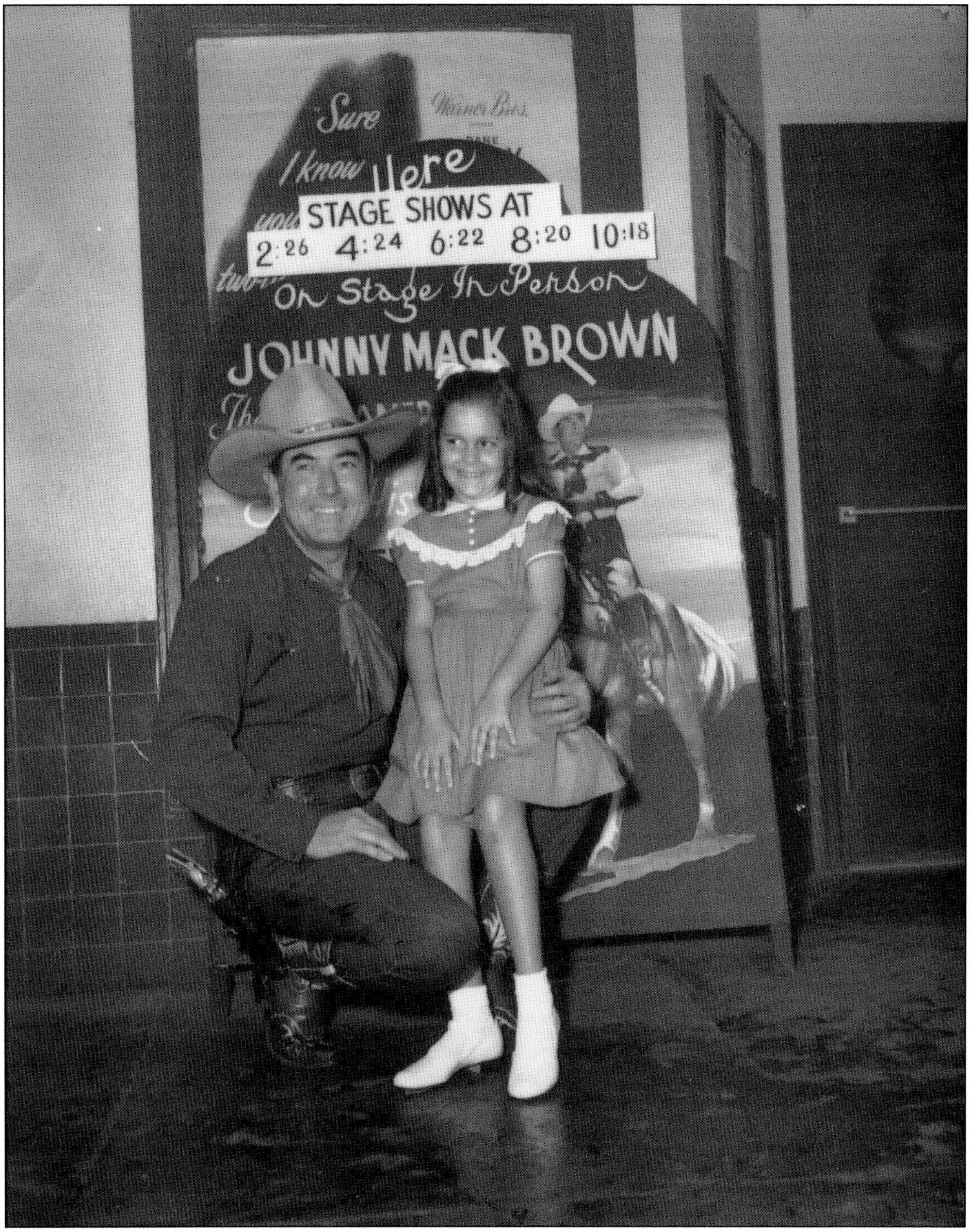

During this era, you could see your heroes up close and in person, even in a town as small as Winder. Many of the cowboy movie stars toured the country doing stage shows, including Johnny Mack Brown, shown here with an unidentified Barrow County girl. Brown, who was born in 1904, grew up in Dothan, AL. He graduated from the University of Alabama, where he was an All-American halfback. He could have gone on to professional football, but instead took his good looks and athletic ability to Hollywood and a movie career that spanned more than 40 years. He had roles in 168 movies and starred with many Hollywood greats, including Greta Garbo, Joan Crawford, John Wayne, and Tex Ritter.

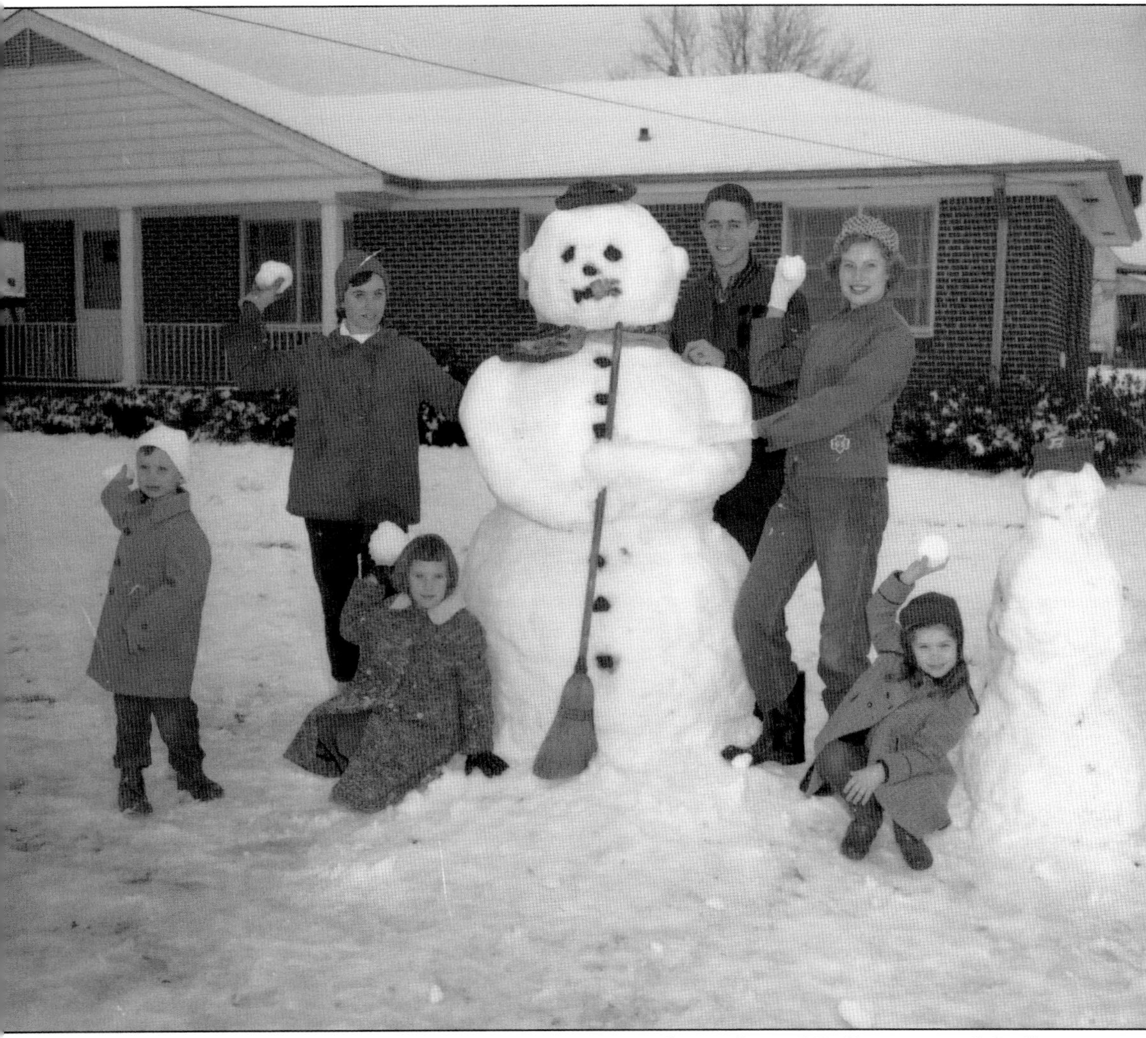

On Saturday, February 15, 1958, Barrow County received 4 inches of fluffy snow, and Stell and Kilgore were on hand to join in the fun while capturing the memories. This photo shows, from left to right, Douglas Osborne, Nancy Osborne, Susan Smith, Richard Hostetter, Peggy Thornley, and Barbara Westberg.

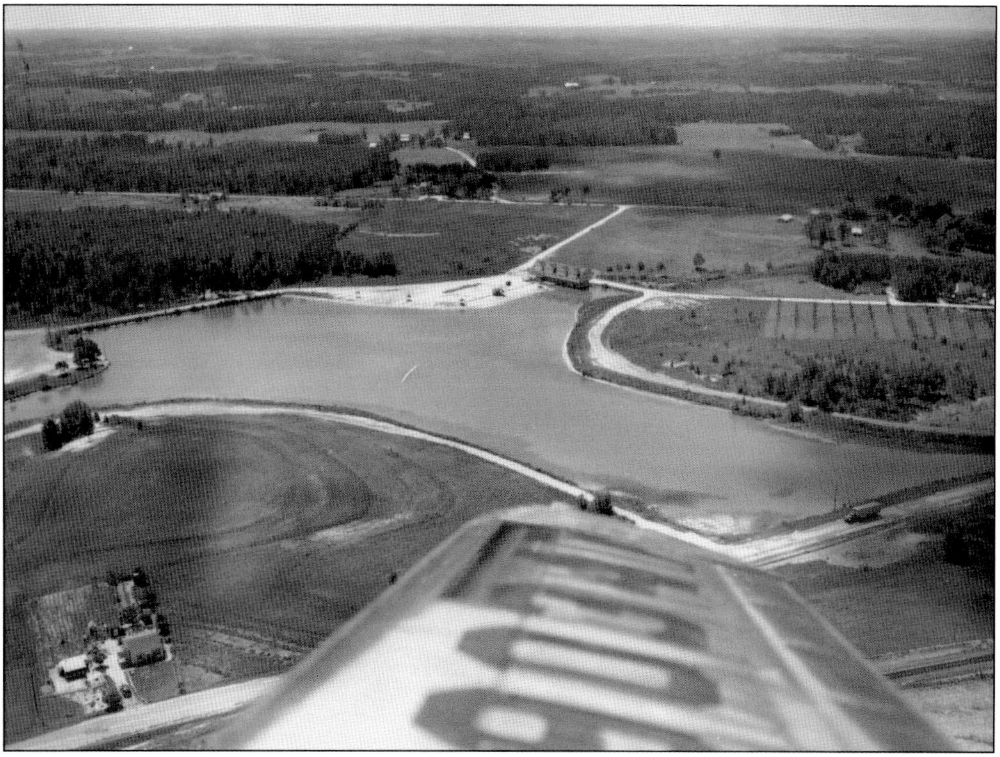

Lake Elder was a popular, privately owned recreation center on the Winder side of Auburn. The lake still exists today, but the building and beach shown here have been gone for many years. At one time the owners even planned a hotel on the property.

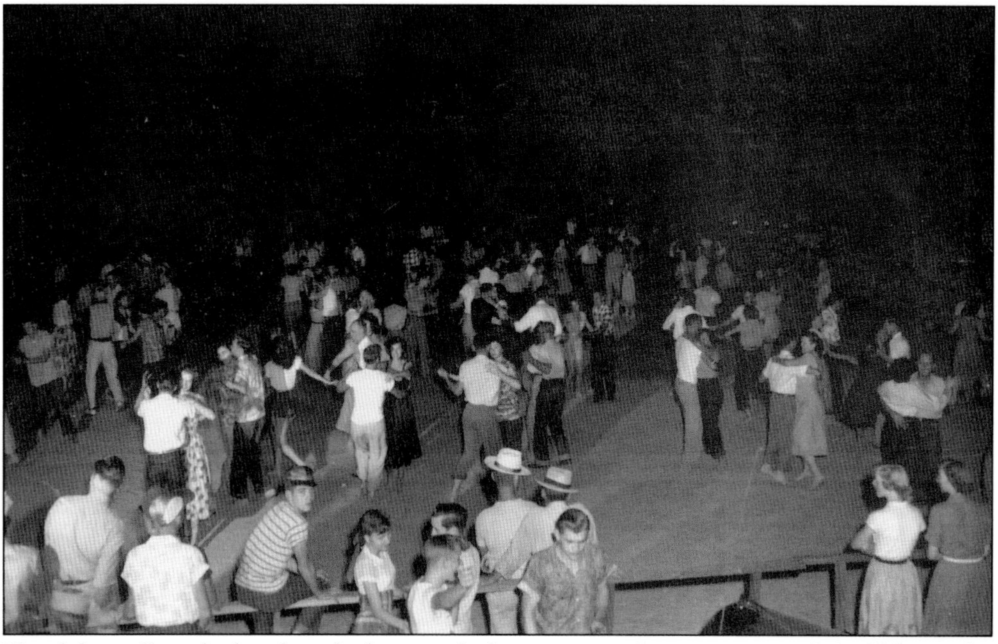

"Sand dances" on the beach and adjoining deck were a popular attraction at Lake Elder in the early 1950s.

Eleven

HEALTH ISSUES

The Stell-Kilgore photos help to illustrate many important advances in health care during this period, as well as the day-to-day work of health professionals to keep Barrow Countians as healthy as possible.

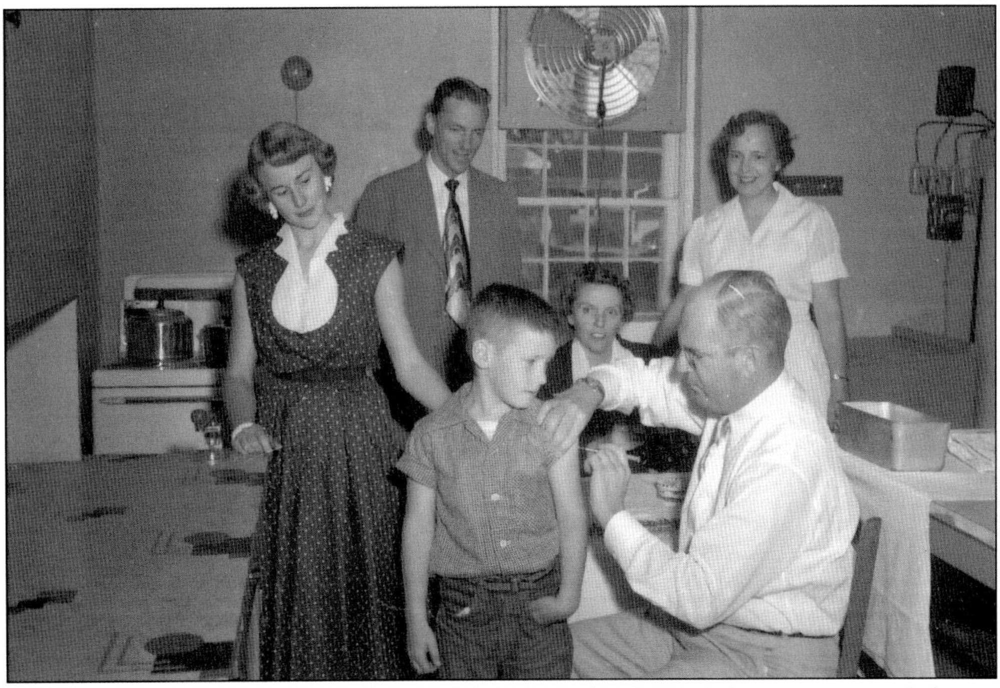

It is almost forgotten today, but polio was a feared crippler. In 1949 the country recorded more than 40,000 victims—nine of them in Barrow County. But Dr. Jonas Salk changed all that. Shown at Barrow's first polio vaccinations, from left to right, are Hazel Gamblin, Fred Hutchins, Lois Patrick, Dr. Alex Russell, and county nurse Lucille Lott. The child is probably one of Mrs. Gamblin's sons.

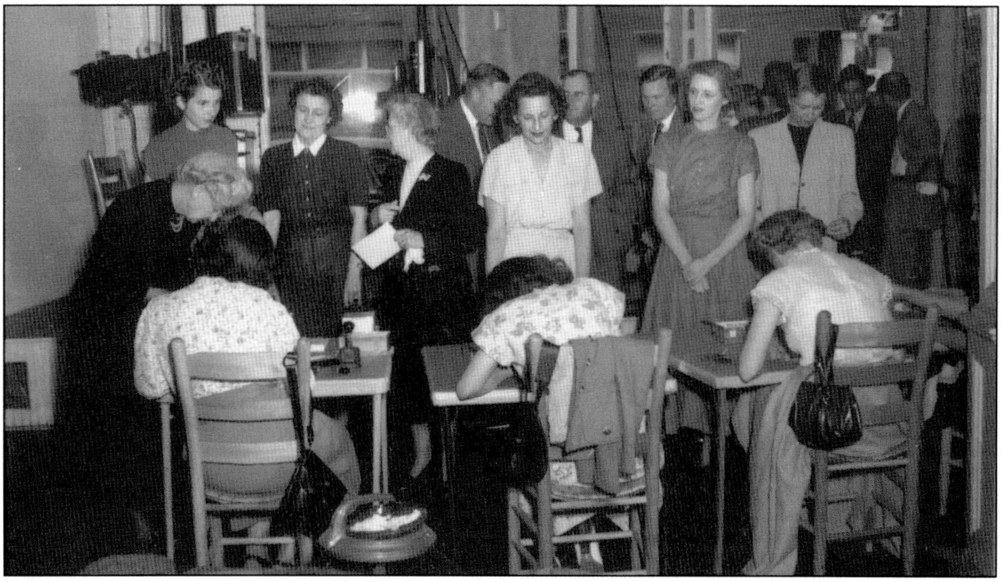

During April 1949, the people of Barrow County were offered free blood tests and X-rays in a state-wide effort to bring tuberculosis and venereal disease under control. Nearly 6,000 people took the tests, and the county turned out to be healthier than average. This photo shows local doctors and their wives on opening day. In the foreground, from left to right, are Mrs. S.T. Ross, Mrs. Ed Etheridge, Mrs. E.K. Harris, Mrs. C.B. Almond, Mrs. Davis Elder, Mrs. Alex Russell, and Mrs. W.T. Randolph. In the background are Dr. Davis Elder, Dr. Alex Russell, and Dr. Ed Etheridge.

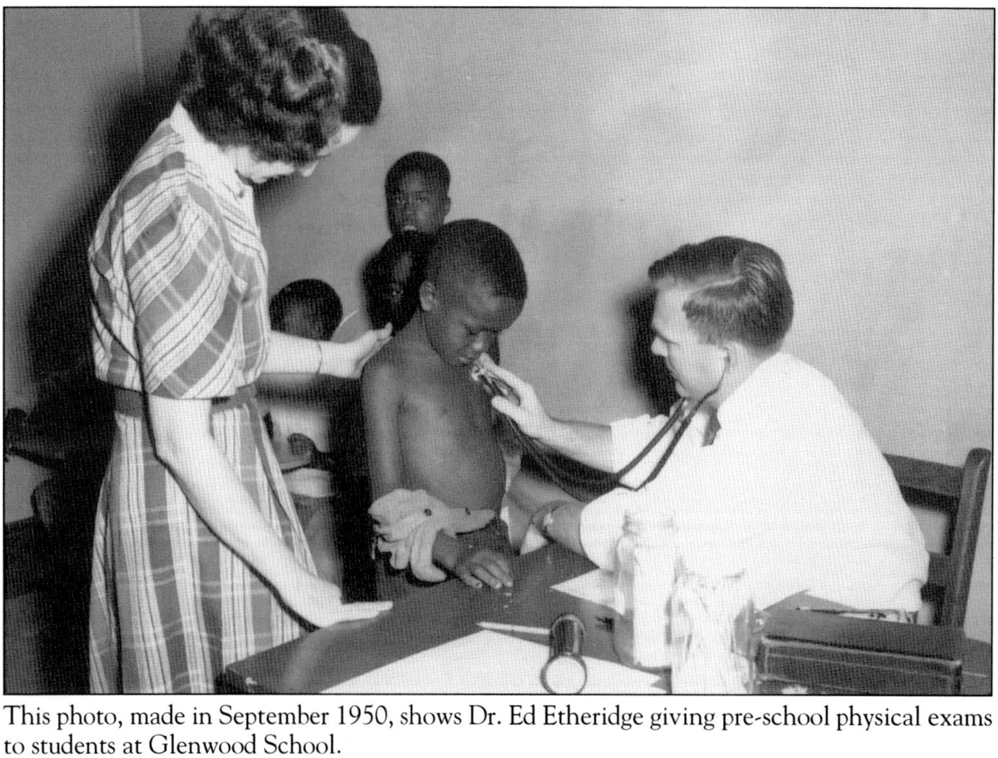

This photo, made in September 1950, shows Dr. Ed Etheridge giving pre-school physical exams to students at Glenwood School.

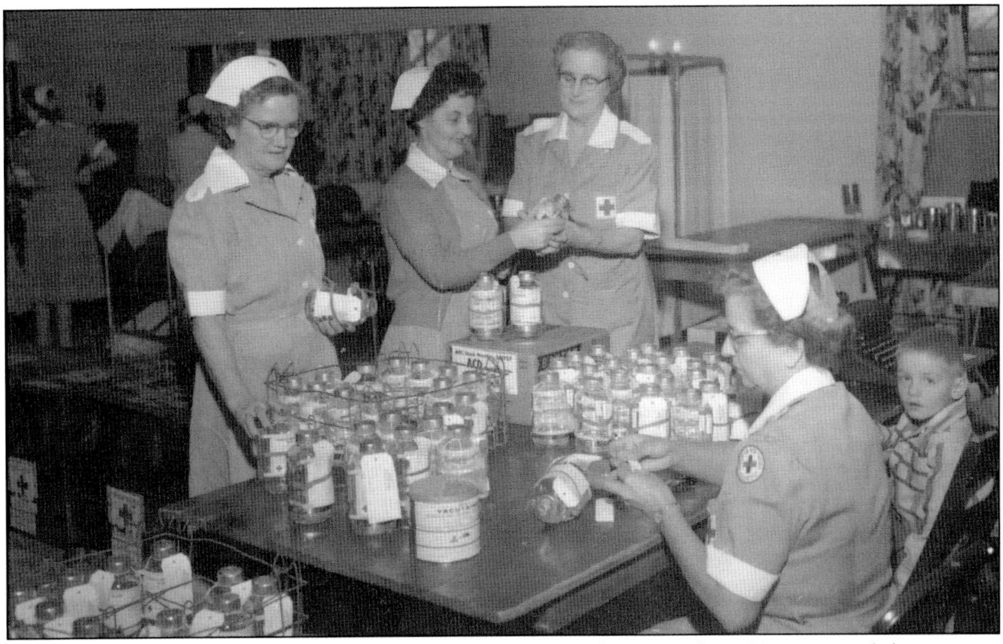

Blood drives have been held regularly in Barrow County for more than 50 years, and the turnout of donors is usually good. This drive was held February 24, 1958. The volunteers, from right to left, are unidentified, Myrtle Dunahoo, Mrs. P.M. Wise, and Elizabeth Williams. The child at right is unidentified.

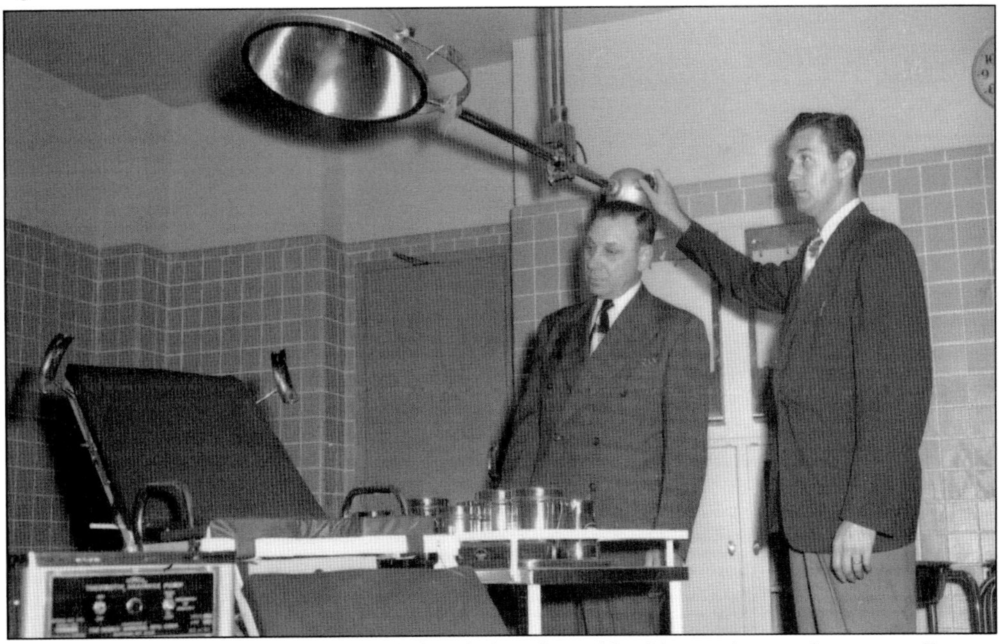

In 1950 the entire community got behind the idea of building a hospital to serve Barrow County. Through dozens of fund-raising drives throughout the county the goal was accomplished. This photo, taken during an open house at the new hospital in November 1951, shows a major contributor, Clair Harris (left), and hospital administrator Dan Barker in the new emergency room.

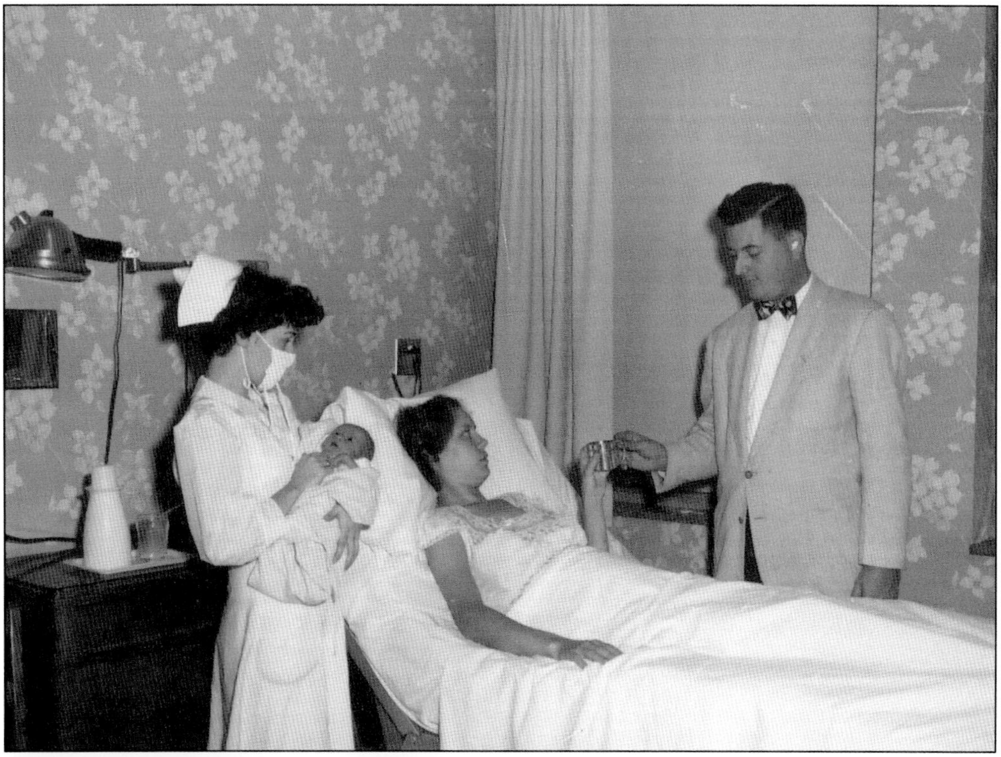

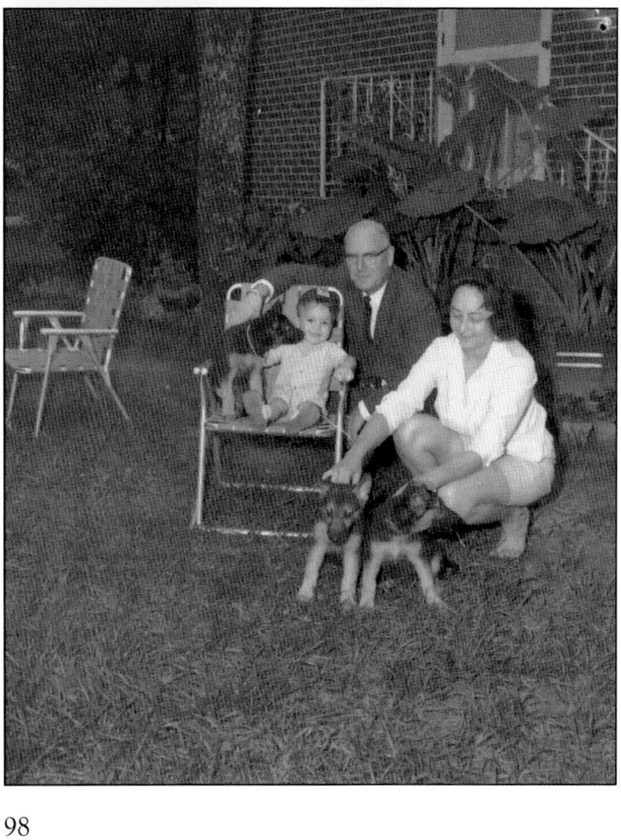

Less than a year after the hospital opened it celebrated its 100th patient. Terry Adams Parker was born at 11:15 a.m. on October 23, 1952. The son of Almond and Louise Roberts Parker of Monroe, he weighed 6 pounds and was delivered by Dr. E.H. Etheridge. Hospital administrator Billy Smith is shown presenting the new mother with a commemorative silver cup.

Stell and Kilgore had to be pioneers in the field of "pet portraits." Their files contain dozens of photos of dogs and other family pets. This photo of Dr. Alex Russell and his wife, Kate, was taken in June 1965, after photographing their German shepherds. The child is Billy Ray White Jr., a neighbor.

Twelve

Law and Order

Stell and Kilgore took hundreds of photos of Barrow County's law enforcement officers during their careers. Some were posed, some were casual, and many were taken when they were on duty enforcing the law. They were also the forensic photographers for the sheriff's departments, and made crime scene photos to be used in solving crimes or as evidence in trials. Their files contain many gruesome photos of murders and suicides.

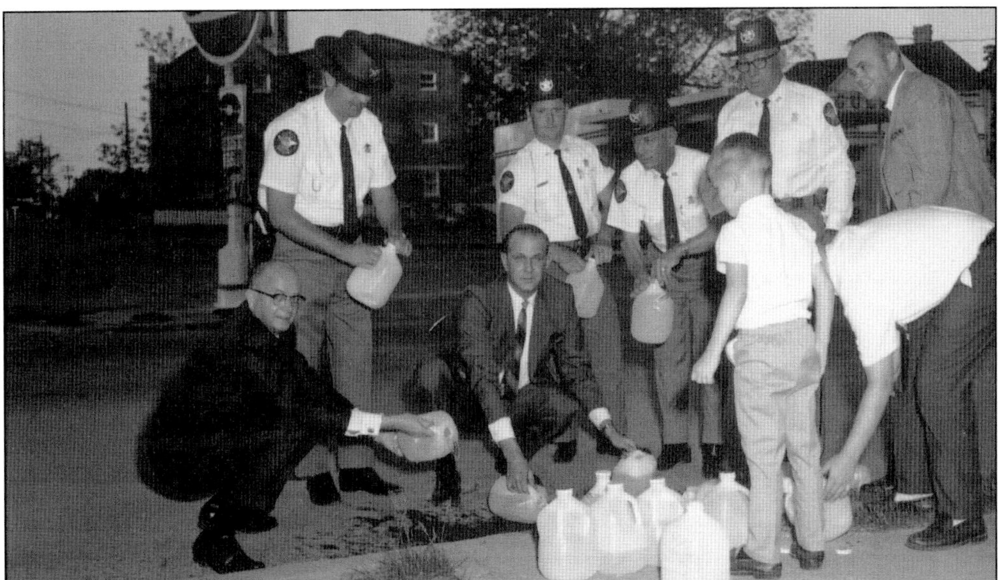

Gov. Lester Maddox, then a candidate for lieutenant governor, was in Winder helping pour out bootleg whiskey on May 4, 1969. From left to right are as follows: (kneeling) Maddox and Sheriff Howard Austin; (standing) Frankie Dunagan, James Teal, ? Doster, Spear McElroy, and Skeet Clack. The child is unidentified. It is said that certain people with a deep love of alcohol would be waiting about a block away, where the drain ran into a creek. There they would scoop the whiskey back out.

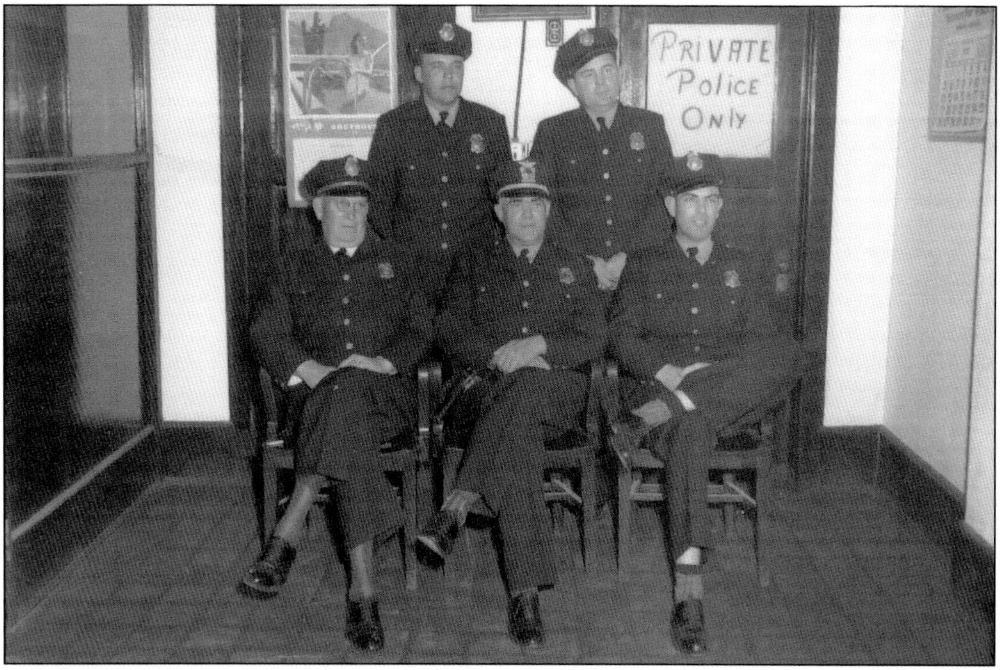

The Winder Police Department was a small one in 1950, consisting of only four officers and the chief. Shown seated, from left to right, are Tom Brewer, Chief Mack Perry, and Donald Hardigree. Standing are Bill Brock and S.A. Campbell.

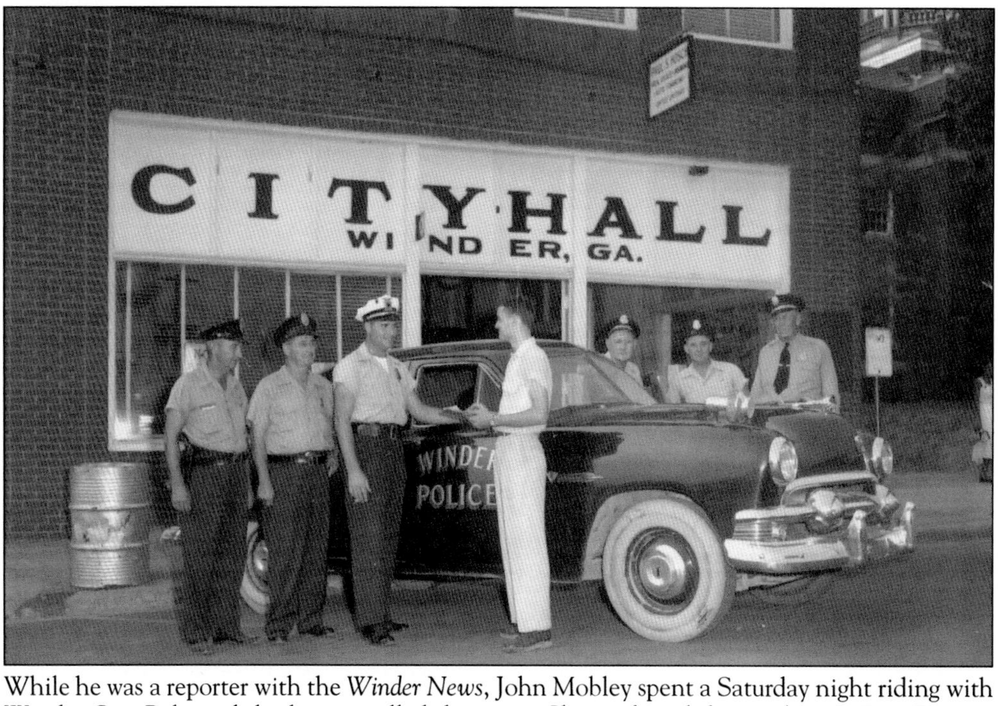

While he was a reporter with the *Winder News*, John Mobley spent a Saturday night riding with Winder City Police while they patrolled the town. Shown from left to right are Tom Brewer, Daniel Deaton, Henry Martin, Mobley, Horace McDaniel, Ollis Evans, and Ben Wardlaw. This photo was made in August 1953.

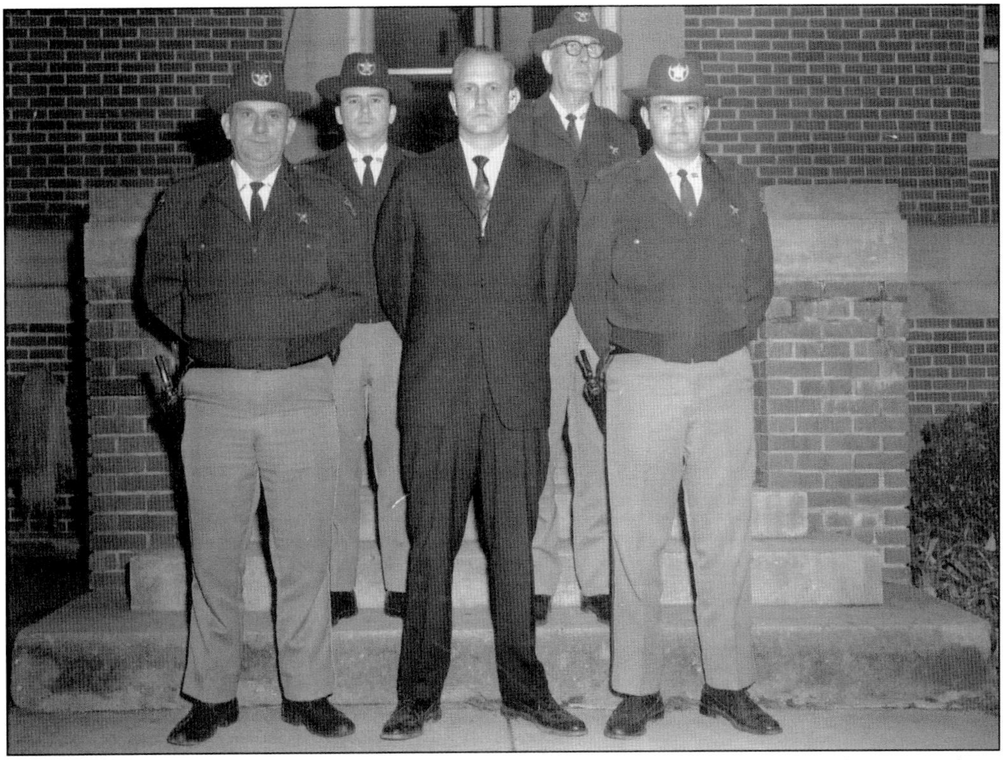

The Barrow County Sheriff's Office was indeed a small force in 1969. In the front row, from left to right, are Leon Skinner, Sheriff Howard Austin, and Frankie Dunagan. Behind them are Richard Skinner and Spear McElroy.

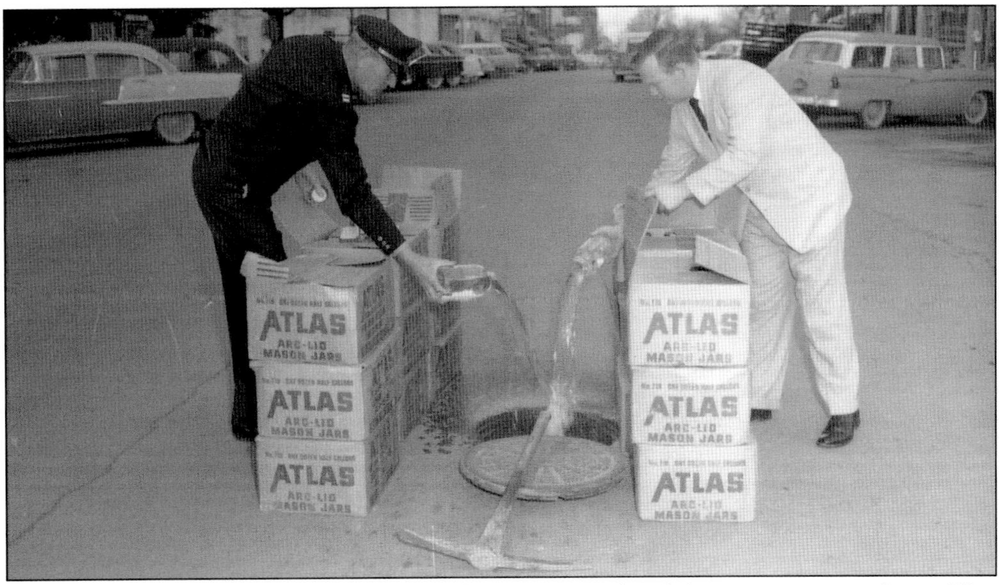

The Winder Police Department also did its part in the fight against moonshine. This photo, made on January 21, 1958, shows Spear McElroy (left) and Deward Clark pouring out liquor in front of the police station. It was located on Broad Street, site of the present courthouse addition.

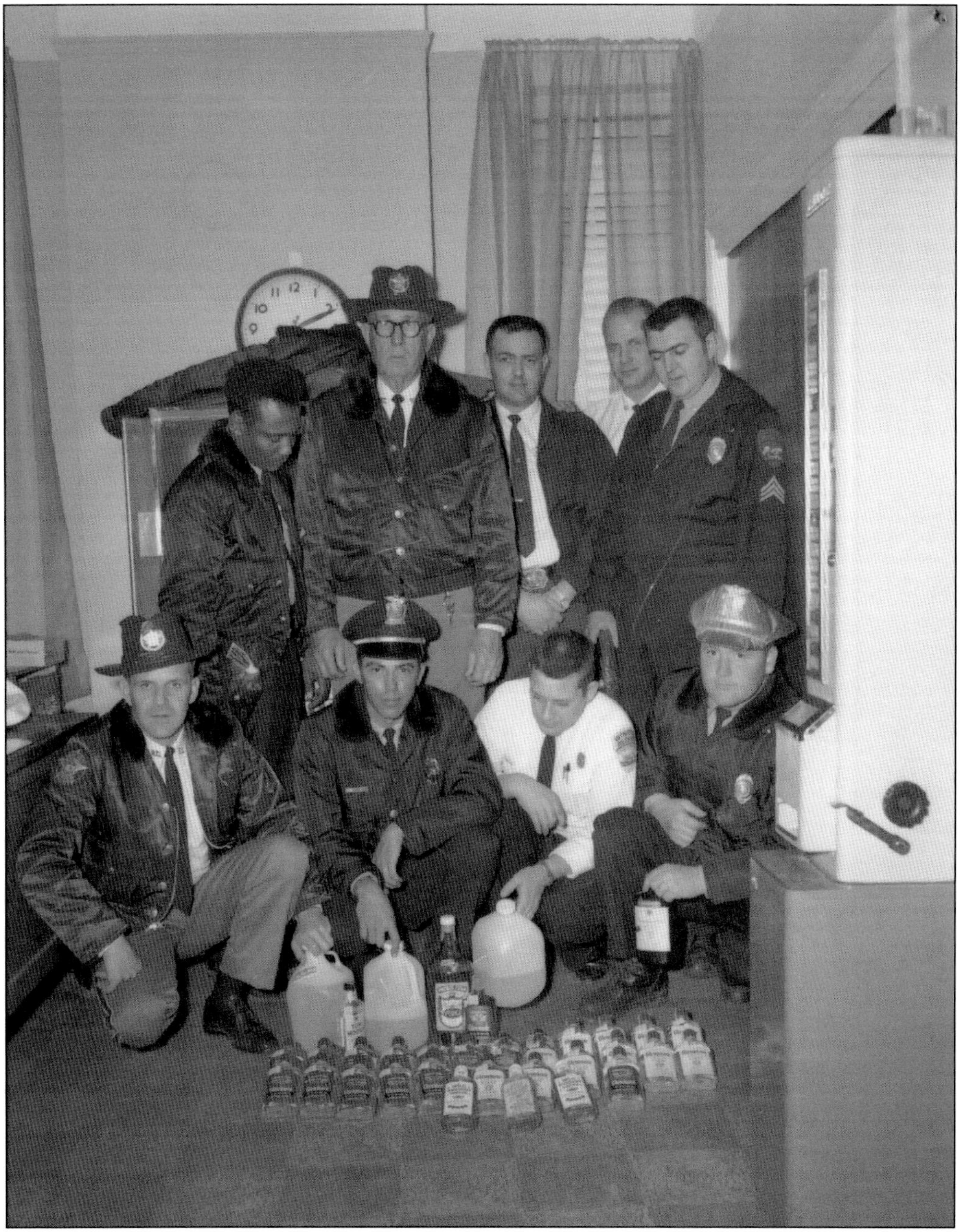

Law enforcement officers also seized their share of "tax paid" whiskey in dry Barrow County. Obviously, some folks had better taste than to drink "white lightning." This photo was taken after a raid on bootleggers in February 1969. From left to right are the following: (kneeling) Gordon Talley, Nelson Huff, Gerald Thomas, and Pee Wee Teal; (standing) Willie Smith, Spear McElroy, Frankie Dunagan, Sheriff Howard Austin, and Jerry Smith.

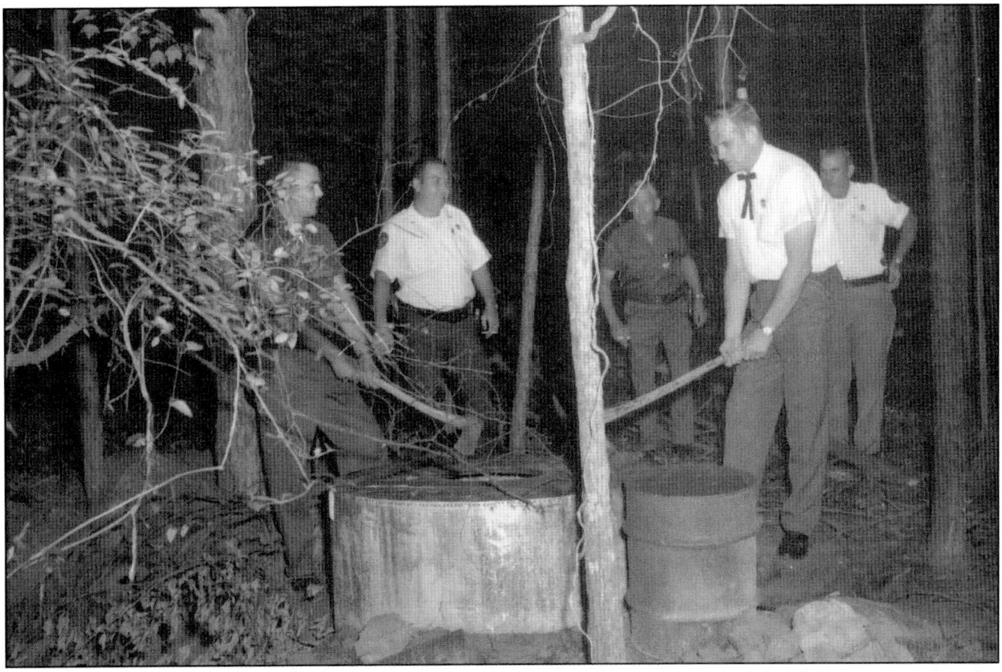

This still was found on the Russell farm, but was obviously not operated by that pioneer family. Shown "busting it up" are, from left to right, Frankie Dunagan, Ralph Canup, Lewis Doster, Sheriff Howard Austin, and Leon Skinner. The photo was made August 4, 1969.

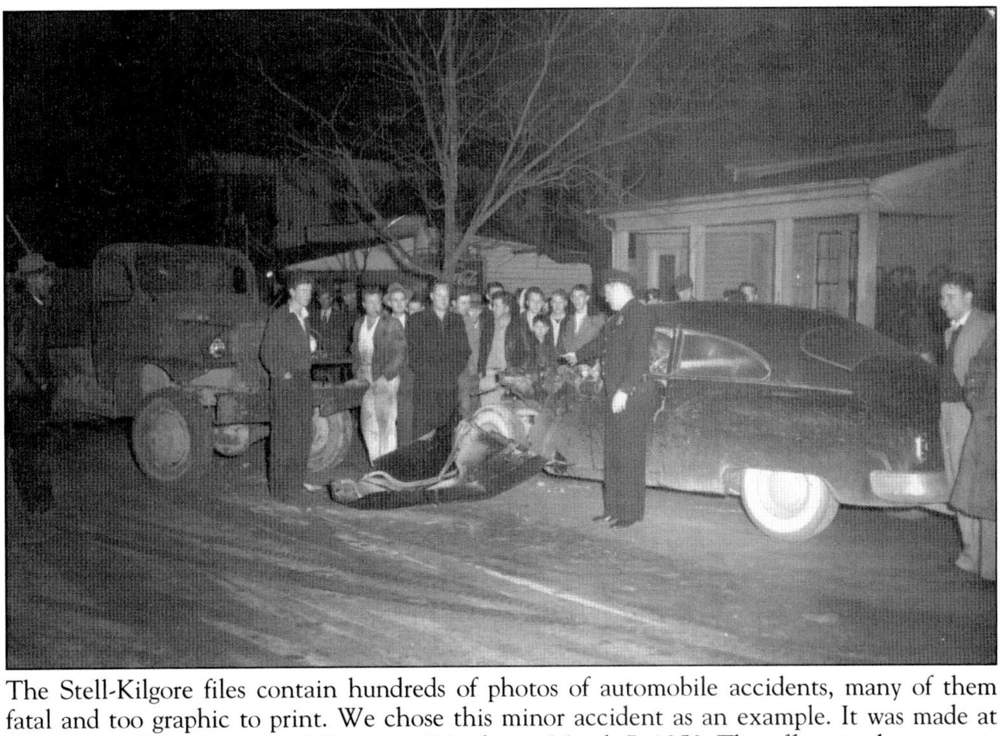

The Stell-Kilgore files contain hundreds of photos of automobile accidents, many of them fatal and too graphic to print. We chose this minor accident as an example. It was made at the corner of New and Broad Streets in Winder on March 7, 1950. The officer in the center is Tom Brewer.

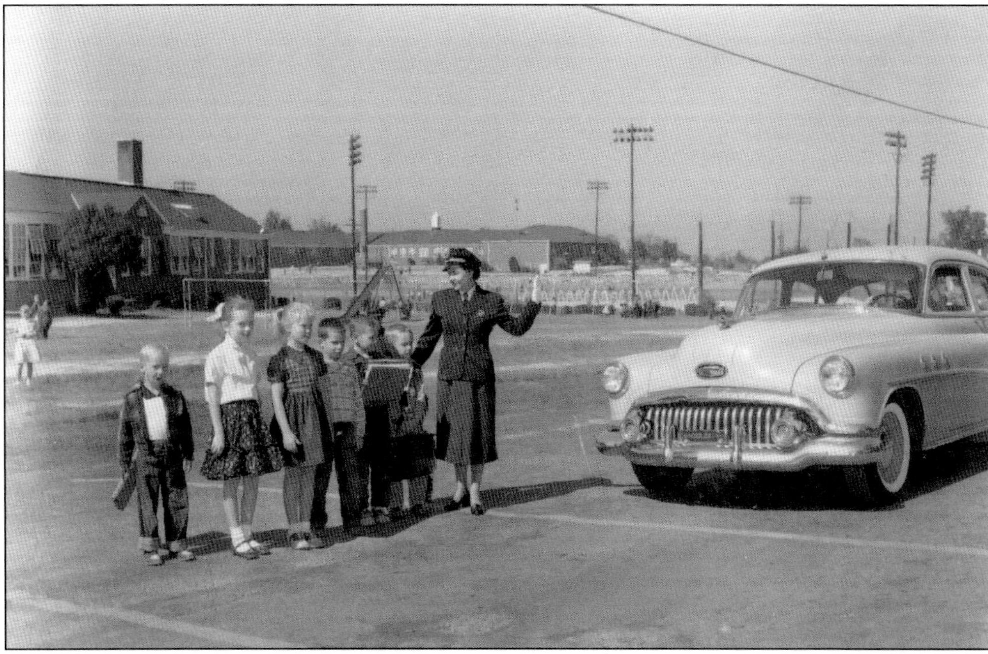

Josephine Moon was Winder's first female police officer. This photo, made in October 1955, shows her escorting children across Midland Avenue in front of the old Winder School. The football field can be seen in the background.

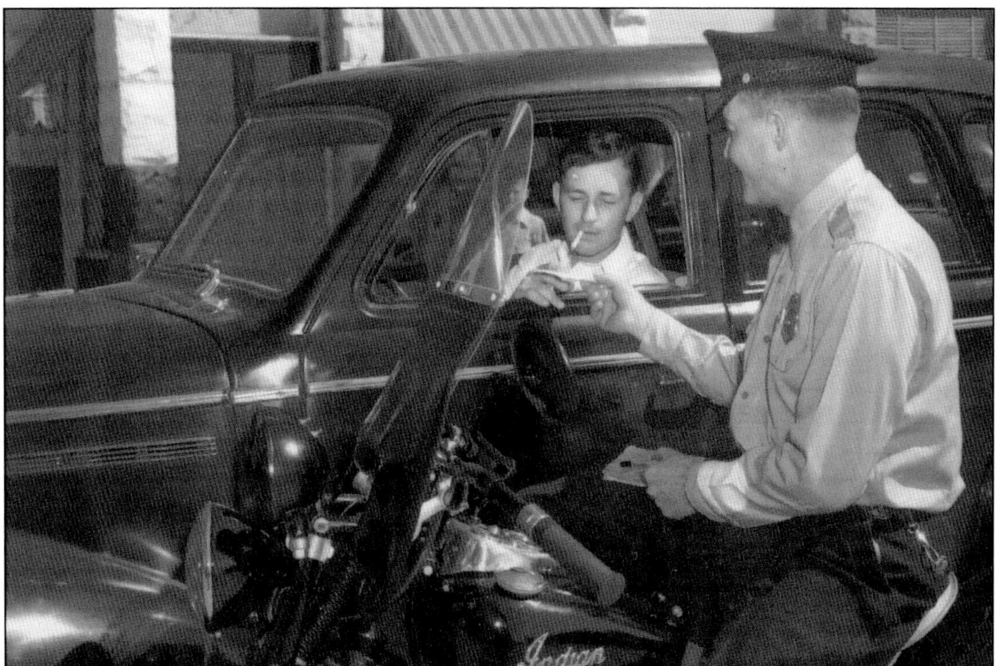

Officer C.M. Mooney, shown here writing a ticket, was probably Winder's first motorcycle police officer. This Indian motorcycle was later wrecked during a chase, as was the next one the city bought. After that they decided to go back to automobiles exclusively. The photo was taken June 18, 1947.

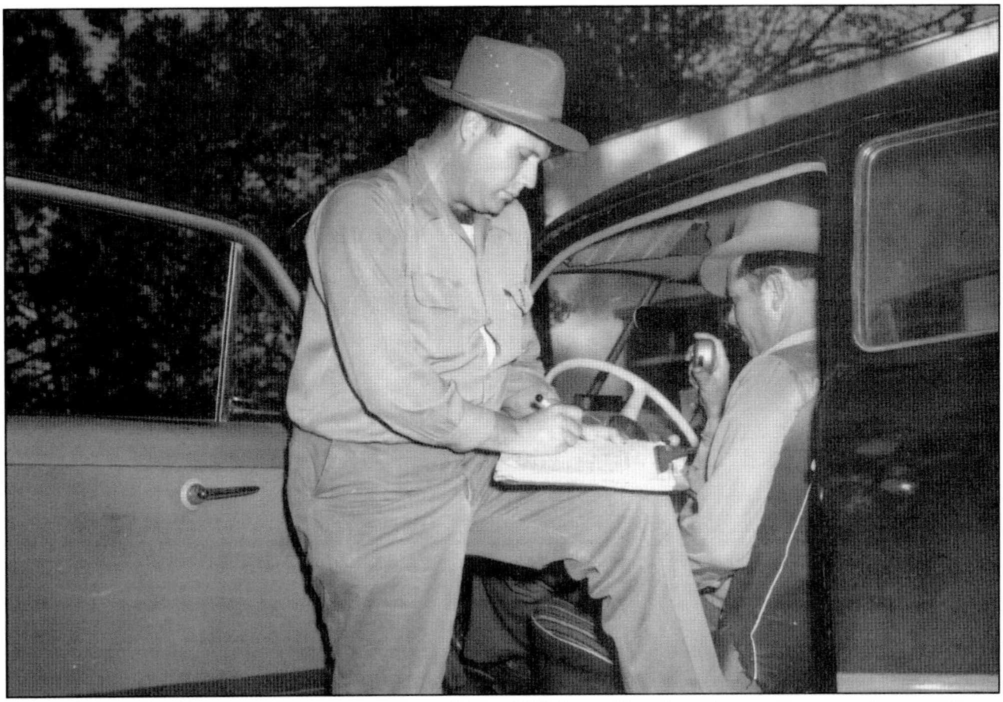

Deputy John Robert Austin takes notes as Sheriff Delmar Smith talks on the patrol car radio at a crime scene near Winder. The photo was made October 20, 1952.

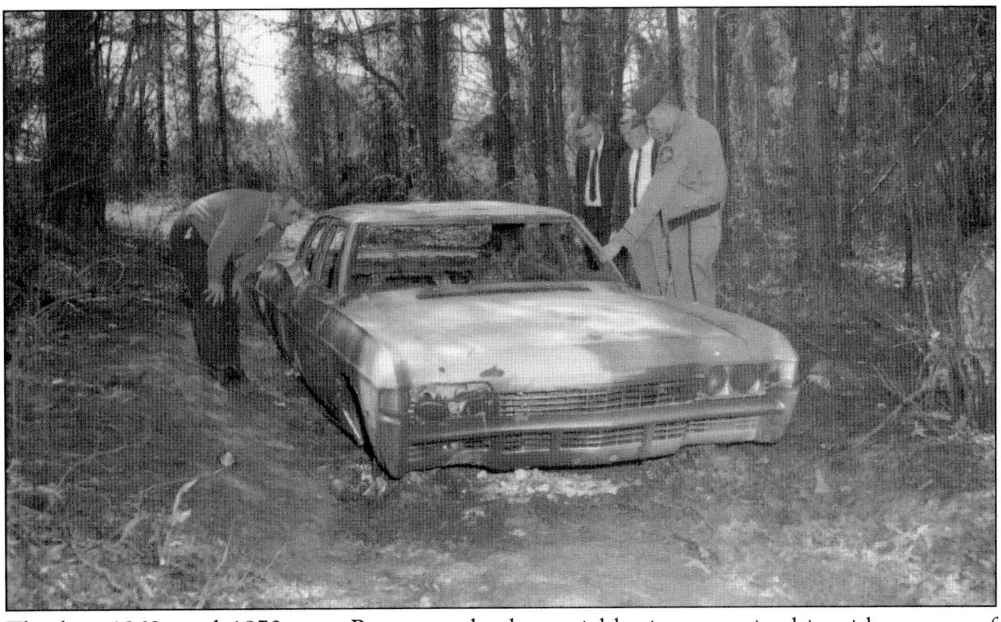

The late 1960s and 1970s saw Barrow and other neighboring counties hit with a wave of crime, including bootlegging, robberies, and burglaries, but car theft seemed to be the crime of choice. The organized ring would steal cars almost nightly. The next day they would be found stripped and burned. This one was found in a wooded area off Highway 82. Shown investigating the incident are, from left to right, Leon Skinner, Jimmy Barnes, Jimmy ?, and Sheriff Howard Austin.

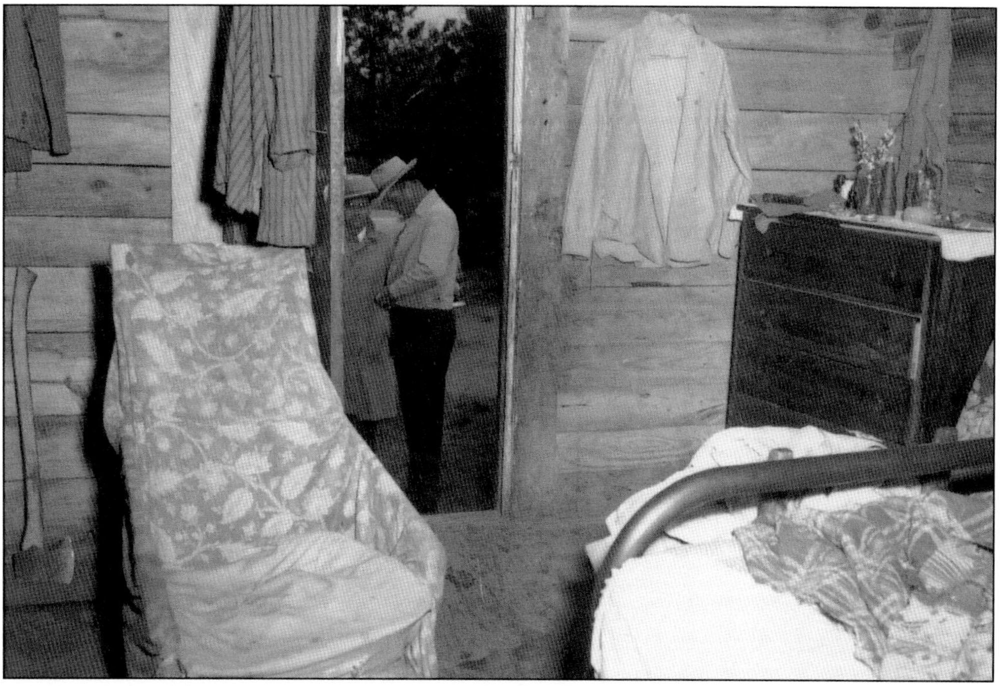

During much of their careers, Stell and Kilgore were the forensic photographers for local law enforcement agencies. Their files contain hundreds of photos of crime scenes including many brutal murders. This is the only that seemed suitable to print here. The body of the murdered woman, Hattie May Riley, was inside this small house in Russell. Shown at right outside the door is Sheriff Delmar Smith. The murder was committed on March 27, 1954.

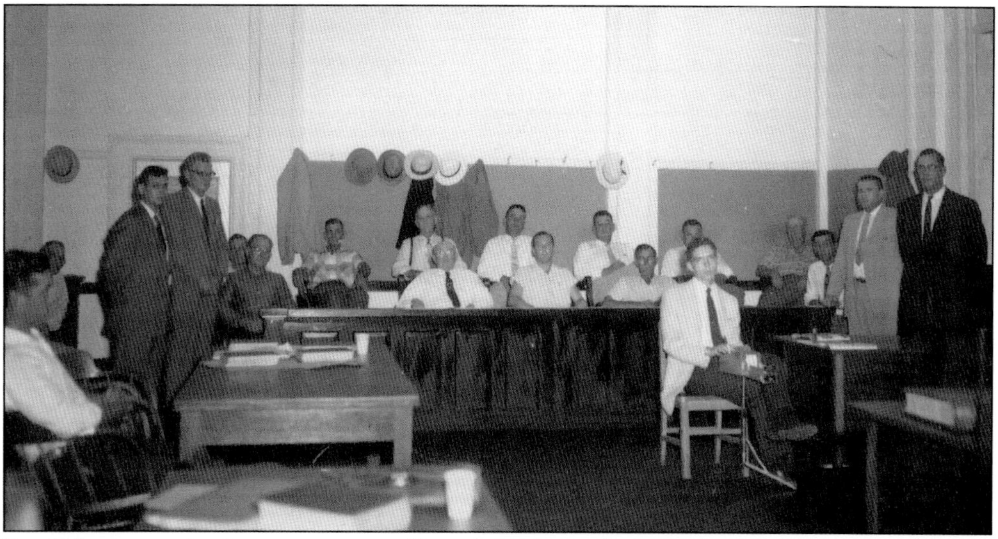

Ray Kilgore was the first person ever allowed to take a photo in the Barrow County Superior Courtroom during a trial, in August 1958. On trial for murder was J.T. Huff, accused of beating and stomping his 24-year-old pregnant wife, Mary Katherine Brown Huff, to death. Judge Maylon Clinkscales found Huff guilty and sentenced him to life in prison. Shown standing at left are Alfred Quillian and Dumont Harrison, clerk of court. Standing at right are Deputy John Robert Austin and Sheriff Delmar Smith.

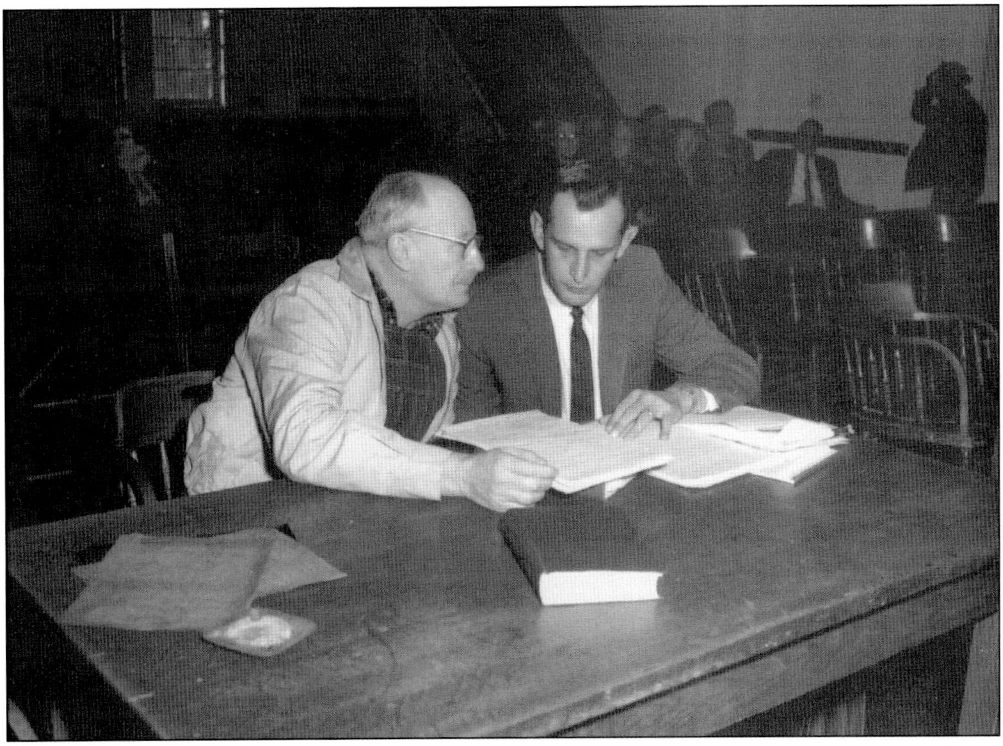

In another courtroom drama, this one in 1960, Ernest McDaniel (left) was on trial for murder, being defended by Richard Russell III (right). McDaniel's wife had been shot in the back with a shotgun while the two were picking berries. McDaniel testified that he had leaned the shotgun against a fence, that their dog knocked it over, and that it accidentally discharged.

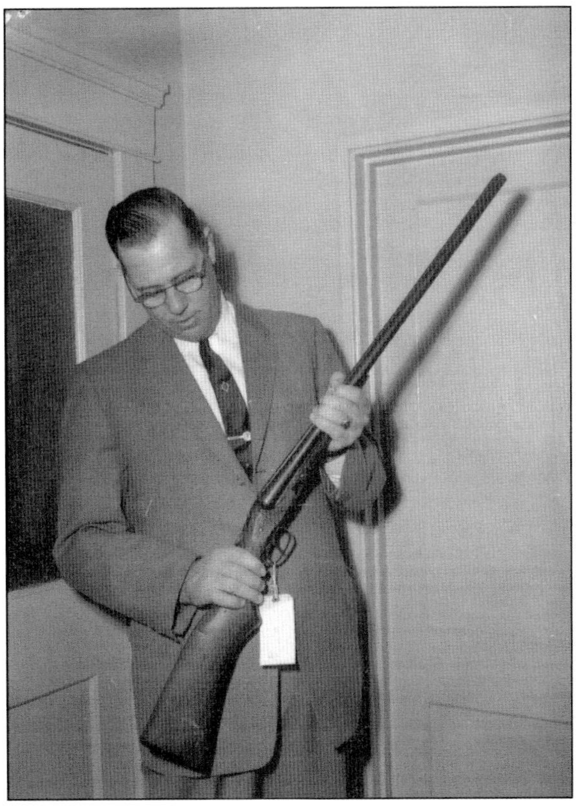

Sheriff Delmar Smith, shown holding the shotgun, threw it to the floor in the courtroom, in an effort to prove that it couldn't misfire in that way. Mrs. McDaniel, however, had been alive when she arrived at the hospital, and was given emergency care by Dr. C.B. Skelton. He was called as a witness. Dr. Skelton testified that just before she died he asked her what happened, and that she had replied, "That old shotgun went off." After two mistrials, McDaniel was found innocent at a third trial.

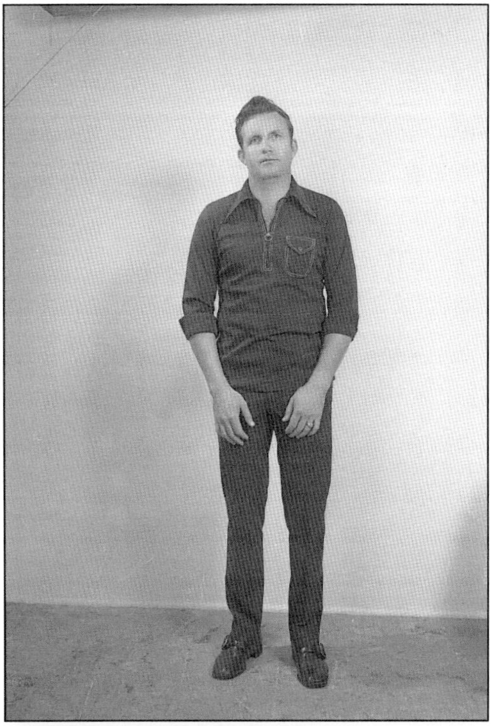

When Billy Sunday Birt came to Pierson Stell for a portrait session on April 22, 1972, many people suspected he was involved in criminal activity. The extent of that activity turned out to be horrendous. He was, in fact, the deadliest man in Georgia history. Birt was convicted, along with several accomplices, of the December 1973 torture and murder of an elderly couple in Wrens, GA. Birt was sentenced to death, but the sentence was overturned and changed to life in prison without parole. Later investigations implicated Birt in at least 28 killings in Georgia. In an *Atlanta Journal-Constitution* article, retired Georgia Bureau of Investigations inspector Bob Ingram said that an accomplice of Birt "told me that he and Birt were responsible for 52 homicides" all over the South. "If that was an exaggeration," Ingram said, "it was only barely so."

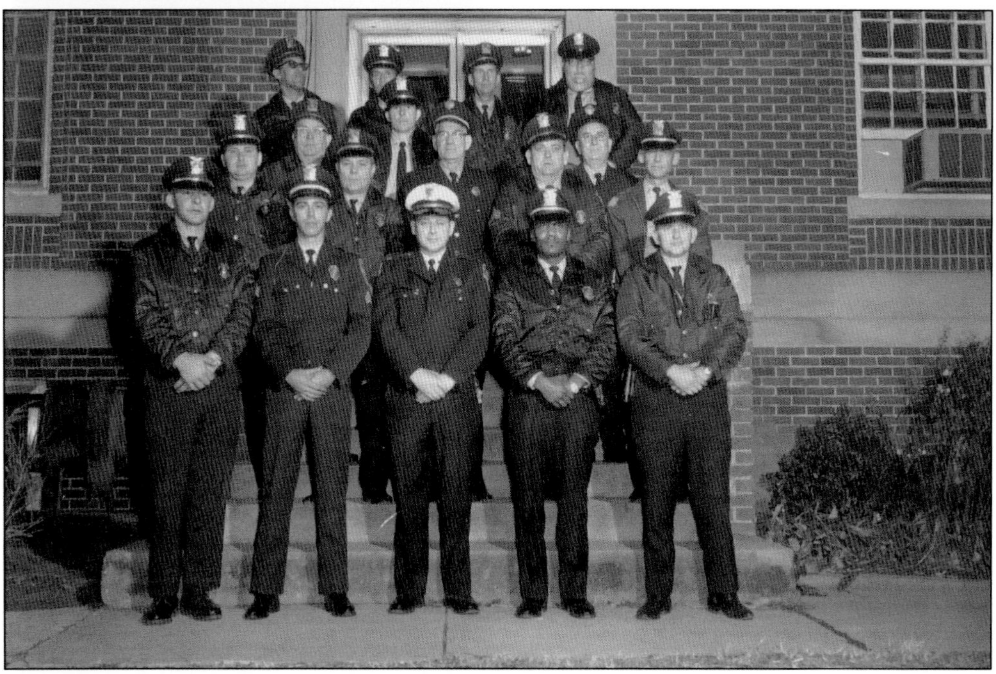

The Winder Police Department had grown considerably by the time this photo was taken in December 1969. From left to right are as follows: (first row) Billy Emmett, Nelson Huff, Chief Gerald Thomas, Willie Smith, and Jerry Walls; (second row) Gene Wall, Clifford Sikes, Tom Bailey, Billy Patrick, and Ted McDaniel; (third row) Hubert Deaton, Ralph Langley, and Robert Howington; (fourth row) Paul Teasley, William McEver, John Stowe, and "Tiny" Love.

Thirteen

SNAPSHOTS OF LIFE

The photos in this chapter don't fall into any specific category, but will serve to illustrate the wide range of subjects found in the Stell-Kilgore files—from political to personal. The two men photographed the famous, the infamous, and the ordinary.

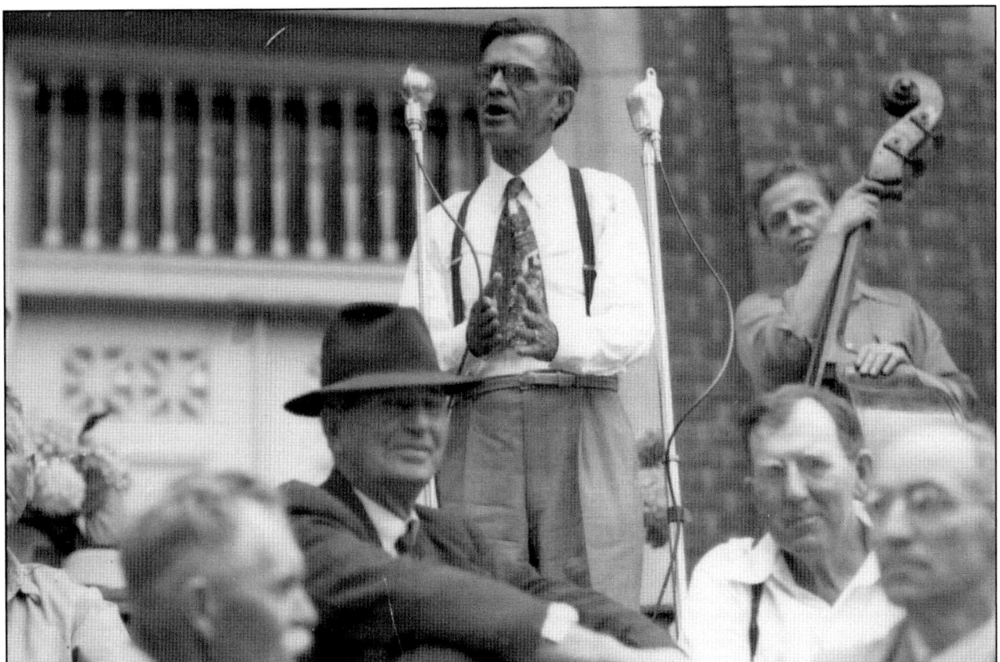

This photo is one of a series made of Georgia governor Gene Talmadge during a campaign speech. They testify as to his speaking technique. In the first photos he has on a coat and tie. Later, as he warmed up, he is shown taking off his jacket and handing it to someone. Then, as this photo testifies, he would get down to business. An unabashed segregationist, and many would say a racist, he fought to hold African Americans down throughout his political career.

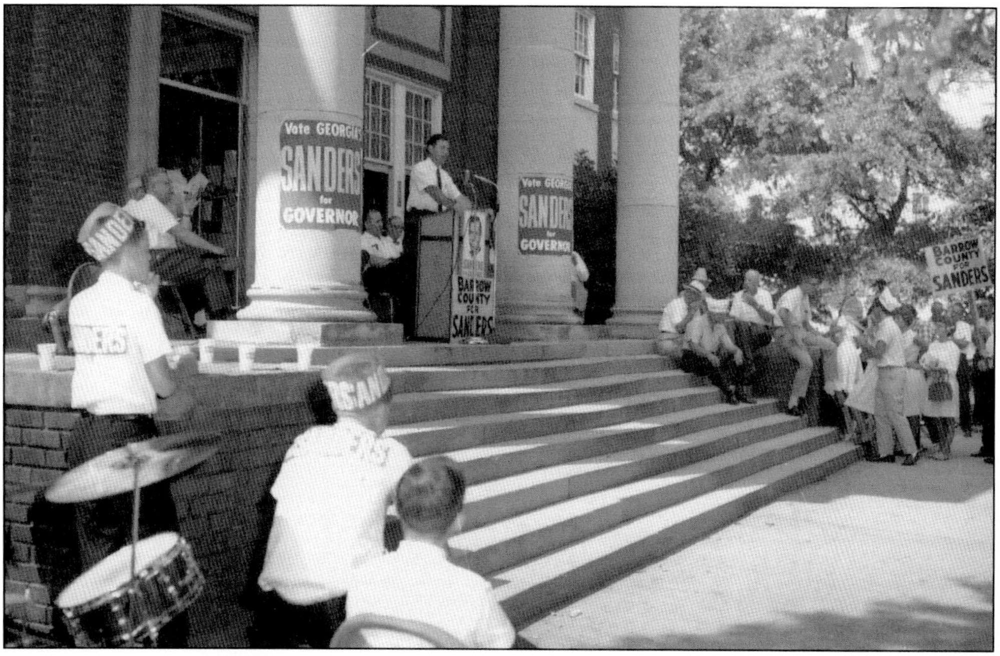

State Senator Carl Sanders made a stop in Winder while running for governor in 1962. He spoke to a large crowd from the courthouse steps after being introduced by Harold Harrison, who was chairman of the local campaign committee. Sanders carried Barrow County as he won the governorship over incumbent Marvin Griffin. In the lieutenant governor's race, Peter Zack Geer prevailed over Lester Maddox after a run-off, but Maddox carried Barrow County in both elections.

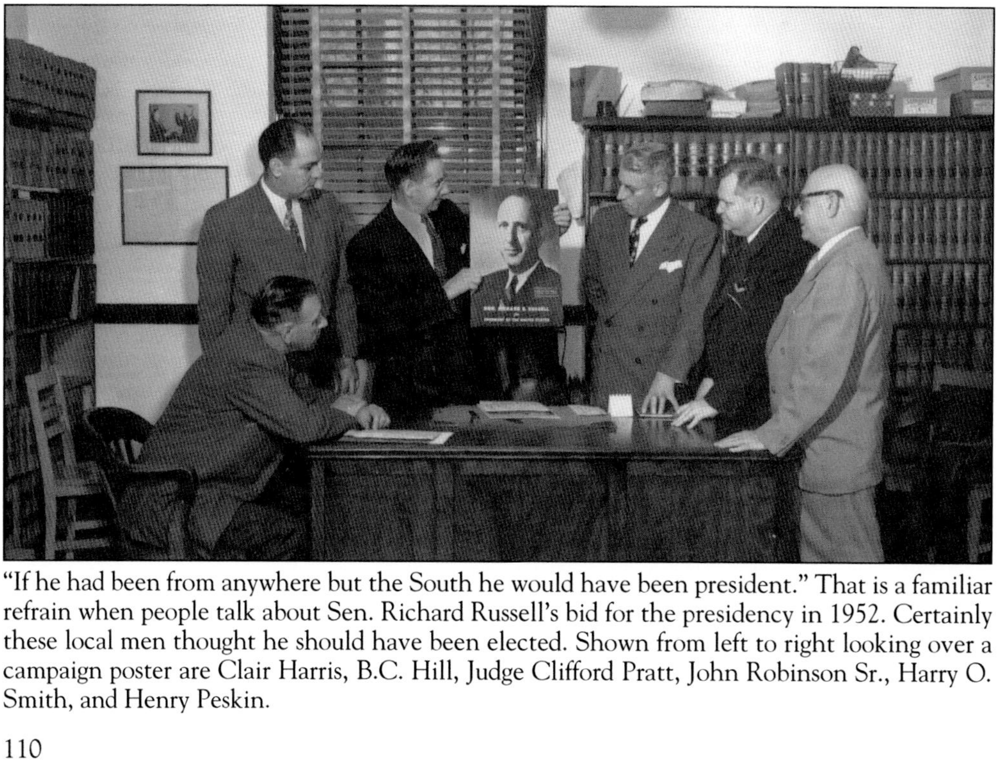

"If he had been from anywhere but the South he would have been president." That is a familiar refrain when people talk about Sen. Richard Russell's bid for the presidency in 1952. Certainly these local men thought he should have been elected. Shown from left to right looking over a campaign poster are Clair Harris, B.C. Hill, Judge Clifford Pratt, John Robinson Sr., Harry O. Smith, and Henry Peskin.

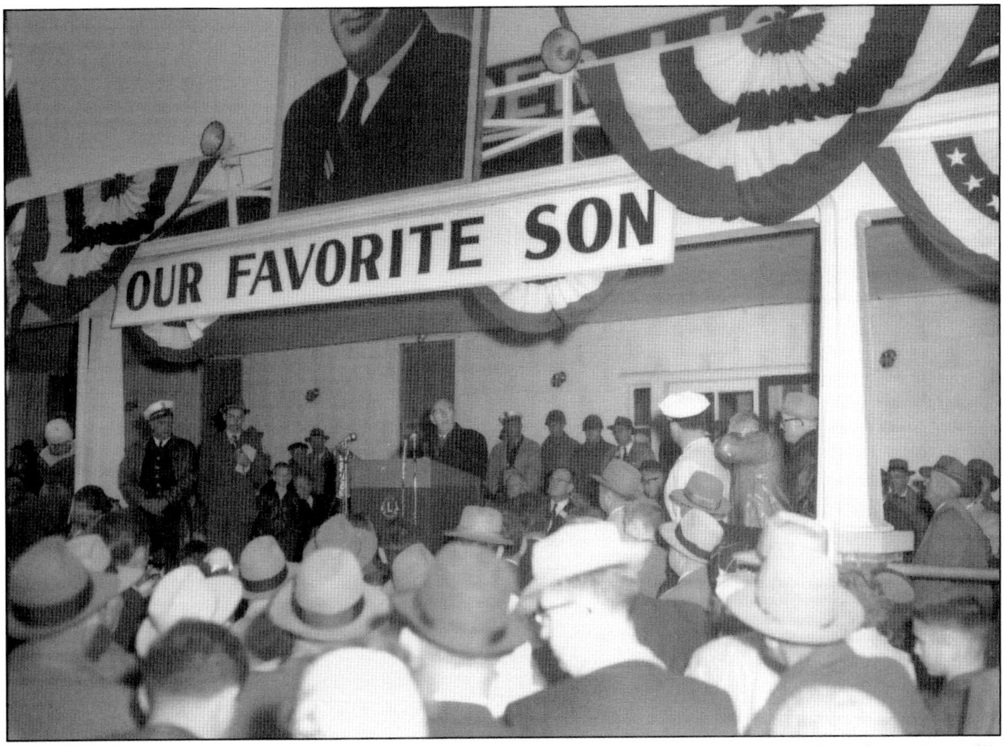

Barrow County turned out in force on "Senator Russell Appreciation Day," October 26, 1957. There was a parade followed by a barbecue at the Winder Lions Club, where Sen. Herman Talmadge was the featured speaker. This photo shows Senator Russell expressing his appreciation to the huge crowd. The community also presented the senator with the keys to a new car.

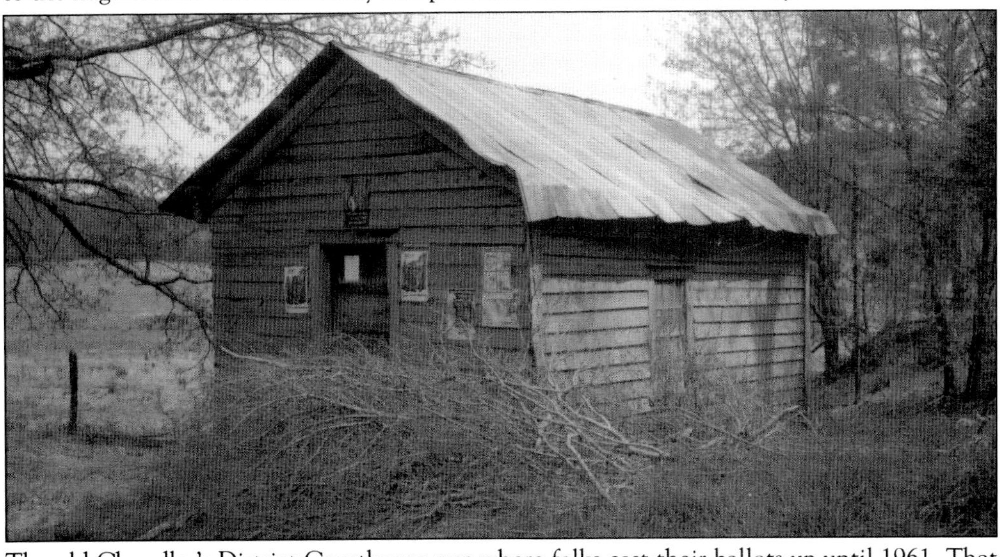

The old Chandler's District Courthouse was where folks cast their ballots up until 1961. That year a new polling place was built, this time of concrete blocks. Both buildings were located on Highway 82, across from Segars' Store in the area popularly known as "Struggleville." Without restrooms or access for the handicapped, the second building was not used very long. New rules forced the voting to be moved to another location.

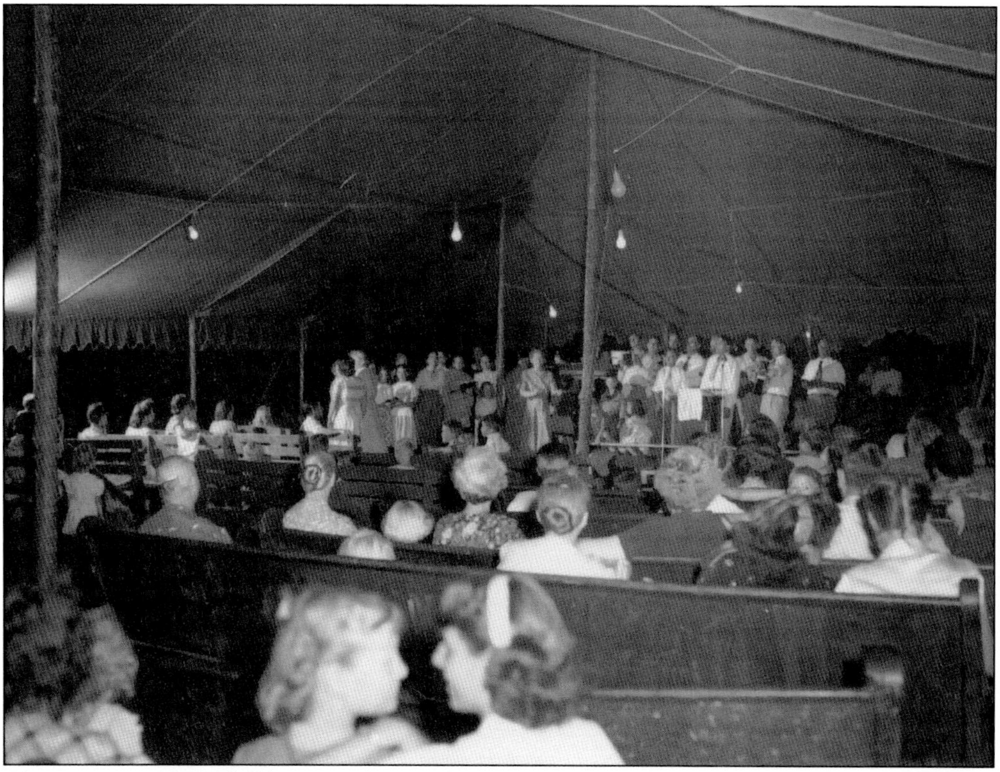

This tent revival was held in Winder in July 1951. It is included as a reminder of the role such events played in local lives 50 years ago.

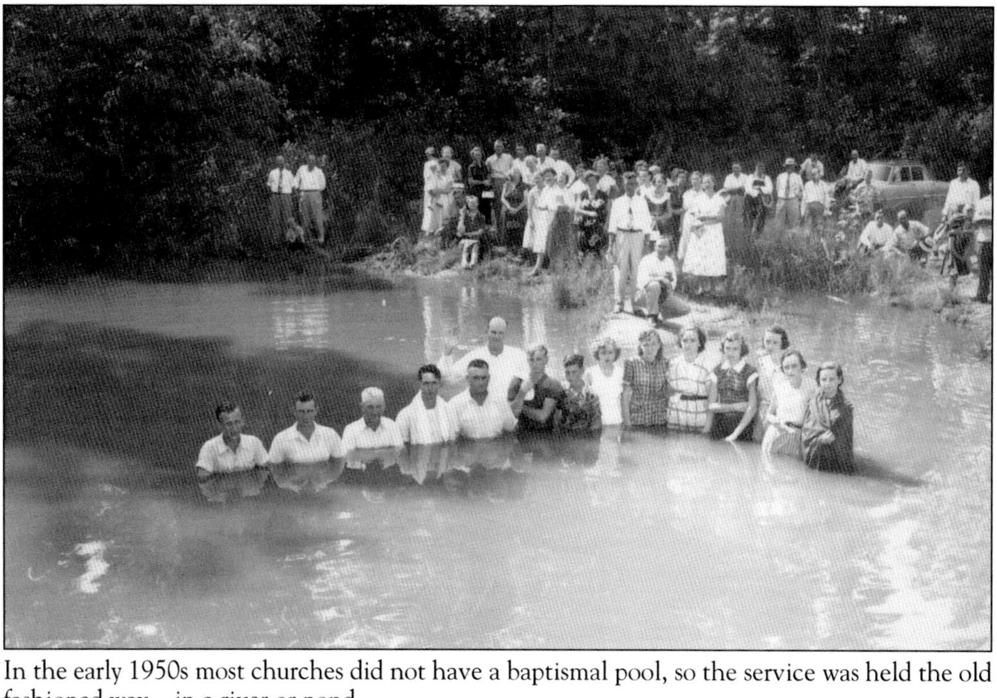

In the early 1950s most churches did not have a baptismal pool, so the service was held the old fashioned way—in a river or pond.

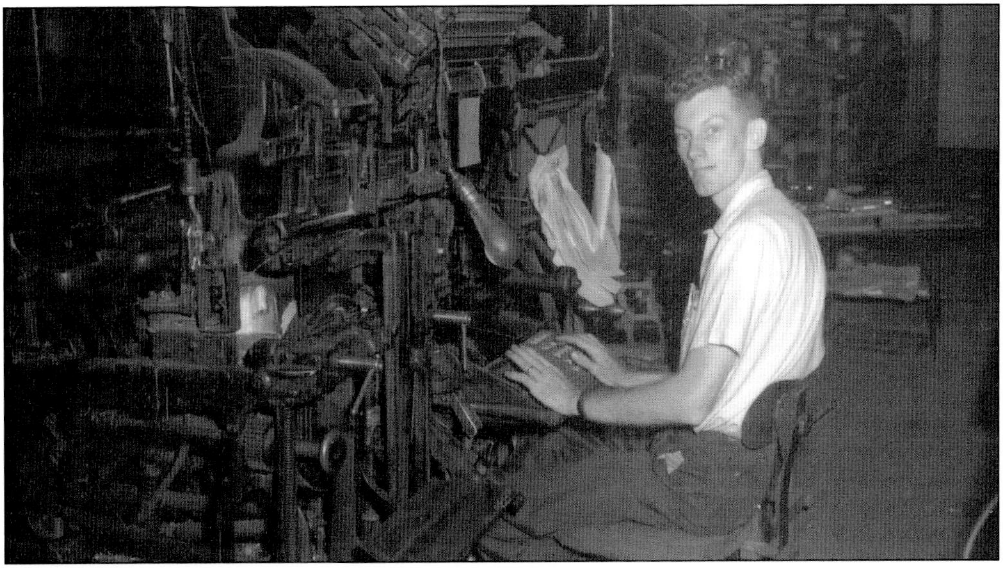

Dub Atkinson is shown setting type the old-fashioned way at the *Winder News*. The newspaper used Linotypes until their conversion to offset printing in the early 1970s.

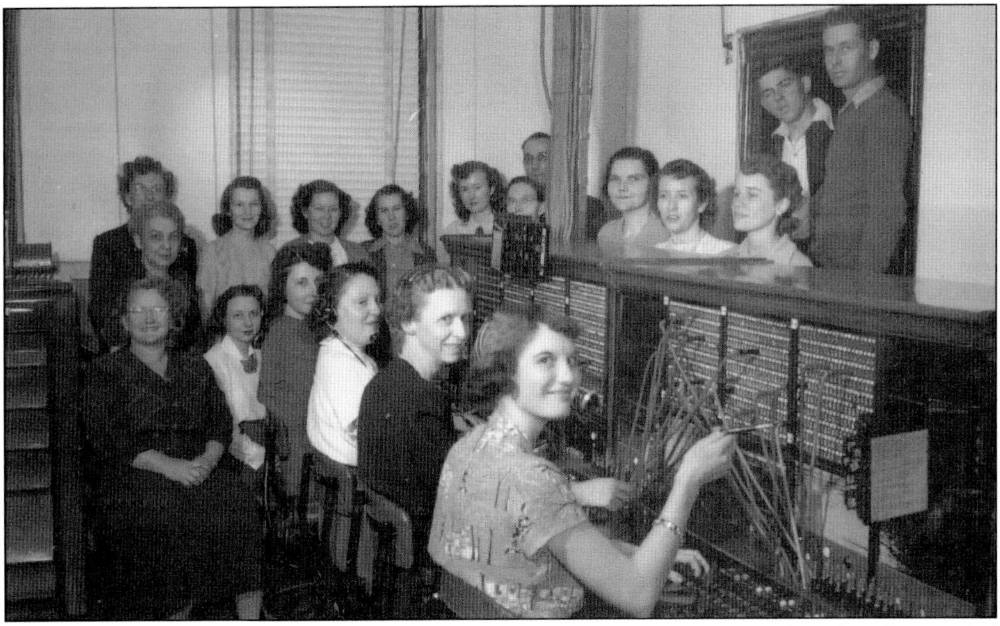

This photo is from an era when callers actually talked to an operator. Although today we dial 911, back then people would pick up the phone and talk to the operator when an emergency arose. She would then call the sheriff, police, or an ambulance. In the event of a fire, she would call the volunteer firemen individually. Manning the phone lines in 1951 were the following, from left to right: (seated) Mary Robison Hopkins, Muriel House Griffin, Dorothy Peppers Thomas, Dorothy Maynard, Jimmie Ruth Hunter, and Betty Teal Treadwell; (standing) Anna Beckman, Louise Robison, Lou Nell Adcock, Clara Watson, Betty Patrick House, Dot Segars Patrick, Fannie Lee Elder, Raye Horn, Jeanette Stewart, Evelyn Thomas, Faye McElhannon, Robert Greeson, and Dorsey Suggs. Men did not work as operators then; they maintained the lines and equipment, and installed telephones.

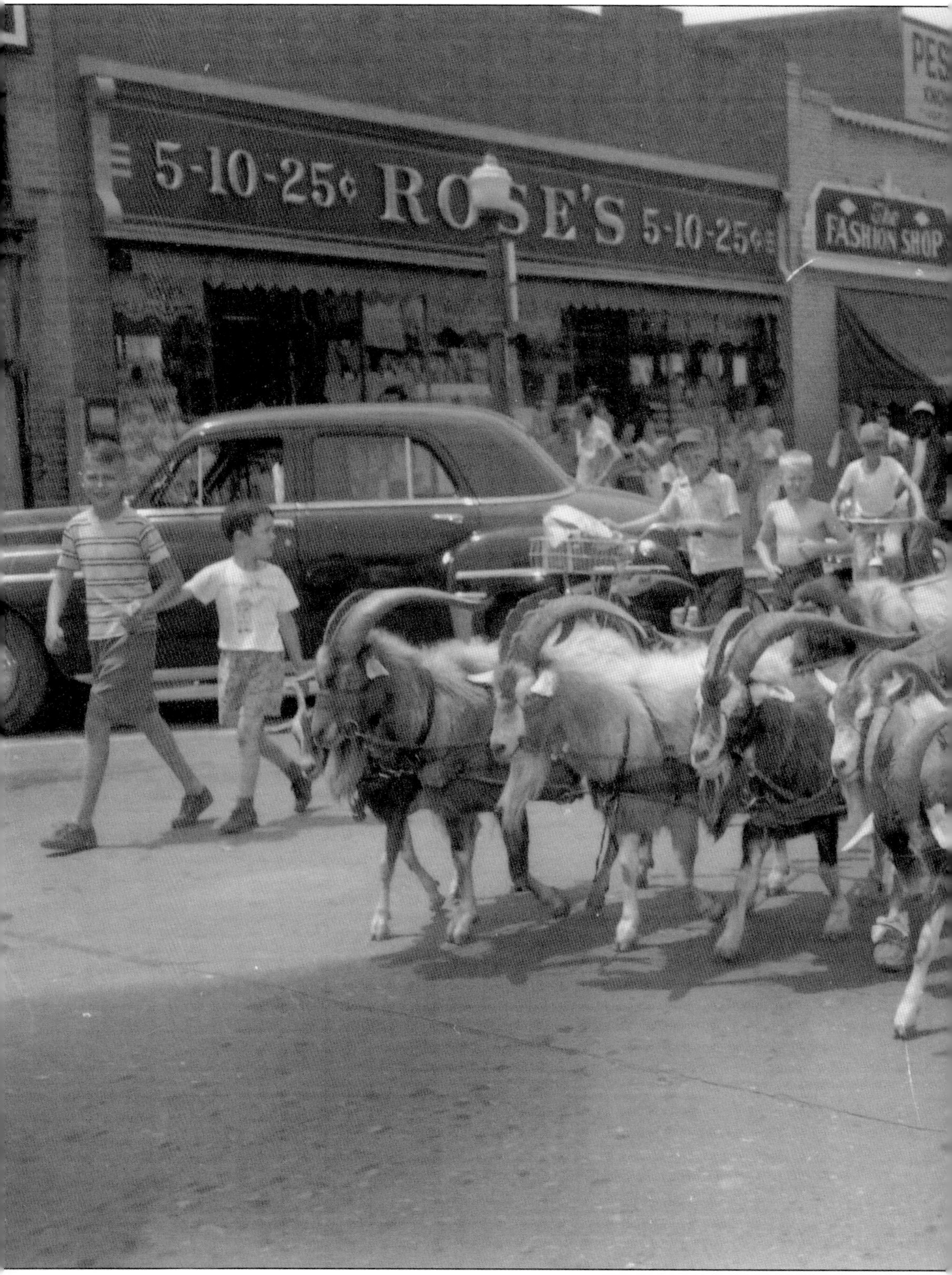
5-10-25¢ ROSE'S 5-10-25¢
FASHION SHOP

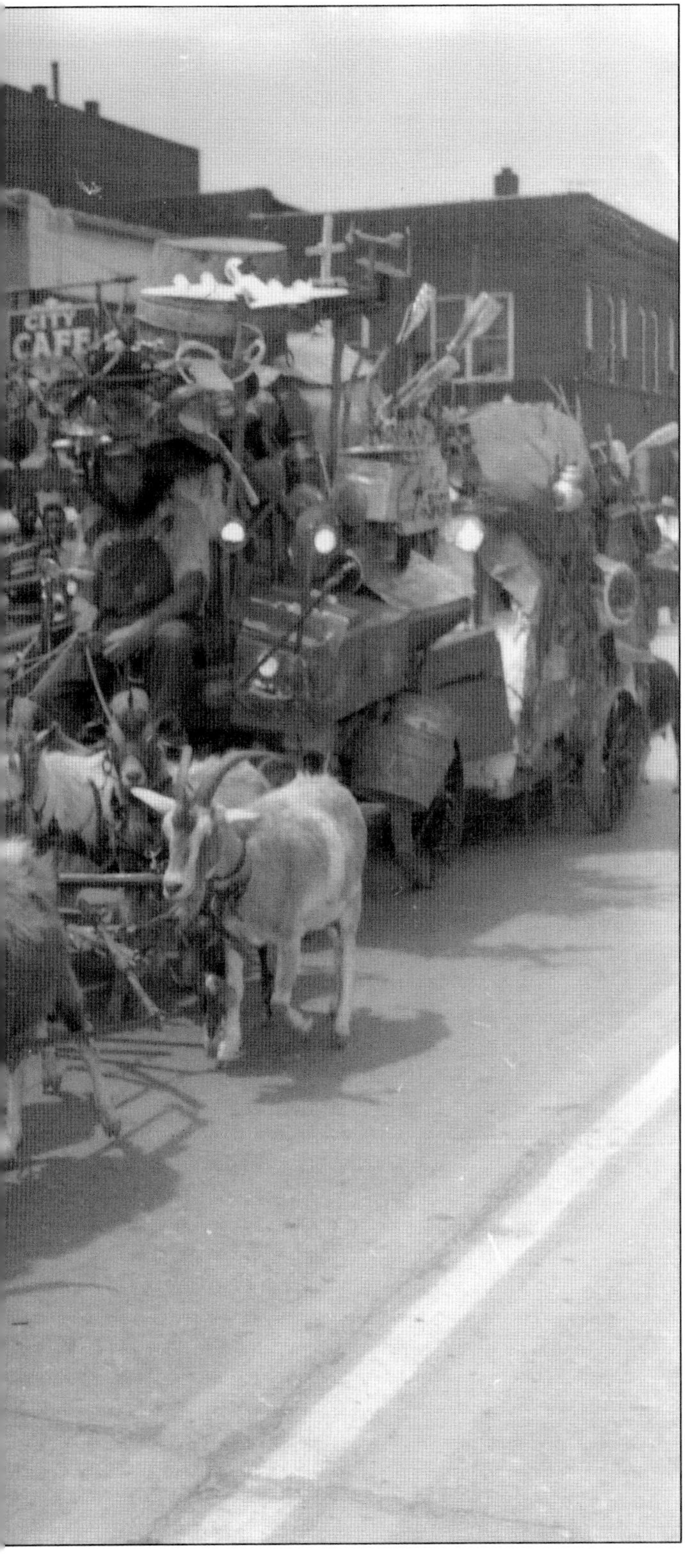

Ches McCartney, known far and wide as "The Goat Man," spent the better part of 30 years roaming the highways of America, in a wagon pulled by a herd of goats. He is shown here traveling up Broad Street in Winder. McCartney would travel 5 to 10 miles a day, then set up camp in a field. He would then feed and milk his goats, and light a bonfire fueled by an old tire. When the spectators came, and they always did, he would preach the gospel and sell postcards of himself. He did not, however, spend all his time on the road. His "home" was a broken-down school bus near Macon. After he came off the road for good he lived there until he was forced to enter a nursing home, where he lived to age 97. This photo was made in June 1951.

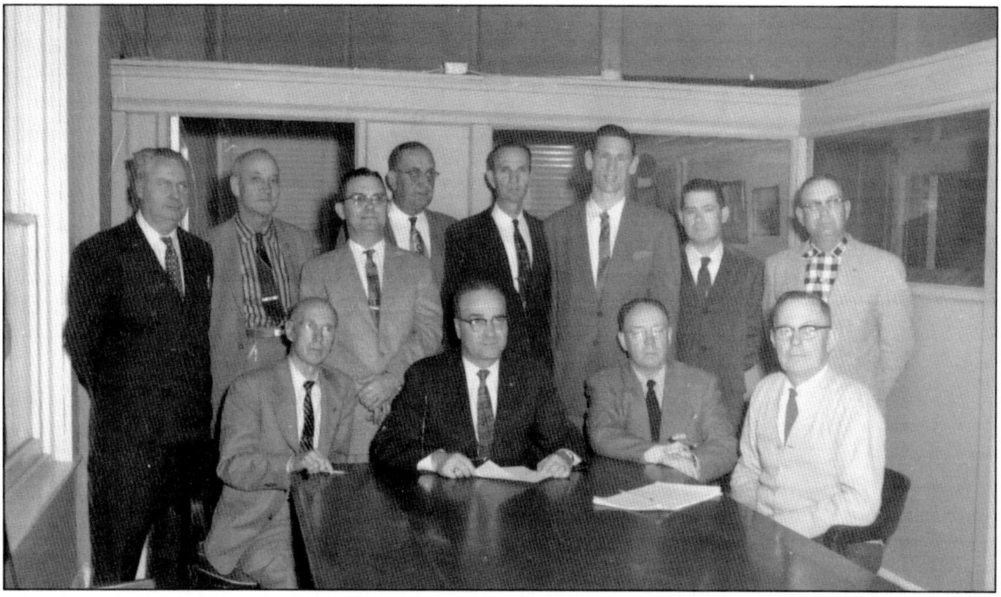

The leadership of the city of Winder is shown in this January 1958 photo. From left to right are as follows: (seated) John Carrington, Mayor John Kelly, City Attorney Nick Rainey, and City Clerk Mark Sims; (standing) Herman Shedd, Walter Youngblood, S.F. Doster, Cliff Rutledge, Harvey Woodward, Jim Harwell, James N. Sheets, and J.D. Cook.

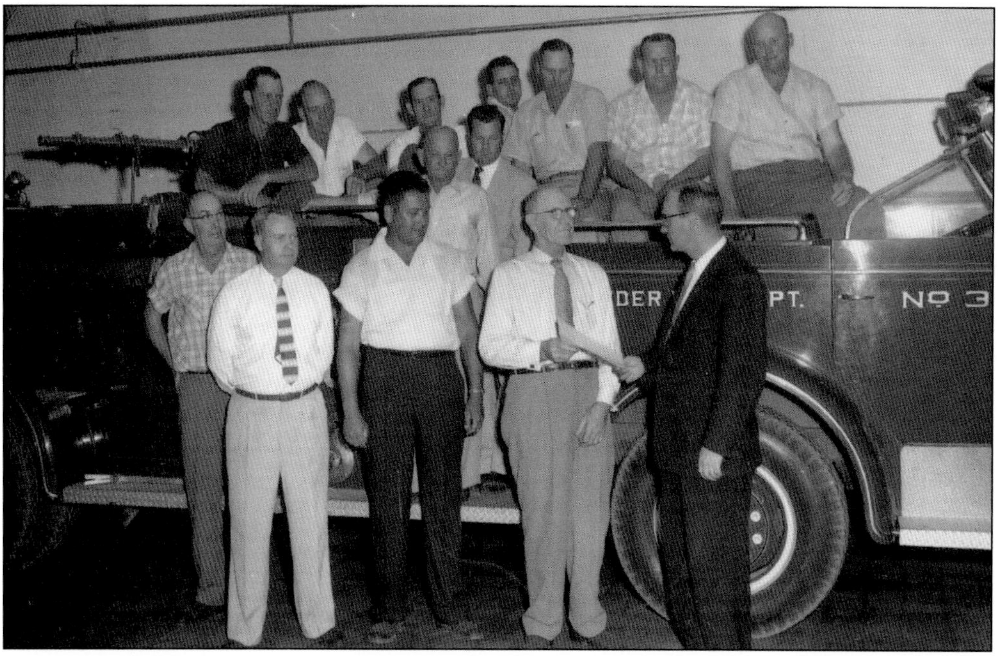

Albert W. Williams Sr. was honored upon his retirement after 50 years as a Winder volunteer fireman. Shown standing, from left to right, are Robert Settle, Herman Shedd, Ludger Lanthier Sr., Albert Williams, and Mayor John Kelley. Standing behind Lanthier are Ambrose Jackson Sr. and Monroe Wise. On the fire truck, from left to right, are Albertus Rutledge, Clyde Doss, Roy Whitley, Clyde Wiley, ? Kesler, Troy Whitley and ? Kesler. The photo was made May 23, 1957.

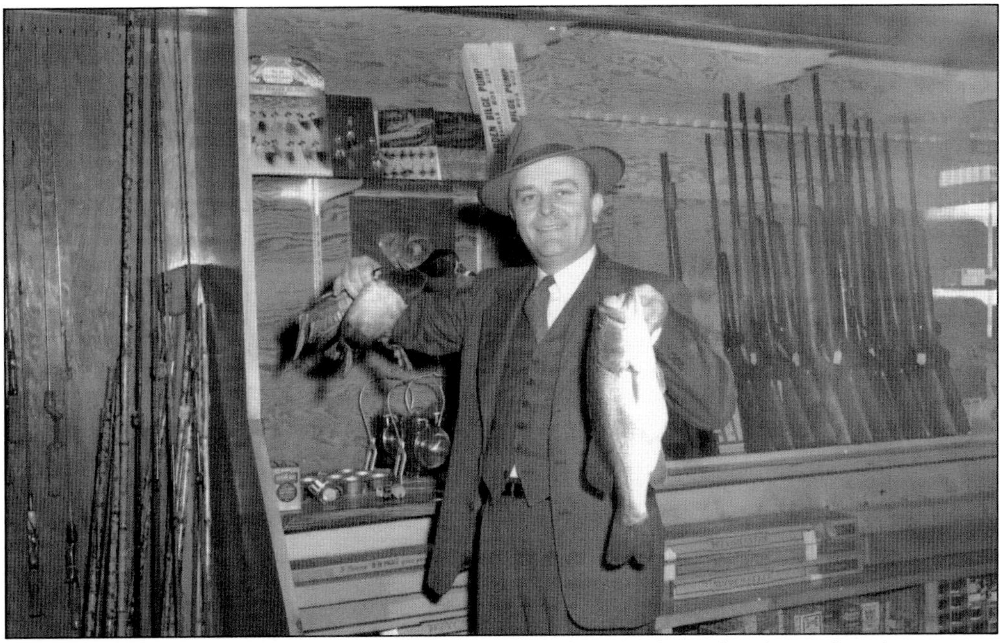

Folks often brought big fish or hunting trophies to Stell and Kilgore for photos, but this one was a little unusual. Brother Nixon A. Taylor of the Christian Church is holding a nice bass, but in his other hand he is holding a mallard duck. We were unable to determine how he bagged both on one trip.

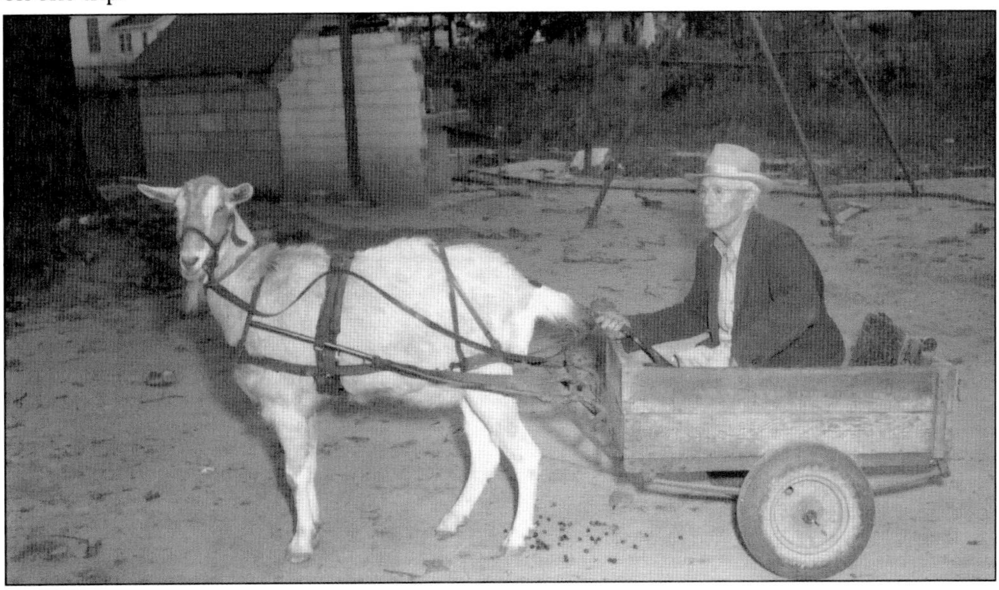

This photo, made in October 1953, is of a man who refused to think of himself as handicapped. When Henry Hill Wages lost both legs due to blood clots, he built this wagon and trained goats to pull it. He used it to get around the large farm he ran near Bethlehem. He would also carry a hoe and crawl in and out of the wagon if he saw any weeding that needed tending. Wages developed his upper body strength to the point that he could climb up into the barn loft to shuck corn. Mr Wages died in June 1964, but one of his grandsons, Randall Wages, still has the cart.

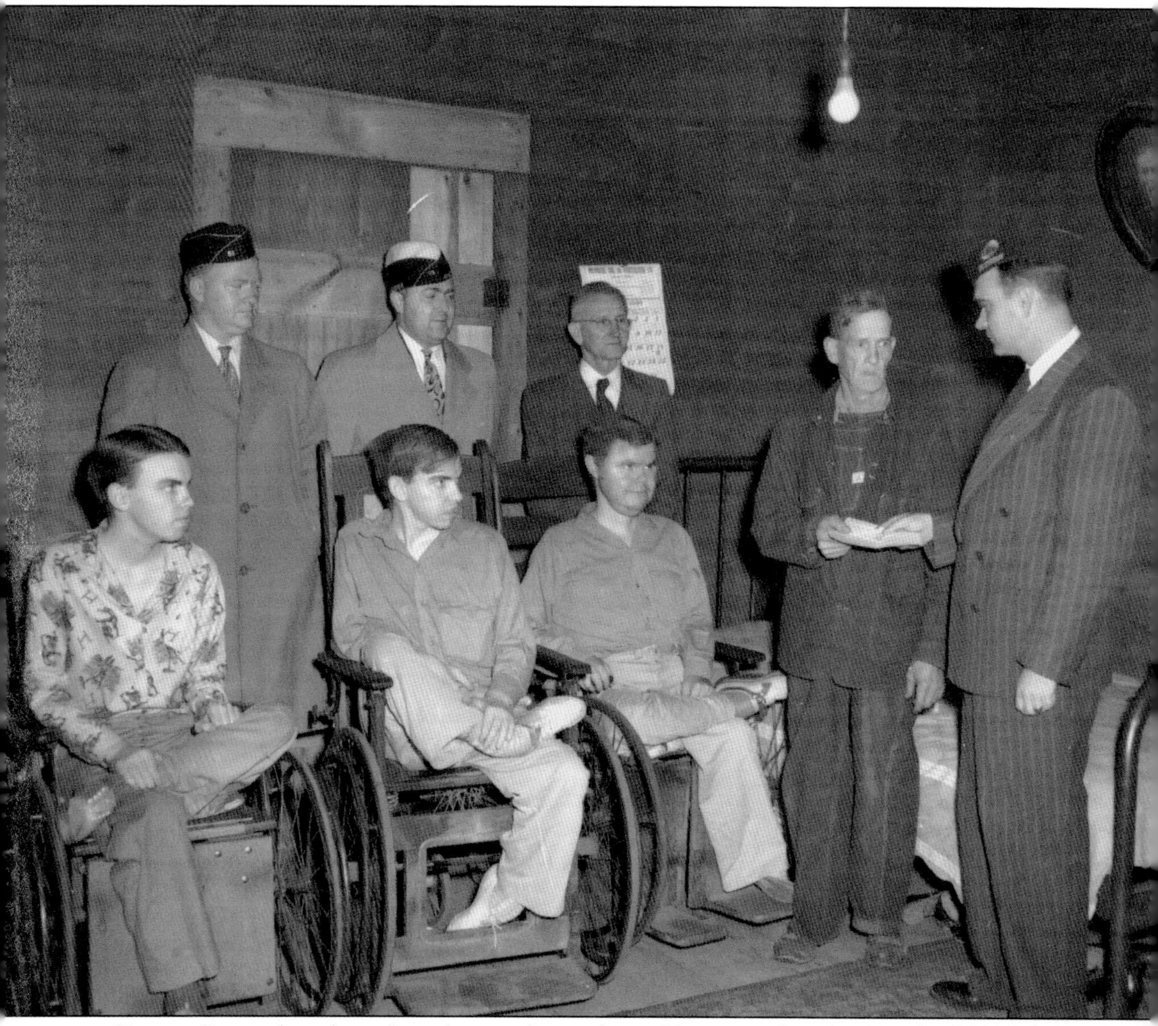

Barrow County has always been known for its charitable nature, but this March 1950 photo is of a particularly compelling campaign. The three Casey brothers were victims of an incurable bone disease and would never be able to leave their wheelchairs. They lived in a small shack that was completely unsuitable for the handicapped, so the people of Bethlehem decided to build a new home and donate it to the family. The rest of the county soon joined in the successful drive. John Kelley of the American Legion is shown presenting the deed to the property to Henry Casey, father of the boys. Looking on, from left to right, are Buster Robison, Jim Griffith Sr., and Rev. L.G. Marlin.

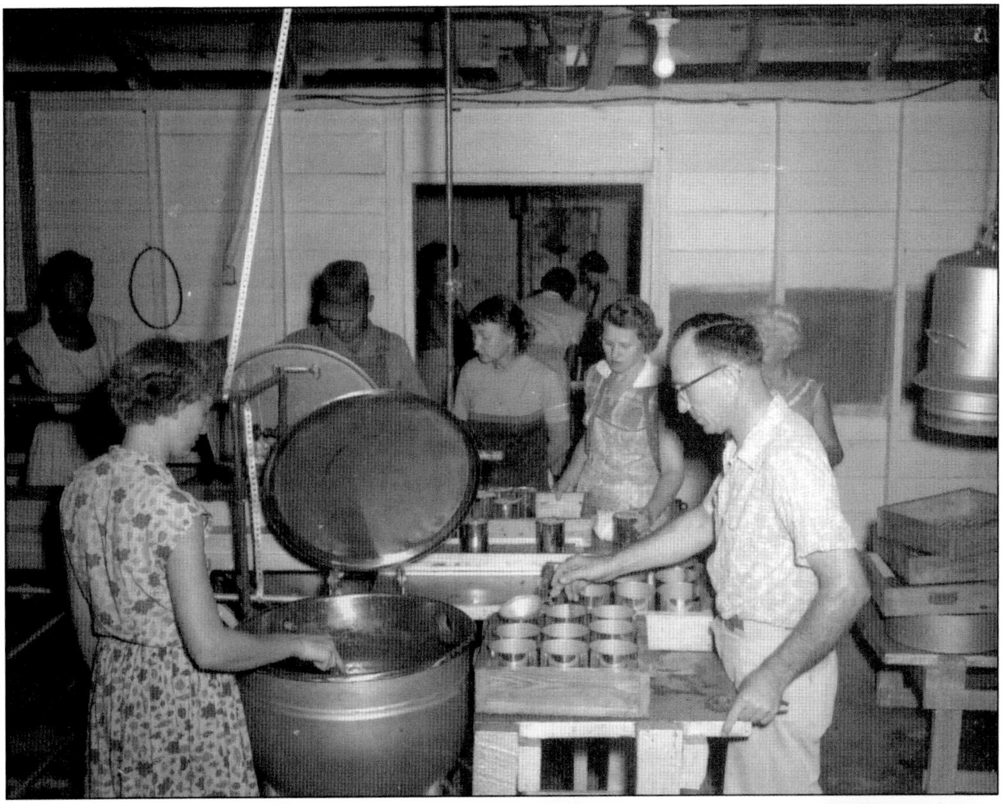

In 1955 Barrow County offered its citizens a cannery, where you could take your garden fresh vegetables and can them—not in glass jars, but in cans exactly like you buy today in the grocery store. It was located on Candler Street in the area of Rose Hill Cemetery. Fred Ingram (right) was on hand to show how it was done.

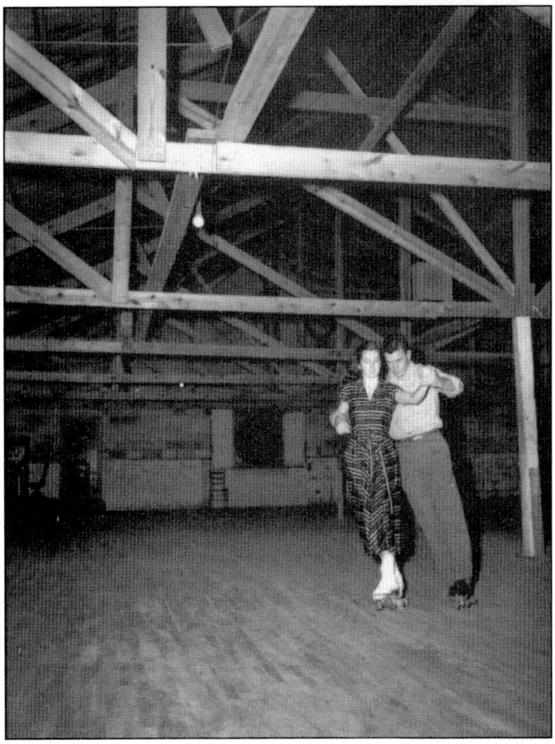

Hamilton's skating rink was a popular place to gather in 1949. It was located on Highway 8 (the Athens Highway) in the area across from Russell Nursing Home. Shown gliding across the floor are Pat Hamilton and Doug Ensley.

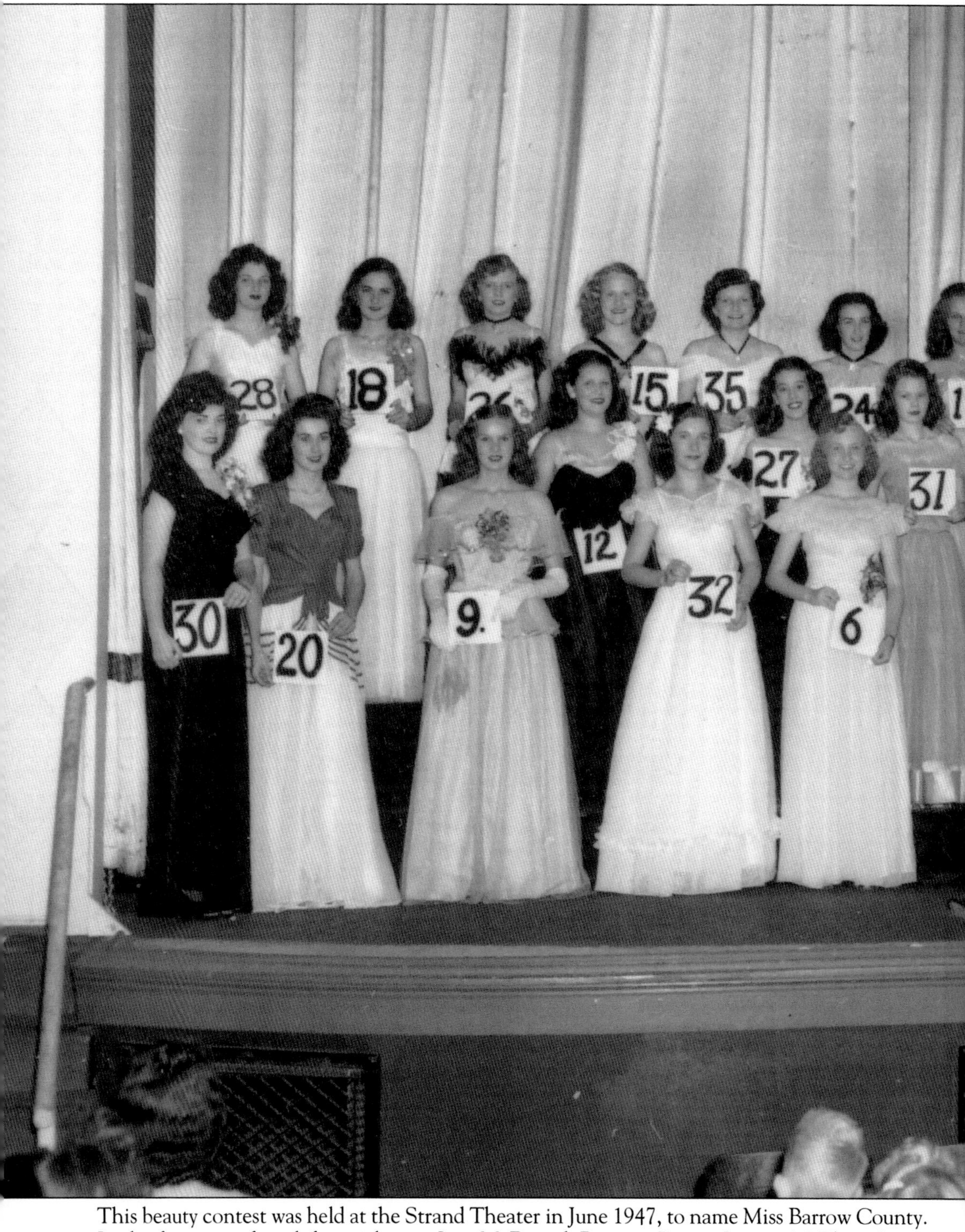

This beauty contest was held at the Strand Theater in June 1947, to name Miss Barrow County. In the front row, from left to right, are Lois McDaniel, Runette Pierce, Joanna McElroy, Jerrye Johnson, Deweylene House, Barbara Tanner, Jean Thompson, Mary Sue Pirckle, Dorothy Higgins, and Very N. Bailey. In the second row (beginning with No. 12) are Joan Robinson,

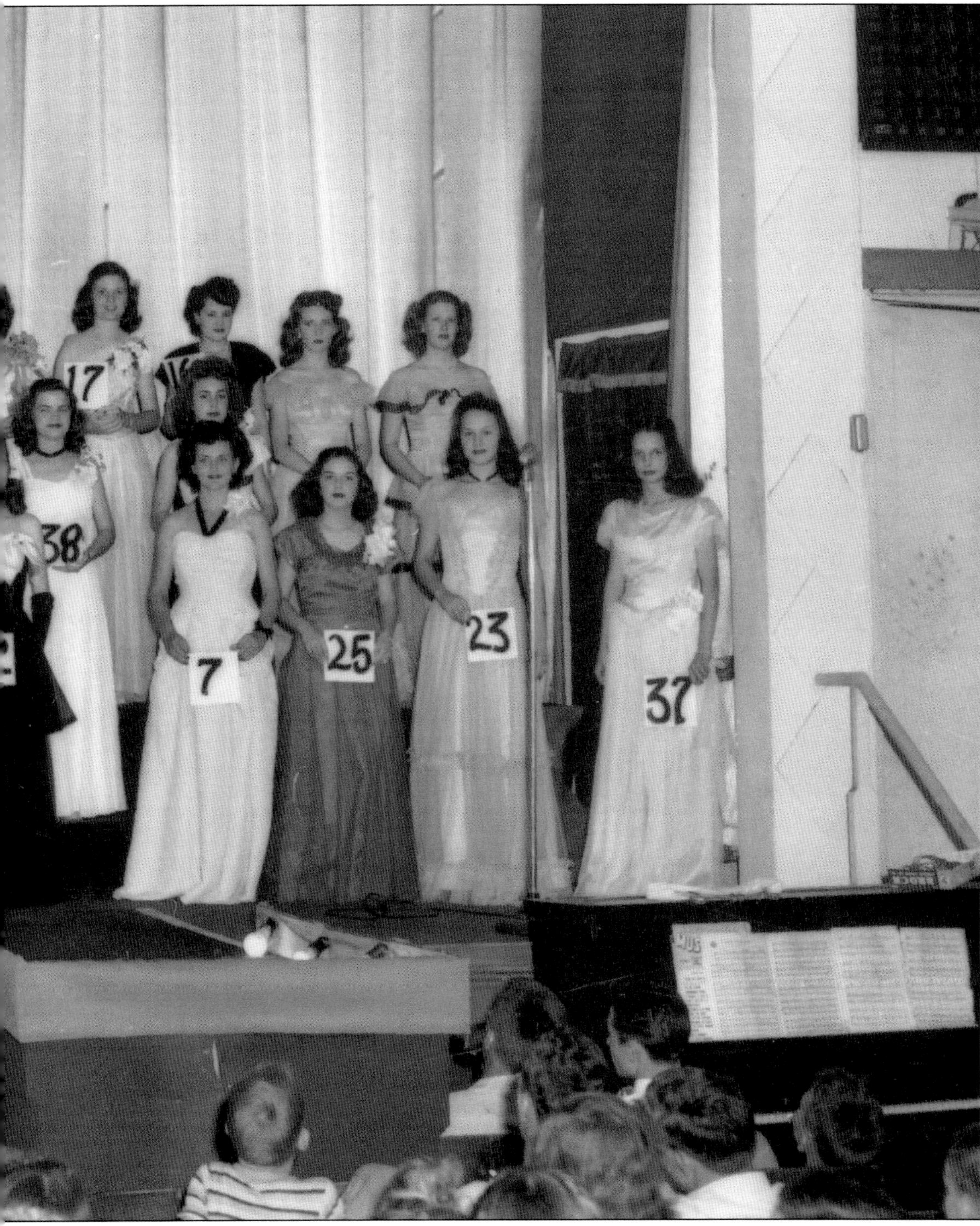

Joan Good, Carolyn Wise, Naomi Matthews, Anita Wayne, and Edna Chancey. In the back row are Phoebe Cook, Carolyn McElhannon, Betty Esco, Peggy Waddell, Robbie Jackson, Ladye M. Arnold, Betty Freeman, Bobbie Page, unidentified, Edith Daniel, Helen Waddell and Janie King. Anita Wayne (No. 38) was the winner.

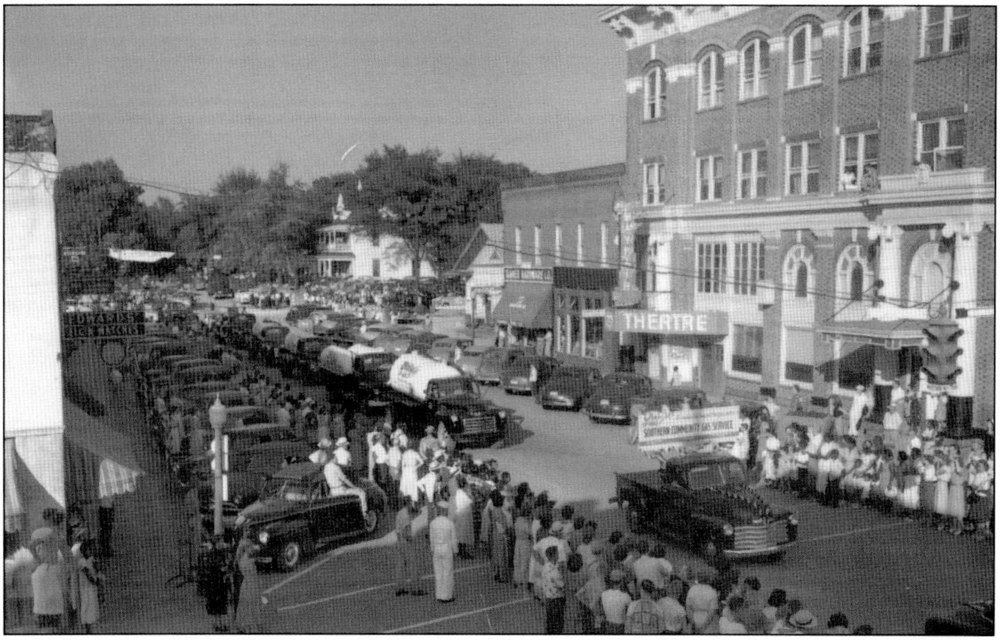

This parade through downtown Winder was held to celebrate "Homecoming Day" in August 1951. It is interesting because it shows two structures that no longer exist. The Mayfair Theater building now houses part of The Peoples Bank. In the background, at the corner of Broad and Midland, is the old Gainesville Midland Railroad depot.

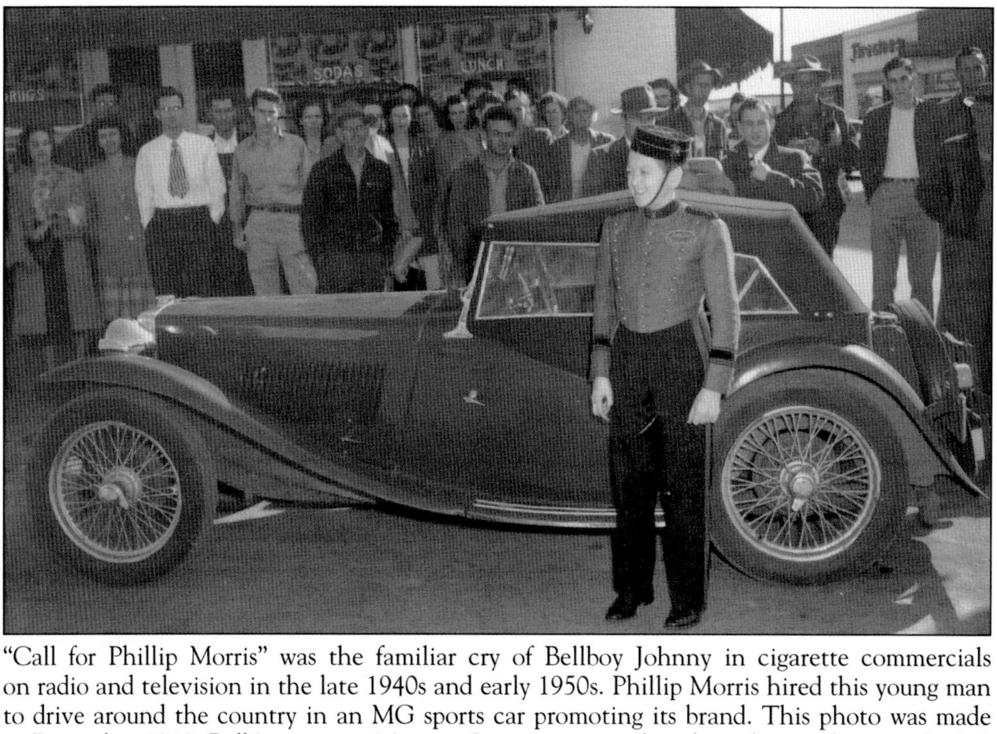

"Call for Phillip Morris" was the familiar cry of Bellboy Johnny in cigarette commercials on radio and television in the late 1940s and early 1950s. Phillip Morris hired this young man to drive around the country in an MG sports car promoting its brand. This photo was made in December 1949. Belk's manager Maurice Sims is seen in the white shirt and tie, to the left of Johnny.

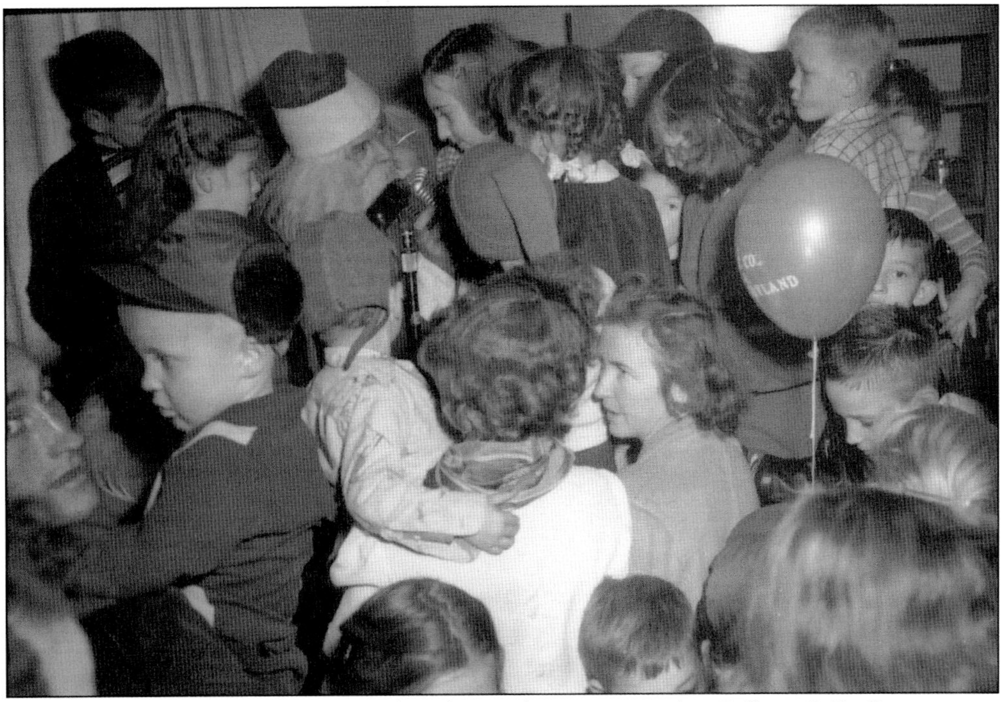

Children swarmed around Santa when he made a visit to the Gallant-Belk Company in downtown Winder on December 6, 1952. The event was also carried on local radio station WIMO, which would qualify it as a very early remote broadcast.

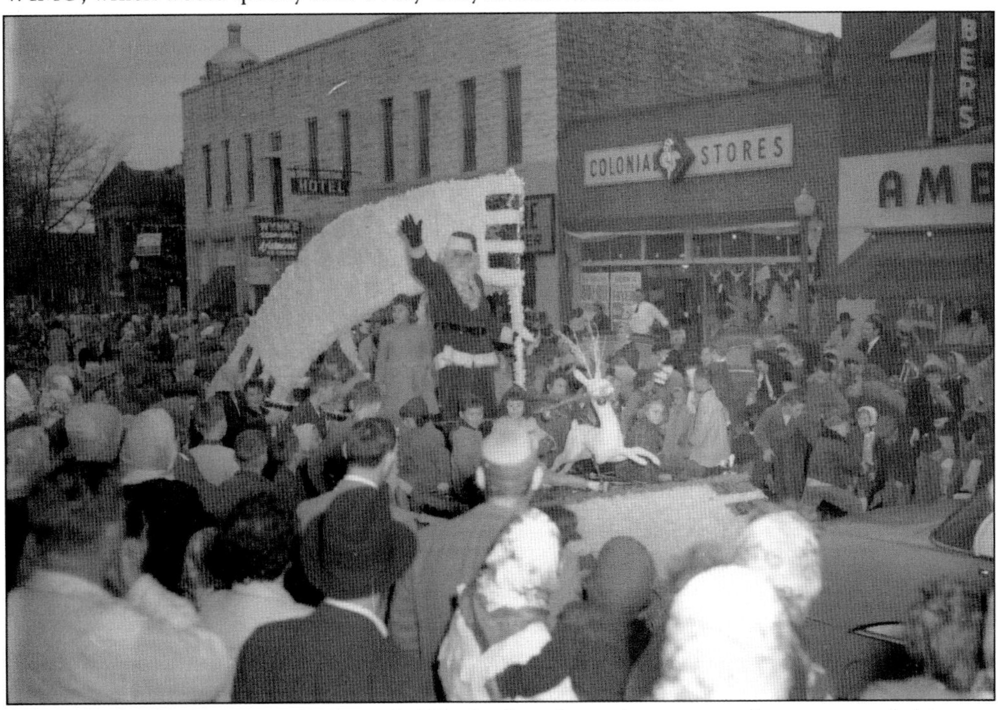

The annual Christmas parade through Winder has always been a popular event, and this one, in 1957, was obviously no exception.

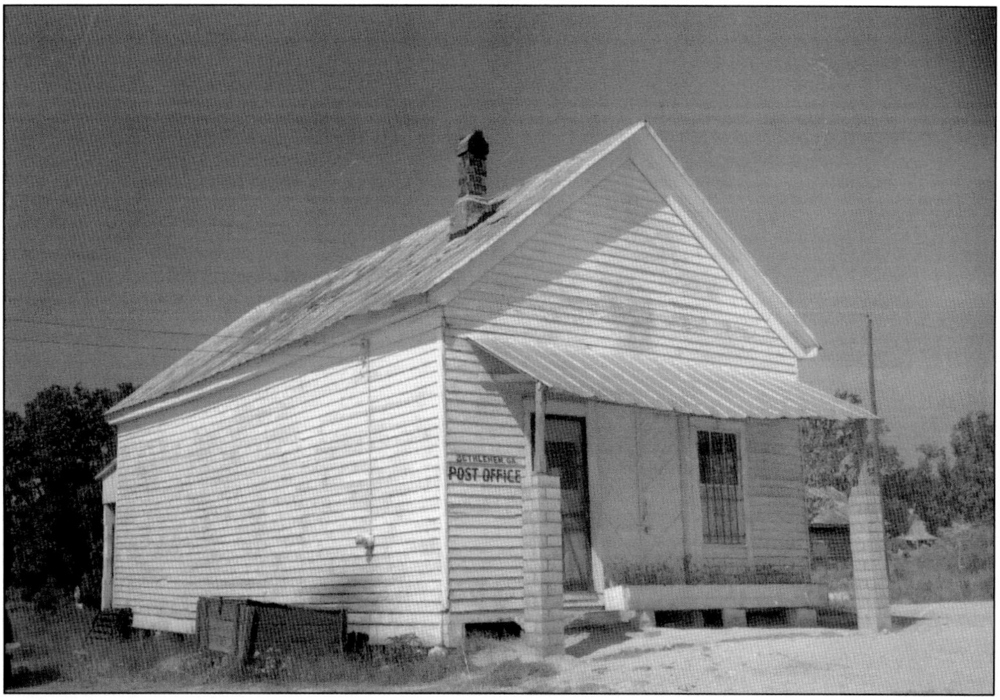

This building served as the post office in Bethlehem in 1951. Even then it was a popular postmark for Christmas cards.

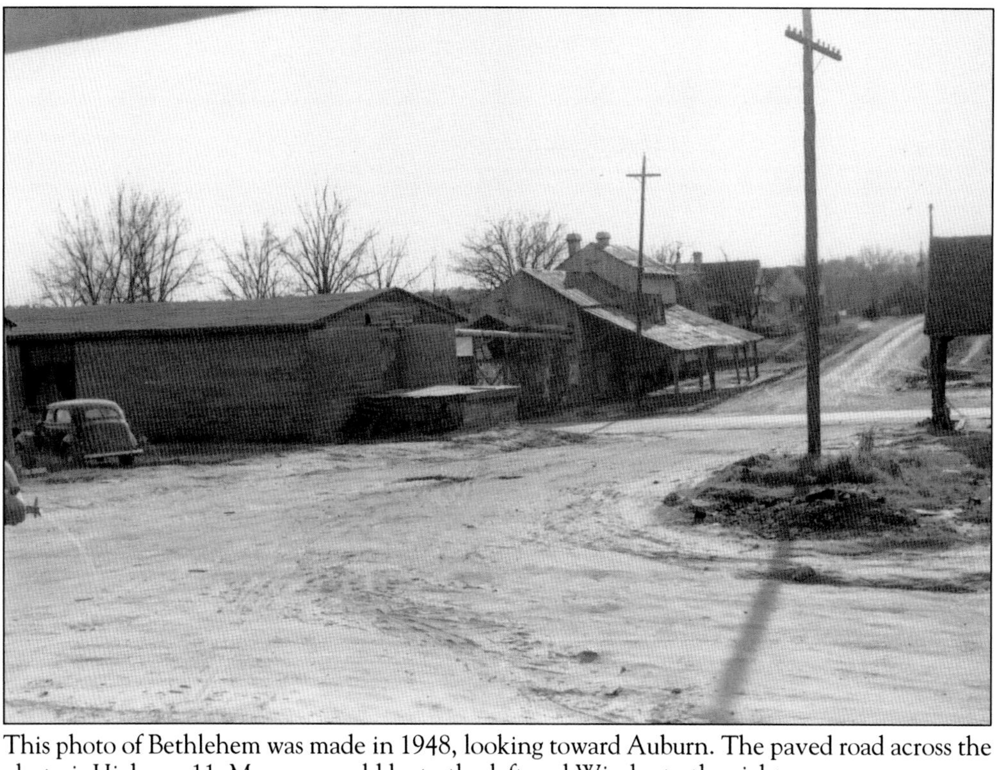

This photo of Bethlehem was made in 1948, looking toward Auburn. The paved road across the photo is Highway 11. Monroe would be to the left and Winder to the right.

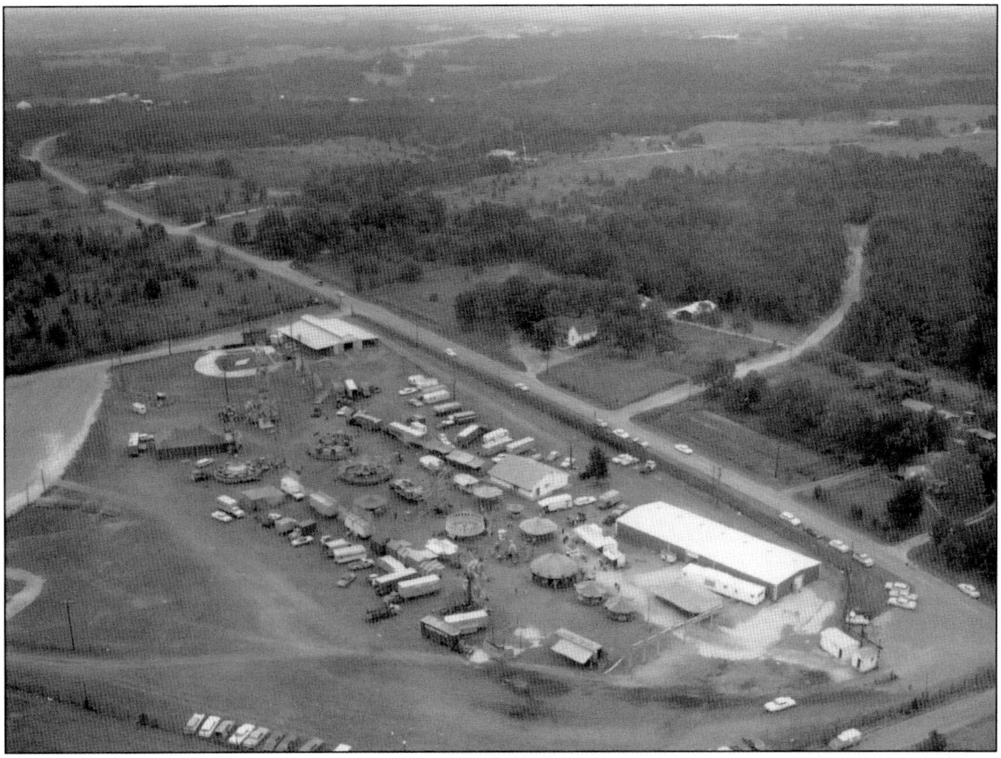

For more than 50 years the Winder Lions Club sponsored the Barrow County Fair at its grounds on Highway 82 near Winder. This photo, made in 1966, shows the midway, the exhibit building, and the livestock exhibit area. The Lions Club discontinued the fair in 1999.

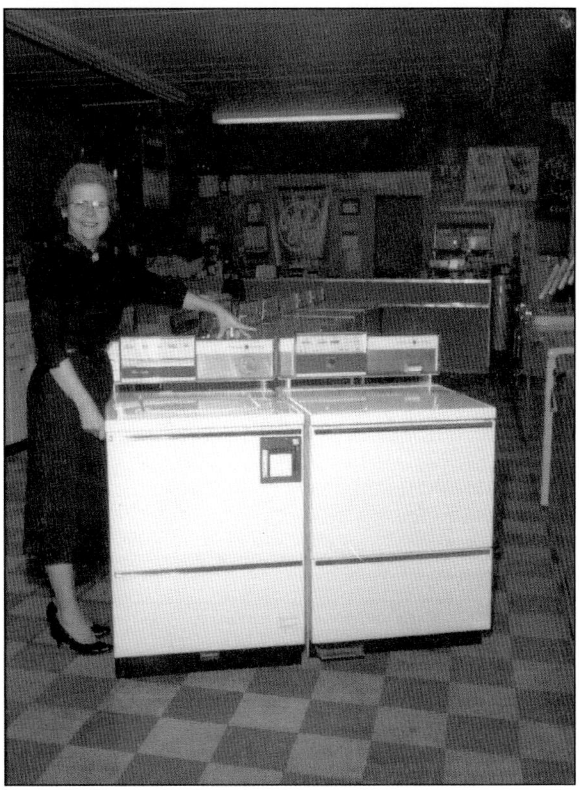

Mrs. E.V. (Evelyn) Harris was the "Electrification Advisor" for Jackson EMC when folks still had to be encouraged to use electricity. Here she is demonstrating a new electric washer and dryer. She also edited *Watts Cooking*, a cookbook that has sold more than 150,000 copies with proceeds benefitting local churches and charities. The photo was made in September 1960.

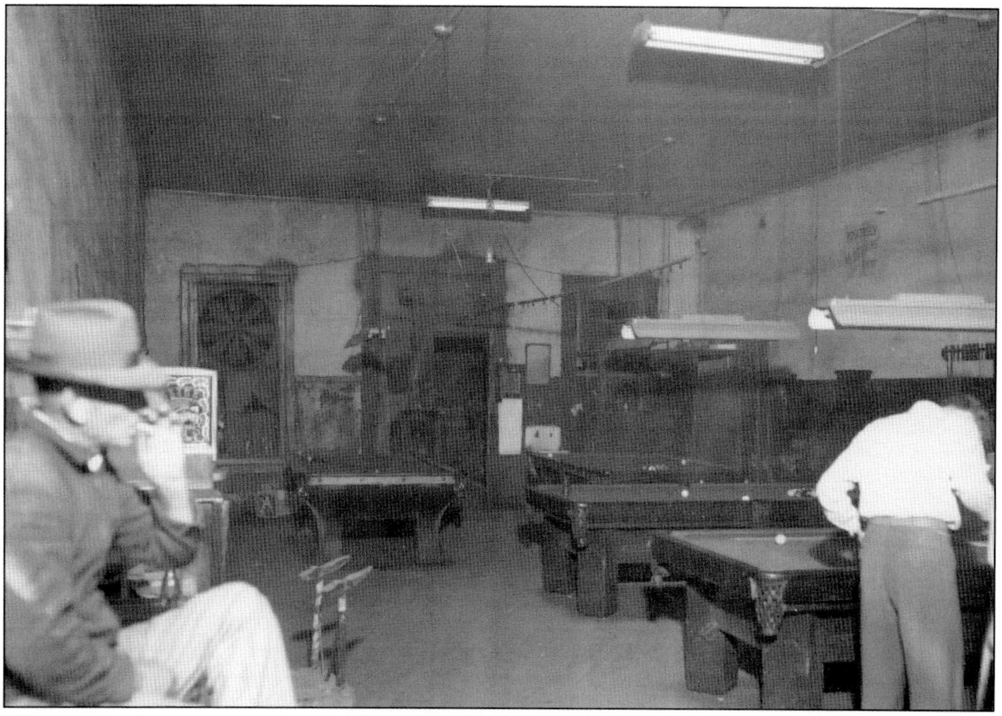

When this photo was made in 1949, Winder had two pool rooms—one on Candler Street and the other behind it facing East Athens Street. Most people who were familiar with the establishments agree that this is the one on Athens Street.

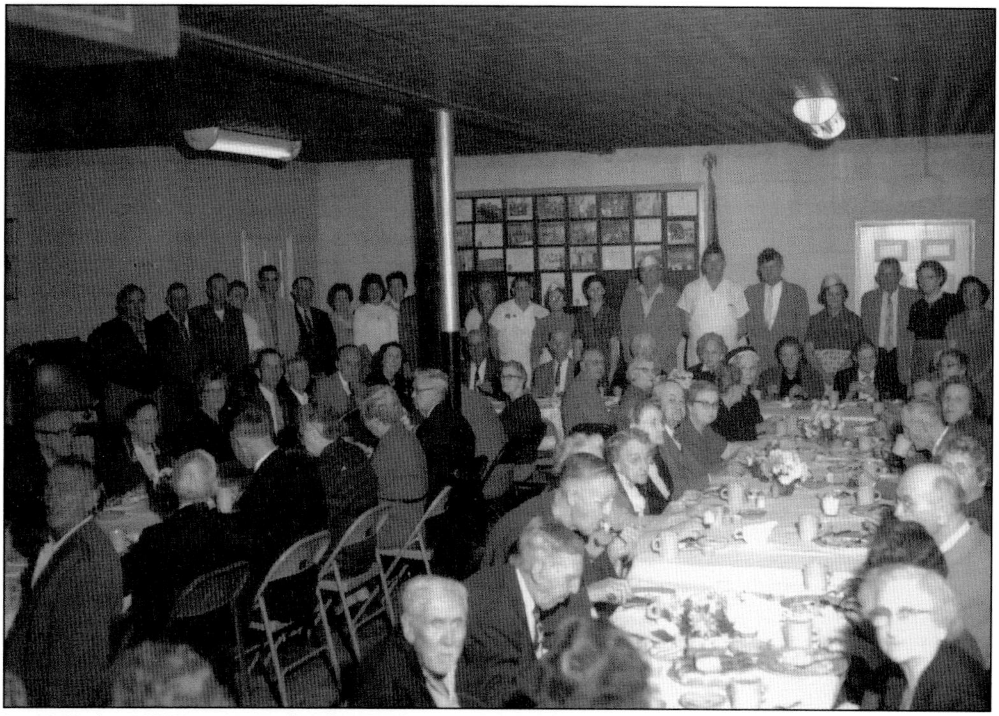

In 1960 the VFW sponsored a dinner for Barrow County's elderly.

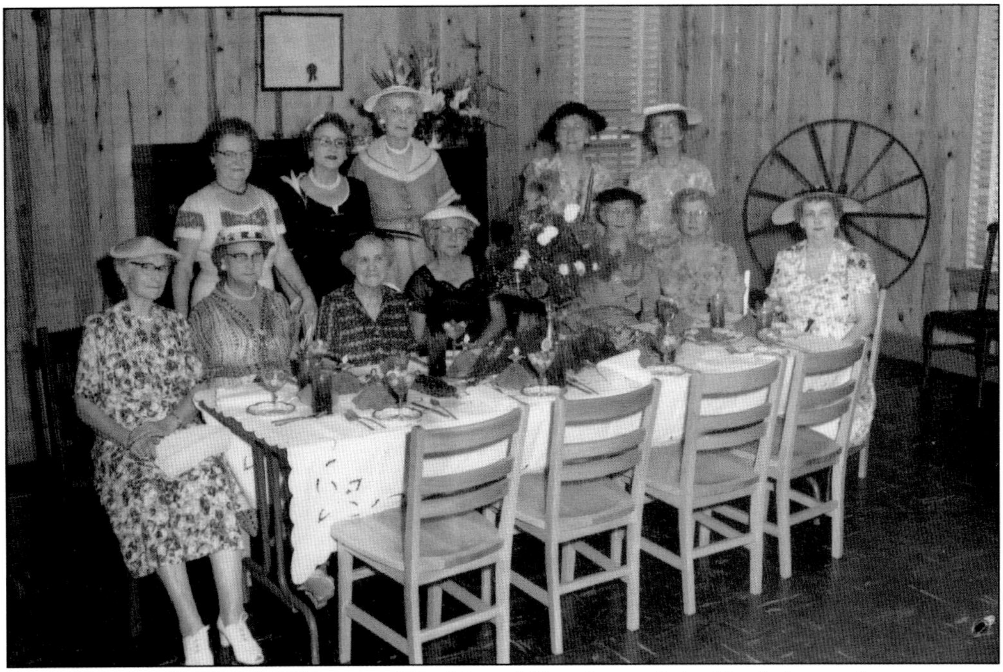

This photo of the Winder Chapter of the United Daughters of the Confederacy shows some of Winder's leading citizens. From left to right are as follows: (seated) Mrs. R.L. Rogers, Mrs. Cleo Roberts, Mrs. Will Herrin, Mrs. Kathleen Moseley, Mrs ? Woodward, Miss Johnnie Lou Smith, and Mrs. A.D. McCurry; (standing) Mrs. Oscar Summerour, Mrs. Launa Williams, Mrs. ? Ware, Mrs. Lavada Holsenbeck, and Miss Cleo Bush. This photograph was taken in June 1956.

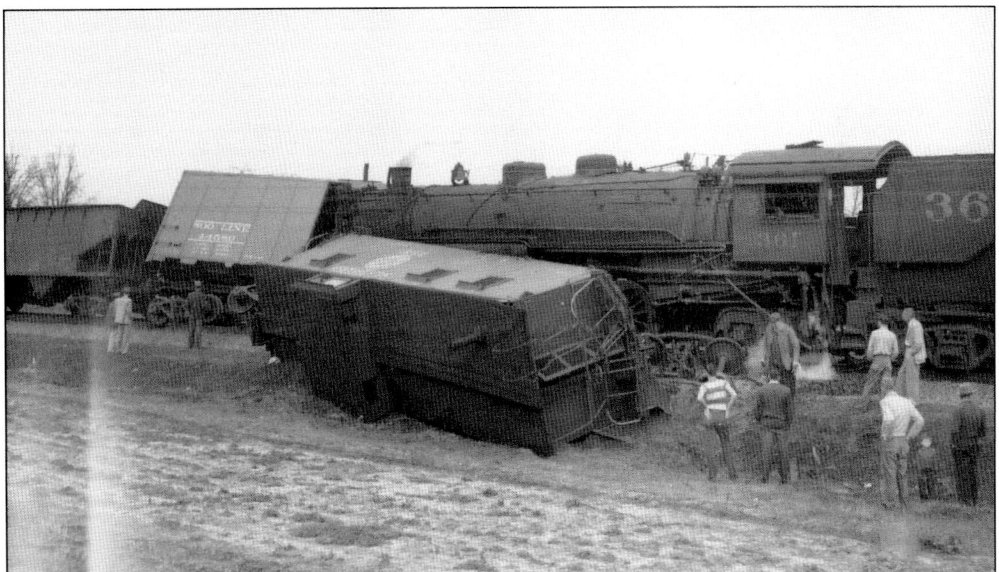

In the 1950s, steam engines still pulled the trains through Barrow County on the Seaboard Coastline Railway. Earlier, the Gainesville Midland Railroad tracks had also cut across the county and through Winder, on the way from Gainesville to Monroe. This photo is of a train accident on the Seaboard line near Winder on February 1, 1950.

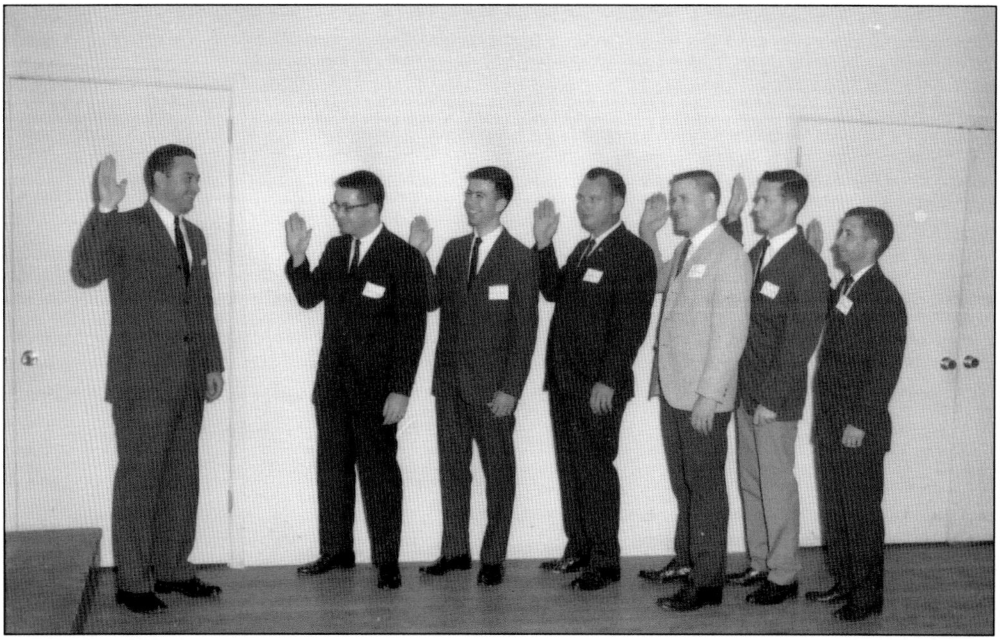

Ben Cheek III (left), region president from Toccoa, was on hand to swear in a new slate of Jaycee officers on May 24, 1964. The officers, from left to right, are Brunell Langford Jr., president; Benton Bowen, internal vice-president; Charlton Wright, external vice-president; Fred Disharoon, director; Don Burrell, treasurer; and Dick Golden, past president and state director. Paul Stallings, who was secretary that year, was not on hand for the photo.

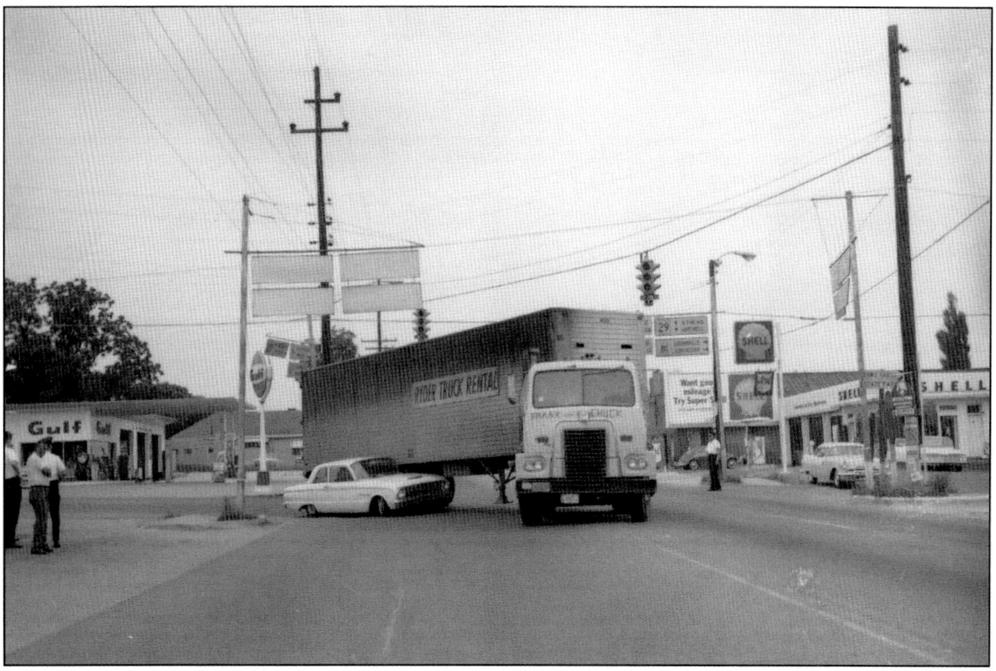

This type of accident at the intersection of Broad and May Streets still happens today with great frequency. The Shell service station shown was replaced by Burger King. This photo was made May 27, 1965.